CHARLES II

Royal Politician

CHARLES II

Royal Politician

J. R. JONES

School of English and American Studies,
University of East Anglia

ALLEN & UNWIN

Boston Sydney

Allen & Unwin, the academic imprint of

Unwin Hyman Ltd

PO Box 18, Park Lane, Hemel Hempstead, Herts HP2 4TE, UK
40 Museum Street, London WC1A 1LU, UK
37/39 Queen Elizabeth Street, London SE1 2QB

Allen & Unwin, Inc.,
8 Winchester Place, Winchester, Mass. 01890, USA

Allen & Unwin (Australia) Ltd,
8 Napier Street, North Sydney, NSW 2060, Australia

Allen & Unwin (New Zealand) Ltd in association with the
Port Nicholson Press Ltd,
Private Bag, Wellington, New Zealand

First published in 1987

British Library Cataloguing in Publication Data

Jones, J. R. (James Rees)
    Charles II: royal politician.
1. Charles II, King of England   2. Great Britain
– History – Charles II, 1660–1685
I. Title
942.06′6′0924   DA446
ISBN 0–04–942196–4

Library of Congress Cataloging-in-Publication Data

Jones, J. R. (James Rees), 1925–
    Charles II, royal politician.
Bibliography: p.
Includes index.
1. Charles II, King of England, 1630–1685.
2. Great Britain – Kings and rulers – Biography. 3. Great
Britain – Politics and government – 1660–1688. I. Title.
DA446.J66   1987   941.06′6′0924 [B]   86–17264
ISBN 0–04–942196–4

Set in 10 on 12 point Bembo by Phoenix Photosetting, Chatham
and printed in Great Britain by Mackays of Chatham Ltd

Contents

Acknowledgements

My greatest debt is to my family, who have borne with my abstraction while researching and writing this study. I also acknowledge with gratitude the stimulation and insights I have received from my colleagues among the historians at the University of East Anglia, and from students who have taken my special subject course. I am very grateful for the comments made on a large part of the text by Professor C. P. Korr, of the University of Missouri, and for the many discussions which we had during my stay in St Louis.

Norwich, *July 1986*

1 Introduction

This is a political study of Charles II, not a 'life' or formal biography. Consequently his private life will not be discussed, except when it impinged on his public attitudes and performance of his duties as sovereign. The treatment of Charles's career is also selective in another sense. The degree of his personal involvement in policy-making, the direction of government and negotiations with foreign states varied considerably from time to time: it is naturally those phases during which he was most closely and actively concerned with these (especially 1650–1, 1660–2, 1668–73, 1678, and 1679–85)[1] that receive the most detailed attention. So this study does not try to give a blow by blow account of the reign, particularly of those periods in which Charles virtually delegated control over at least routine administration to a single minister. One of its main theses is that the conditions affecting government and political activity were constantly changing during the reign, making it impossible to generalize about Charles's methods and objectives as a ruler and royal politician. It has been claimed that the key to understanding Charles II is to see him as a post-revolutionary ruler, limited by the fundamental changes effected by the English Revolution of the 1640s and 1650s.[2] However, it will be argued that these earlier changes had only a comparatively minor influence, and that essentially new (post-1660) developments and changes had a far greater impact, creating new situations and new sets of problems for the restored monarch and his ministers.

Charles and his ministers found themselves under almost constant pressures – from parliament, the church, foreign states, organized public opinion – which differed essentially from those that previous rulers had encountered. It is the main thesis of this study that these pressures proved to be the most important influence on Charles, making him concentrate almost entirely on short-term tactics and engage in complex manœuvring in order to achieve mainly defensive objectives. The title contains the words 'royal politician', indicating a very different interpretation from that advanced by the only previous major study that attempts to present Charles as seriously active and indeed successful in his political activity, Arthur Bryant's *King Charles II*.[3] Bryant depicts Charles as a strong and well-intentioned sovereign, deeply concerned with the interests of his people, the effective founder of the British Empire and the Royal Navy, opposed by a narrow, corrupt, self-perpetuating oligarchy, including an emergent plutocracy. These conclusions were perhaps heavily influenced by the political context and fashions of the 1930s, but they had the merit of breaking with the traditional picture of Charles as an immoral and frivolous king, who possessed neither principles nor objectives and refused to commit himself to the tedious business of governing.

Once he had consolidated his position in England, Charles began to experience, and resent, the restrictions on his freedom of action represented by his first set of leading ministers, Clarendon, Southampton and Ormonde. Men of an older generation, they stood in the way of his appointing untested contemporaries of himself, and they disapproved of any attempts at political innovation (such as parliamentary management) and of the adventurous foreign policy that produced the second Dutch War in 1665. By the time that war ended in catastrophe, in 1667, Charles had become aware of the extent to which his powers were restricted in more fundamental ways, and especially by comparison with those of his peers, the contemporary kings and princes of Europe and, above all, his cousin Louis XIV, who assumed the personal direction of policy in 1661. This raises a question of importance. It is quite wrong to describe Charles and those ministers who served him after the fall of Clarendon as reactionaries. Charles rarely looked back across the gulf of the Civil Wars. He never set himself the task of recovering those powers and rights (for example, the prerogative courts) that his father had lost in 1641–2. Neither he nor the new ministers whom he appointed from 1662 on had personally participated in decision-making processes under Charles I. Understandably, considering their disastrous outcome, Charles never took any of his father's policies or methods as a model or guide. He frequently referred to the malice of those who had destroyed his father and plunged the nation into the miseries of civil war, but (unlike the Anglican clergy) he maintained a revealing silence about his father's reign and failures.

The restored Church of England, rather than the restored monarchy, provided the vehicle for post-Restoration reaction and conservatism – and continued to do so until the 1720s.[4] Under the extremely effective leadership of Gilbert Sheldon, the church acted as the main limitation on the king's freedom of action. It made him live and rule (if not die) as an Anglican. The alliance of the Anglican clergy with the gentry, and their influence in the Commons that was elected in 1661, produced an ecclesiastical settlement in 1661–5 that differed fundamentally from Charles's wishes. After 1673 he finally had to abandon all public attempts to introduce religious toleration. Clerical unity proved to be sufficiently strong to render largely ineffective the intermittent use of the powers of royal patronage to try to create diversity among the higher clergy. On the other hand, loyalty to the church, and a determination to defend its exclusive

and legal rights against encroachment by the king and his ministers, legiti-
mized the revival among former Cavaliers of attitudes associated with the
Country critics of early Stuart administrations. The alliance between church
and Country was actually strengthened by Clarendon's fall: in the years
1668–71 independent peers and MPs constituted the dominant interest, ready
to work with Charles, but only on terms acceptable to themselves.

The most obvious restriction that Charles experienced derived from his
need to secure the collaboration of parliament. Never before had parliament met so frequently – he had to call a session every year (except 1672
and 1676) between 1660 and 1681. The main reason was his need for
extraordinary grants of supply, but especially in the early 1660s he also
needed parliament to pass a heavy programme of statutes. However,
Charles in his formal relations with parliament did not diverge from the
traditional forms. Almost invariably he made a speech to both Houses at
the start of each session, outlining his expectations but leaving the detail to
the lord chancellor or keeper. He received addresses from both Houses, or
from either, which were discussed at council before a formal reply was
formulated and transmitted. These replies called for care, since they were
likely to form the basis for a debate, and Charles frequently ordered their
publication, so as to counter any impression made by propagandistic
addresses. He took the initiative on occasion, sending messages that asked
for the expediting of supply or of a specific Bill. These too were increasingly used for propaganda, to vindicate the king's intentions, or to try to
expose parliament, or usually the Commons, to charges of being
obstructive. During the session of 1670–1 Charles began to attend Lords
sittings regularly, renewing a custom of his predecessors that had been
discontinued: the Lords thanked him, and he made it clear that he did not
intend to 'interrupt' their proceedings. However, it is clear that his presence during the crucial debate on Exclusion (15 November 1680) had a
decisive effect on the outcome.[5]

After 1667, and even more after 1673, Charles and his ministers became
increasingly involved in attempts to organize and influence both Houses of
Parliament. From as early as 1662, the king, unlike Clarendon, saw the need
for systematic management, and significantly the two earliest pioneers of
management successively rose to the very top of the ministerial structure:
Clifford (originally Arlington's lieutenant) and Osborne (Buckingham's)
each became lord treasurer. The latter (as Earl of Danby) proved particularly
to be an innovator in developing the techniques of dispensing patronage that
made it practicable to organize a working majority in the Lords and
Commons. But his organization was still primitive in comparison with the
political machines controlled by eighteenth-century ministers, and neither he
nor Charles had the capacity to influence general elections. During the three
Exclusion Parliaments (1679, 1680–1 and 1681) the Whigs overwhelmed the
Court interest in the Commons.[6]

Charles's long dependence on parliament had one unexpected and bale-ful effect: it facilitated foreign intervention in English politics in new and potent ways. The frequency and effectiveness of intervention by France and William III represent a new and random force in English politics.[7] Traditionally, the great powers, France and Spain, had concentrated on attempts to influence the sovereign personally and to build up parties among ministers and at Court. But from 1670 until the climax of the Revolution of 1688 foreign states intervened on a far wider front. Their agents and diplomats worked at Westminster as well as at Whitehall. They used clandestine propaganda to influence popular as well as parliamentary opinion. These interventions frequently produced decisive results. Louis XIV vetoed the idea of dissolving the Cavalier Parliament in 1673, which had been proposed so as to prevent the passage of the Test Act. William III forced Charles to abandon the third Dutch War in 1674. Four years later French intervention initially prevented William and Danby from pushing Charles into a war against France, and later precipitated Danby's downfall. Charles's ability to rule without Parliament during the last four years of the reign largely depended on the financial subsidies he received from Louis in return for pledges not to interfere with French policies in Europe.[8]

At the Restoration, conservatives like Clarendon and Nicholas thought that the return of the legitimate monarch and the constitution would put an end to 'politics', in the sense of ordinary and unofficial people concern-ing themselves with affairs of state, and criticizing those who held offices under the Crown. They also believed that parliament should restrict its proceedings within narrow limits. It should grant extraordinary supply and enact (after debating and possibly amending) the Bills drafted by the privy council. If there were grievances, it could humbly address the king for their rectification, but the proper channels for the presentation of grievances were bodies that derived their authority from the Crown: grand juries, empanelled from substantial landowners by the sheriff, who was named by the king; corporations, whose charters were granted by the king, and could be forfeited in case of abuse; JPs meeting in quarter sessions, who could be dismissed at will. Unofficial public opinion on public matters had no legitimate existence and so no right to information: the Licensing Act imposed strict controls over printing and publishing.[9]

Several developments frustrated these conservative hopes. Despite its self-proclaimed loyalism, the Cavalier Parliament, and especially the Commons, did not wait for the council to transmit drafts of Bills, but frequently initiated legislation, and on matters of the first importance, including the first Uniformity Bill and the prohibition of Irish cattle imports. Moreover the controversial character of much of its legislation in the first years (particularly on religion), and the stubborn opposition staged by a comparatively small but highly articulate minority, focused public attention on the annual sessions. Furthermore the Commons received more frequent demands for extraordinary grants of supply than had ever been made before. Charles had to justify these demands. The criticisms of extravagance and mismanagement with which the Commons responded, even when granting supply, were widely echoed outside Westminster by taxpayers. Moreover the retention in 1660 of some of the hated excises introduced by the Long Parliament meant that the comparatively poor as well as property owners now paid taxes. However it was the degree of governmental incompetence exposed by the failures of the second Dutch War, and the accusations of massive corruption made by MPs against ministers, officials and contractors, that provoked the greatest and most sustained criticisms of the administration, and Charles's encouragement of attacks on such obvious and easy scapegoats as Clarendon and Peter Pett, the naval commissioner blamed for the success of the Dutch attack on Chatham, educated the public in the failings of their betters.

There are obvious parallels between the political atmosphere generated by the failure of the second Dutch War, especially the alienation of both parliament and the public from the court, and the state of disaffection created by the misrule of the first Duke of Buckingham and the failures of his wars in the 1620s.[10] Then, Charles I had dissolved parliament and as a set policy ruled for eleven years without one. Now, Charles II, because of his precarious financial situation, had no immediate alternative but to continue with annual parliamentary sessions and submit to the restrictions that the Commons imposed on his expenditure of extraordinary supply. The wider consequences were that he had to accept, for the time being until he could gain his independence (and this took much longer – more than a decade – than he expected), a regular interest and concern with public affairs, the forming of opinions and the expression of criticisms, by persons who were not accountable to him and held no official position. Despite the Licensing Act and the attempts to suppress the new coffee houses, unofficial views and criticisms of the administration were increasingly discussed and disseminated. Consequently one can talk of 'politics' and 'public opinion' after 1667 in an almost modern sense.

The Court's political strategy can be seen as a back-handed acknowledgement of the existence and persistence of high levels of political consciousness and the continuation of critical attitudes towards government. Charles could not seriously consider dissolving the existing parliament, even before Danby began to construct working majorities. Particularly after 1673 the Country opposition tried repeatedly to force a dissolution. The joint assumption, which the next general election confirmed in 1679, was that the electorate would now be influenced at least as much by national and political issues as by local obligations and alliances, territorial connections and corruption. The second and third Exclusion elections (August–September 1679, February–March 1681) demonstrated another major development, the emergence for the first time of party politics. Under Shaftesbury's leadership the first Whigs organized, manipulated and exploited public opinion and prejudice – especially the powerful currents of anti-popery. Charles was the first king who had to face organized political activity, in the country and at elections as well as within parliament, by a party committed to forcing through major statutes of the highest impor-tance. In repulsing the Whig attempts to change the succession, and then in eliminating them as a party, Charles had of necessity to rally all who opposed the Whigs. With his encouragement and help, but not directly under his leadership and control, the Tories contested the Whig claim to represent the interests of the nation and to defend the Protestant religion.

The activity of the political parties, which sharply divided every section of the population (including many of those outside the 'political nation' – that is without rights as electors or qualifications to hold office), is one of the distinctive characteristics of late Stuart Britain.[11] But for Charles it represented a development that he saw as incompatible with royal authority and effective government. His objective during the years after 1681 was to eliminate all forms of independent and unofficial political activity, Tory as well as Whig. Charles did not intend to call another parliament. He reimposed control over publishing and discouraged addresses (however loyal) and representations of a political character. By 1685 he had largely succeeded: politics in a popular sense no longer existed. Charles had had no choice but to act as a royal, although never as a party, politician, but he regarded the abnormal conditions of the years 1679–81 that made him undertake this form of activity as not only a threat to monarchical authority but likely to provoke another rebellion.

It can be seen, then, that conditions affecting government differed very significantly from one phase of the reign to another, and that Charles's attitudes and the extent of his involvement in administration and politics varied as considerably. For lengthy periods he gave the appearance of authorizing a single minister to direct the administration, deal with parlia-ment and even formulate policies; although attending council regularly and keeping himself well informed, Charles allowed Clarendon (1660–7), Buckingham (1667–8) and Danby (1673–9) to assume day to day control over affairs. But during these ministries Charles deliberately generated uncertainty about his intentions, by frequently consulting men outside the ministry and by considering alternative policies from those being officially pursued. At other times Charles deliberately employed composite min-istries, in which no individual enjoyed supremacy. The first, the so-called Cabal of 1668–73, had a relatively fixed composition, but the mixed administrations of 1679–85 were constantly changing in membership.

No minister at any time could be confident that he possessed the king's full confidence or support. Daily he could see the king talking with rivals and aspirants for office at Court. No minister had the ability to control access to the king. All suspected the existence of secret discussions, by the back-stairs controlled by Chiffinch, about changes in policies and appointments.[12] A minister who ran into serious difficulties, like Clifford in 1673 and Danby in 1678–9, could not expect Charles to make serious efforts to retain him in office. At best he might get a pardon and compensation, at worst he could be thrown to the wolves, as Clarendon was in 1667, lucky to escape with his life into exile.

During composite ministries Charles systematically encouraged and exploited tensions between rivals – Arlington and Buckingham in 1668–73, Hyde and Halifax in 1680–4 – so as to reserve ultimate control for himself. Nor did he commit himself to continuing to support policies that he had allowed or even encouraged a minister to initiate. Buckingham was pursuing Charles's own wishes, privately agreed between them, when he introduced proposals for religious toleration in 1668. When the Commons rejected them, the king not only acquiesced but accepted instead the opposite policy of new repressive religious statutes that parliament demanded. In 1668 Arlington was permitted to negotiate the Triple Alliance, committing Charles, in alliance with the Dutch (and Sweden), to preserve the Spanish Netherlands from French aggression, at the same time as Charles was deciding on a totally contrary policy, of a secret alliance with France to destroy the Dutch republic. Charles engaged in another set of contradictory diplomatic policies in 1678, when he allowed Danby to negotiate alliances with the Dutch, and raise an army, for an immediate war against France, while he simultaneously negotiated with Louis for subsidies, in return for an undertaking not to enter the war. He continued until the end of his life to puzzle and confuse ministers and servants as well as opponents of the Court. When he died, Charles was in the middle of another labyrinthine manœuvre: having just given associates of his brother James important ministerial offices, he strengthened the alternative Court faction headed by Halifax, and began clandestine negotiations with Monmouth for his return to England – at the very moment when James was about to depart for Scotland.

It is this simultaneous pursuit of contradictory lines of policy on so many occasions that makes it difficult to say categorically whether Charles actually attempted to make himself absolute, or authorized or encouraged his ministers to make the attempt.[13] Certainly the ministers whom he encouraged to attack and ruin Clarendon gave him undertakings that they would greatly increase his effective authority. However, their new policies ran into insuperable opposition in parliament, where a majority of peers and MPs attached to traditional principles provided a far more formidable barrier to the realization of Charles's wishes than Clarendon had ever done. The policies of the so-called Cabal ministry, which came nearest to constituting an attempt to make Charles absolute, never got beyond the first stages. They were essentially an attempt to release the king from dependence on a parliament dominated by a majority who proclaimed their own loyalty to the Crown but expected Charles in turn to be loyal to their traditional constitutionalist and Anglican principles.

The ministers of 1668–73 certainly hoped to make it possible for Charles to rule without parliament, as all his predecessors had done. Religious toleration was established through use of the suspending power. The dismissal of JPs who refused to accept its legality would produce an obedient local administration. Large-scale expansion of the army would deter popular protests. Use of the dispensing power enabled the king to get round legal restrictions. French subsidies and an indemnity from the defeated Dutch, together with taxes voted for the war, would give the king financial independence, and the dissolution of parliament would make it practicable to dismantle much of the existing patronage system, which was largely geared to parliamentary management.

The failure of the Dutch War, and William's propaganda offensive, forced the abandonment of these policies, but they never progressed further than the preliminaries necessary for the establishment of absolutist methods of government. Even a victorious war would have meant the end of French subsidies and the eventual expiration of the extraordinary taxes voted in 1670–1. How would Charles then finance a greatly expanded army? He could expand his army at short notice by recalling his subjects who served in continental armies, and this would make it easy to disband, but where was he to obtain the bureaucrats (who before 1640 were trained in the prerogative courts) to man a professional administration at the centre and in the localities? There is little evidence that such questions were even formulated, or seriously considered, by the ministers (above all Clifford, who most exactly expressed James's views) who had promised to increase royal authority.

Yet most of Charles's subjects, influenced by lethally effective Dutch propaganda in 1673–4, firmly believed that the infamous 'Cabal' ministry had planned to 'establish' both popery and arbitrary government.[14] Public disquiet became so strong that Charles had to abandon both policies and ministers, and turn to Danby, who promised to return to conservative principles and policies acceptable to the Anglican majority in parliament – from which the previous ministers had tried to release the king. It is not surprising, then, that Charles never associated himself completely with Danby and with policies that the former had had to accept only because of the failure of alternatives that he undoubtedly preferred.

However, after the collapse of Danby's position in 1679 the king had no choice but to associate himself totally with conservative principles. Coming under intense and continuous Whig pressure to accept the Exclusion Bill that would put James out of the succession, Charles never flinched in his determination to defeat what he saw as an attempt to reduce the Crown to a permanent state of dependence on parliament. But he had to recognize that this determination was doubted by most of his subjects. He had acquired a damaging reputation for inconstancy by frequently giving way under pressure, enabling Shaftesbury to argue that eventually Whig unity and determination would force Charles to concede passage of Exclusion. The Whigs also used the king's recent association with Danby, his pro-French sympathies and his support of Lauderdale's repressive methods in Scotland, to advance the claim that they were defending the nation's constitutional liberties as well as the Protestant religion. Consequently it was incumbent on Charles to prove to his potential supporters that he was struggling not just to defend the rights of James or the Crown but to uphold the integrity of the constitution.

Charles had to prove the interdependence of the lawful rights of the monarchy and those of the nation. He and the Tories argued that the passage of an Exclusion Act would necessarily be followed by further legislation transferring prerogative powers to parliament and unbalancing the constitution. Many of the Whigs' principal arguments were turned against themselves: the standing army would need to be expanded in order to enforce Exclusion, not least because an Act passed at Westminster would have no force in Scotland. In the later stages of the crisis, Charles, in his declaration issued after the dissolution of the Oxford Parliament, made the intransigence of the Whig leaders the basis for warnings either that they were disregarding the consequent risk of civil war or, in the charges levelled at Shaftesbury, that they were actually preparing another rebellion.[15]

The Exclusion crisis clarified the question of the king's political objectives. Whatever these had been in the years after 1667, he was content, after defeating the Whigs, to have survived their challenge and to have preserved intact the prerogative powers that belonged to the Crown. In his last years Charles governed strictly, and at times – as in 1683, when the Rye House conspiracy was uncovered – with considerable severity, but he did not attempt to increase his royal authority beyond its legal limits. He ignored the law in only one important respect. The Triennial Act, which the Cavalier Parliament had emasculated by removing the sanctions imposed by the Act of 1641, still required a general election to be held in 1684.[16] Charles ignored it, but otherwise he was satisfied by the disappearance of the pressures which he had experienced in various forms since 1649. At long last Charles became the master of all his subjects. He no longer needed to seek their assistance; instead he could now demand obedience. In his last three years Charles treated his ministers as pawns. Subjects who broke the law – dissenters generally, Whig plotters in 1683 – suffered severely in exemplary fashion. All forms of independent political activity – even by Tories – virtually ceased. The Whig hold on the government of the City of London was destroyed, and the forfeiture of its charter reduced the City to a state of dependence.

These last years of ease and security represented a hard-won achievement, and Charles paid a heavy personal price in terms of character and personality. Although his early and bitter experiences had led Charles to trust no one, but instead to rely on his own skill as a practitioner of the techniques of machiavellian statecraft, his surface amiability and apparently careless hedonism as a young man had concealed his ruthlessness, cynicism and opportunism. In his last years, and as a result of the strains imposed upon him during the struggle against the Whigs, Charles discarded his disguise of *faux bonhomme* to reveal (as can be seen in his later portraits) a cold streak of cruelty and indifference. He allowed Catholic priests whom he knew to be innocent of plotting to be executed, because it suited his political purposes. He was undoubtedly disappointed by the failure in 1681 to obtain Shaftesbury's conviction and execution, but in compensation he had Russell executed in 1683 outside his own front door, and put Armstrong to death in 1684 without trial.[17] Similarly Charles behaved in increasingly dominant and masterful fashion towards his ministers and courtiers. He humiliated Monmouth when the latter refused to submit unconditionally, but seems to have thought in his last weeks of bringing him back so as to make James feel insecure. Charles deliberately maintained tension between the rivals Rochester and Halifax, before finally punishing the former for his presumption (in aiming to become chief minister) by proposing to exile him to Dublin, where he would have found himself in an artfully contrived false position with insufficient powers to check a pro-Catholic line of policy.

There is little evidence to suggest that Charles ever 'loved' or even respected his people. He established a unique relationship with them in 1660, by pardoning all of them, with the exception of the handful of regicides. But Charles never trusted them, and all his experiences after 1660 confirmed and strengthened his determination to try to rule without having to obtain their consent for his acts of state. In the last phase of his reign Charles asserted his authority; apart from the Whig hard core, the nation acquiesced. Charles owed his final success to the skill with which he used two decisive advantages during the Exclusion crisis of 1679–81, a crisis comparable in intensity with those which destroyed his father and his brother James. The king's prerogative vested in him the power to call, prorogue and dissolve parliament, but in practical political terms everything depended on the timing of the exercise of this power. In the early stages of the crisis Charles could do no more than hold back the tide of Whig power, but in 1681 the surprise dissolution at Oxford proved to be the turning point. Moreover by then Charles was able to persuade the nation that Whig intransigence endangered peace and stability. In the last stages of the crisis fear of another civil war, with all its incalculable consequences for everyone, effaced the popular fears of popery and absolute government that the Whigs had exploited.

2 Charles in Scotland, and in Exile

Born on 29 May 1630, Charles was just too young to be marked for life by his experiences during the Civil War, in which he did not play an active part. Even when Charles I sent him to the west country as nominal general, with a council of his own, the real purpose was to ensure the prince's safety. With no real authority he presided over a series of reverses and retreats until he was forced to leave England, first for the Scillies, then in April 1646 for Jersey. He could not control his divided and demoralized generals and council, and had no opportunity of developing independent powers of judgement and decision.[1] His final move from Jersey to Paris (June 1646), which meant quitting his father's dominions for a foreign kingdom, was not militarily necessary. It was decided for him by those councillors who were linked to the queen, his mother, who had established herself in France as the king's overseas representative. Edward Hyde, later Earl of Clarendon and Charles's principal adviser after 1651, vainly opposed the move.[2]

Charles stagnated during the two years that he remained in Paris. The queen's main concern was to attempt to make use of him in order to establish closer links with the French Court, both in the long term and so as to obtain additional immediate aid. She tried to marry him to her niece, Mademoiselle, daughter of her brother Gaston. She did not consult her son on major matters of policy, and did not involve him in the secret and complex negotiations that enabled Charles I to make an attempt to recover his kingdoms by force, and that provoked the second Civil War.[3] The prince's first opportunity for action came in May 1648, when Hamilton, the leader of the Scottish party that now declared for the king (the Engagers), invited him to accompany the army that was about to invade England. Charles and his mother were willing, but the queen's associations with those in the French Court who opposed Mazarin led the all-powerful minister to delay giving the prince permission to leave France.[4] This proved to be fortunate. The Scottish invasion was bitterly resented in northern England, and Hamilton attracted little support even from former royalist activists. Cromwell destroyed his army in Lancashire (17–20 August); five days later Hamilton surrendered.

Charles left France in early July. When he arrived at The Hague he found that by accident he was now the right man in the right place. He was faced by an extremely fluid situation which was constantly changing, and which necessitated decisive action on his part. The royalist rebellion in Kent had virtually collapsed. Fairfax was besieging the main royalist army in Colchester. On the other hand half the English fleet had mutinied and now crossed to the Dutch coast. Ironically their action had been sparked off by an imposter, Cornelius Evans, claiming to be Charles. It was immediately clear that offensive action by the fleet represented the royalist last chance of saving their cause from total collapse. Charles assumed personal command, displacing (and offending) his 15-year-old brother James, who had arrived before him, and quickly displayed his ability to use his judgement and make crucial decisions.[5] For the first time in his life Charles had personal authority, but he soon found himself encountering a succession of intractable difficulties which foiled all his vigorous efforts. Charles deployed the fleet to establish a blockade of the Thames estuary, stopping the movement of parliamentarian transports and supply vessels. However, he decided to allow merchant ships to pass freely in and out. This was a very difficult decision to take. An economic blockade could only have very long-term effects, and the alienation of mercantile interests that it would infallibly cause would rule out any chance of London declaring for the king. He chose not to seize and confiscate ships and cargoes but instead to levy quite modest payments in return for allowing free passage, money which he used to finance provisions and furnish pay for officers and seamen. This politically prudent behaviour infuriated the latter. They felt cheated of the prize money which they had expected from wholesale seizures of 'rebel' ships.[6]

Charles encountered a series of problems in dealing with his senior commanders, Rupert, Batten and Willoughby, who constantly quarrelled with each other and were also at odds with his councillors Colepeper and Long.[7] Lacking naval expertise, Charles necessarily relied on them to enable him to force an engagement with Warwick, the parliamentarian admiral, before the latter could concentrate his scattered ships, but they failed him, and bad weather also frustrated Charles's eagerness to attack. In the second week of August political complications increased his problems. Lauderdale arrived as negotiator for Hamilton and the Engagers, with a demand that Charles should sail the fleet to the Firth of Forth to co-operate with the Scots. His real but concealed arguments were political rather than military. Hamilton had invaded England by the west-coast route, so the fleet could not assist him directly. The Engagers wanted the prince to come to Scotland under their patronage in order to strengthen themselves in relation to the intransigent Covenanting party led by Argyll, who had refused to support them. Earlier the queen had not been prepared to accept the Engagers' terms, especially on religious issues, but the precariousness of their position in Scotland made Lauderdale insist on stringent conditions. Charles must discard Rupert and other named royalists, and replace Anglican clergy by Presbyterians. The fall of Colchester, and Warwick's success in concentrating his fleet, removed all chance of a decisive victory in the south-east, but Charles hesitated before accepting all Lauderdale's conditions. Very much against his father's wishes, as he must have known, he was prepared to conform personally to Presbyterianism in Scotland, but he could not persuade his officers and seamen to move north.[8]

The negotiation was in any case doomed by Hamilton's defeat, but for Charles it was an educative experience: Lauderdale's demands were to be reiterated in more stringent form by the Covenanters in 1650. The fleet had to return to the Maas, having accomplished nothing. Lack of money for pay and provisions lowered morale.[9] At this critical moment Charles fell seriously ill with smallpox, and while he was absent Warwick recovered several ships, and a few returned to him voluntarily. The remainder of the royalist fleet eventually escaped to Ireland, and thereafter engaged in a nomadic privateering existence, first in European and then in Caribbean waters.[10] Charles was left stranded in Holland, a helpless observer of the dramatic developments in England. He joined with his brother-in-law, William II the stadtholder, in a series of futile attempts to save Charles I, writing intercessory letters to Fairfax and the army council. He asked Louis XIV to intervene. He and William persuaded the States General to send a special mission to England, but it arrived too late.[11]

On 4/14 February 1649 Charles learnt of his father's execution. He was now king in constitutional law, despite the abolition of the monarchy by a parliamentary ordinance. He learnt that, without prompting, Argyll and the Covenanting party had proclaimed him King of Scotland. On the question of reciprocal recognition Charles now had to make a crucial decision. The king's alliance with the Engagers had divided the ministers whom Charles inherited from his father, with the so-called Presbyterians (led by Colepeper) and the queen's associates in combination against Hyde and Nicholas.[12] The main problem – which continued to underlie all differences among the exiles until 1660 – concerned the extent to which it was legitimate to offer concessions in return for support. During the summer of 1649, which he spent in Paris, Charles also had to demonstrate his independence from his mother, who tried to retain a dominant influence by claiming that she alone could obtain significant aid from the French Court.

The total defeat of the English royalists during the second Civil War, and the severe repression which followed, meant that Charles had to look initially to Ireland and Scotland. He immediately discovered that there was no question of a united effort by the two kingdoms. One of the major demands of the Scottish Covenanters was for Charles formally to repudiate all engagements made with the Catholic parties in Ireland by Ormonde.[13] This meant that Charles had to choose between Ireland and Scotland as the base that he would use in his attempt to recover England. At first the former seemed to offer the more favourable possibilities, since Ormonde had already succeeded in constructing a (fragile) union of all the contending factions. This achievement led the papal nuncio Rinuccini, from the king's point of view a major disruptive influence with whom it would be virtually impossible to negotiate, to depart in February. Forces loyal to the Rump held only Dublin and part of the Pale. Consequently Charles moved to Jersey in September, intending to sail to Ireland.[14] By then the royalist cause in Ireland was already largely lost. In August Ormonde suffered a heavy defeat at Rathmines. In September Cromwell arrived with reinforcements. His capture of Drogheda, followed by the celebrated and never-forgotten massacre, marked the start of an irresistible offensive which quickly broke the back of Irish resistance. It was purposeless for Charles to join his increasingly desperate adherents, although they prolonged their defensive struggles until 1651.

Ormonde had united the Irish factions, but it would be for Charles himself to try to reconcile the equally bitter political, personal and ideological enmities that divided the Scots. Three mutually hostile parties opened negotiations with him. After their defeat at Preston and Hamilton's execution (March 1649) the party of the Engagers, nominally led by the new Duke of Hamilton but actually directed by Lauderdale who had struck up a good relationship with Charles, was the least important for the time being, but could not be ignored since it represented the preponderance of the Scottish nobility. A purer form of royalism was personified by Montrose, the charismatic but impetuous Cavalier, who volunteered to initiate action in the Highlands at the earliest possible date. In terms of personality, courage and self-sacrifice Montrose is probably the most romantic of all seventeenth-century British characters, so that it is difficult to see him as contemporaries did. By 1649 Montrose had largely isolated himself. Nearly all politically active Scots – clergy, Covenanters and Engagers – hated him for having ignited a bloody civil war in Scotland in 1644, and for embodying in his army a formidable contingent of papists from the Western Isles and Ulster. Lowland Scots loathed and feared him: together with his legendary Irish lieutenant, Alasdair MacColla, Montrose was the first leader to realize the military potential of the Highland clans – which was to function as a kind of joker card in British politics until Culloden in 1746.[15] Montrose's campaigns in 1644–5 had been marked by savage brutality, indiscriminate plundering and frequent massacres – such as that at Aberdeen which was comparable in ferocity with Cromwell's at Drogheda.

By commissioning Montrose, Charles gave his authority to a war chief whose primary intention was to renew hostilities as soon as possible, but not against the Rump and the regicides in London. Montrose would continue his blood feud against Argyll and the Covenanting party who, after all, had proclaimed Charles King of Scotland in February. After making Montrose lieutenant-general in May, Charles gave him an undertaking that he would be consulted before any major decision was reached in Scottish affairs.[16] Charles did this before sending Montrose off as ambassador extraordinary to the northern European states in July. The object of this mission was to raise the men and money with which an invasion could be launched.[17] At the same time Hyde and Cottington were sent to Madrid, and later Colepeper went to Moscow, on similar but more general fund-raising missions.[18] In September Charles urged Montrose to 'go on vigorously, and with your wonted courage and care, in the prosecution of those trusts I have committed to you'. The timing and strength of his invasion would depend on his success in northern Europe.

However, the rest of Charles's letter reveals the fatal ambiguity in his Scottish policy that was to lead Montrose to disaster and death, and reduce Charles personally to abject humiliation. Charles asked Montrose

> not to be startled with any reports you may hear, as if I were otherwise inclined to the presbyterians than when I left you. I assure you I am still upon the same principles I was, and depend as much as ever upon your undertaking and endeavours for my service.[19]

What Charles refrained from explaining explicitly was how Montrose's activities fitted into his general political strategy. Charles calculated that Montrose's preparations for an invasion of Scotland would at the least extract more reasonable terms from Argyll and the dominant Covenanting party. Alternatively it was possible that Montrose would repeat the sweeping victories of 1644-5, establishing himself so strongly that Argyll would have to come to terms with Charles in return for the latter restraining Montrose and his partisans. Charles was attempting an almost impossible task, to make use of two parties whose mutual enmity was based not only on strong ideological differences but also on primitive blood feuds. The leaders engaged in mutual denunciation as the king initiated this policy: in March 1649 the Covenanters denounced Montrose (or James Graham, as they called him) as the 'most bloody murderer in our nation'; he replied in May condemning them as traitors who had sold their king to the English regicides.[20]

Charles was deliberately and cynically using Montrose (who, of course, would be running incalculable personal risks) to soften the terms which Argyll's commissioners demanded of him in March 1649. Conscious of both their own rectitude and their overwhelmingly strong bargaining position, the Scottish parliament instructed these commissioners to require Charles to take the Covenant and impose it on all his subjects, to recognize the parliament and accept all its political and religious acts, to banish all 'malignants' (Engagers as well as Montrose's party) and to repudiate Ormonde's treaties with the Irish Catholics.[21] By offering only minor concessions Charles effectively rejected this first formal approach, but he continued to negotiate with Argyll by correspondence, even though the Scottish parliament explicitly refused to abate the demands which Charles had refused to accept.[22] An emissary (Libberton) carrying this message had to chase across Europe after Charles, whom he caught up with in Jersey (January 1650). Despite the harshness of the parliament's attitude, Charles now decided to open serious negotiations with the Scots even though their intransigence showed him that he would have to make important concessions.[23]

Charles's decision to renew negotiations was a personal one. His council was divided on the issue. His courtiers showed themselves extremely hostile, and actually threatened to lynch Libberton. But the impending collapse of royalist resistance in Ireland seemed to leave him with no alternative. The queen mother and her group among his councillors added their influence in favour of negotiations.[24] But the prospect of the Covenanters' intransigence made it all the more important for Montrose to weaken their strength by proceeding with his invasion. Faithful to his promise to consult him, Charles informed Montrose, in a crucial letter of 12 January 1650, that he intended to open negotiations with Argyll's party at Breda in the United Provinces on 15 March.[25] The tone of this letter is understandably defensive. Charles explained his decision by assuring Montrose that it was only his preparations that had induced the Covenanters to agree to reopen negotiations. In fact, as Charles must have known from Libberton, the Scottish parliament was still deeply divided on whether to do so, and news of Montrose's recruiting and fund-raising mission had actually strengthened the intransigents. In this letter Charles told Montrose:

> your vigorous proceeding will be a good means to bring them to such a moderation in the said Treaty as probably may produce an agreement, and a present union of that whole nation in our service.

Charles must have known that these last words were pure moonshine. He knew that Montrose's objective was not union but the destruction of his own personal enemies, justified by the claim that he was revenging the death of Charles I, and the massacre or judicial murder of his own adherents by the Covenanters in 1645.[26]

This letter of 12 January from Jersey is crucial because it illuminates Charles's intentions, but it had no effect on Montrose's actions. It took a long time to reach him in Orkney on 23 March. By then his preparations had reached an advanced stage, and the Breda negotiations had begun (a little late, on 19 March). The king added personal assurances, repeating his pledge that he would never consent to anything that would prejudice Montrose, and as a symbol sent him the Order of the Garter – although he did not add the information that he had conferred another Garter on Montrose's other, lesser, enemy Hamilton.[27] Charles also sent Montrose the Scottish parliament's address inviting the king to return together with his general reply, that is the preliminaries to the Breda negotiations, with a request for his comments. The long delay before the letter reached Montrose meant that his comments arrived too late to have any effect: their tenor was to warn Charles against trusting Argyll.[28] The real reply came in the urgency with which Montrose pushed on with his invasion. On 14 April he landed in Caithness, on the 27th his army was destroyed at Carbisdale and on 4 May the Scottish army took him into custody.[29]

Knowing nothing of these developments Charles agreed on 1/11 May to accept the Scottish parliament's invitation to return, although he declined to accept all the demands – specifically rejecting a repudiation of Ormonde's Irish treaties and refusing to make a personal subscription to the Covenant – nor did the majority of the Scottish commissioners insist on his doing so.[30] They were not being 'moderate' in this, but calculating. They reckoned that once Charles was in their hands in Scotland he would no longer be receiving advice from malignants and could be forced to accept the full demands. On his side Charles seems to have hoped that after his arrival in Scotland he could win for himself an improved bargaining position. Obviously he would be greatly helped if by then Montrose had succeeded in raising the Highlands, but there was no information about the progress of his campaign. Charles therefore sent Sir William Fleming to Edinburgh with letters, dated 3 and 5 May, to cover an extraordinary wide range of contingencies. In the letter intended for publication Charles instructed Montrose to disband his forces, and to withdraw with them from Scotland. The king could not ensure that an armistice would be granted for this purpose, but on 8/18 May he wrote informing the Scottish parliament of his instructions. He asked that Montrose and his men should be given leave to depart, after laying down their arms – that is, when they would be completely at the mercy of their implacable enemies.[31]

Charles struck a very different note in two private letters to Montrose. In the first he explained that Montrose would have to go into exile until Charles succeeded in making his peace for him in Scotland, when he could hope for the restoration of his honours and estates. Then, using Scotland as a secure base, Charles would launch the decisive invasion of England, with Montrose as one of his commanders. The second letter had a less confident tone, Charles stating that his 'real intention' was to provide for 'your interests and restitution', although this might not be immediately possible. However, Charles had to add instructions to Fleming to cover a number of possible developments. By the time of his arrival Montrose might have established himself in a strong position: if so, whatever

Charles said in public, he was not to disband – instead all royalists should be directed to rally to him. Similarly, if Fleming found that royalists opposed the order to Montrose to lay down his arms, the latter was to keep his army intact. Another adverse possibility was that the Scottish parliament would not ratify the Breda treaty, because Charles had not accepted all its demands: in this eventuality Montrose was to remain in arms, clearly for the purpose of exerting more pressure.

All these possibilities were overtaken by events. Fleming reached Edinburgh before Montrose arrived as a prisoner.[32] Argyll and the Covenanting party now knew that Charles was concerned to preserve Montrose's life. Argyll chose not to intervene. He had many hundreds of dead Campbells to avenge. But the general political hostility to Montrose was so intense that even Argyll probably could not have saved his life. Recognizing this hostility Argyll exploited public sentiment. He informed parliament that he knew that Charles was not sorry James Graham (that is, Montrose) had been defeated in an invasion undertaken without, indeed contrary to, his commands.[33] As a face-saver Argyll did not vote personally for Montrose's condemnation, which preceded his execution on 21 May. After this devious performance it is not surprising that Charles, as well as the Scottish royalists, ruthlessly engineered Argyll's execution in 1661 in another round of judicial feuding and blood-letting.[34]

Montrose's death, which many historians have described as a betrayal, remains a slur on Charles II's reputation, like that of Strafford on Charles I's. However, the whole enterprise was doomed from the start by miscalculations on Montrose's as well as Charles's part. The former grossly mistook the likely response to his invasion of the northern clans, let alone the general reaction of the Scottish people. The king used Montrose to try to strengthen a desperately weak bargaining position in negotiations with the Covenanting party. The failure of the invasion meant that Charles was left with no option but to stick to the agreement that he had already concluded with those who now put Montrose to death. The king's conduct was certainly not moral or honourable, but in his state of weakness he had no realistic alternative course of action.

The Breda agreement with the Covenanting party was to lead to an even greater disaster. From the start several of Charles's council members vehemently opposed it on principle. For men like Hyde and Nicholas there were two fundamental objections in principle. First, a promise to establish a Presbyterian system of church government as a replacement for the old Anglican order of episcopacy, not only in Scotland but in England and Ireland as well, contravened the divine order and must weaken the institution of monarchy. Secondly, they believed that for Charles to place himself in the hands of a party that had been formed as an act of rebellion against Charles I was politically unwise: it would disgust and antagonize the king's true servants and followers.[35] However in the spring of 1650 no practical alternative course of action existed. If the Scots were repulsed, the exiled royalists would have to continue to live in a state of demoralizing and defeatist inaction. Charles had little money, no army units at his disposal (unlike in the late 1650s when he disposed of a miniature army in the Spanish Netherlands) and no base other than Jersey. His partisans in England could not attempt any major action without external assistance. Irish resistance to Cromwell was crumbling. The war against Spain still absorbed Mazarin and the French government. Even William II could no longer afford to subsidize Charles, and in June 1649 had had to ask him politely to leave the United Provinces (for France and then Jersey), because the States General feared that harbouring Charles would incite the Rump to acts of hostility against Dutch commercial interests.[36]

There was an almost unanswerable case for accepting the conditional offer made by the Scottish parliament in terms of practical politics, if not in terms of principle. No European sovereign or state would take Charles seriously, or give him significant aid, unless he seized this opportunity of establishing himself in Scotland. Charles ensured a favourable decision by loading his council with new members who supported an agreement with the Scots – Buckingham, the new Duke of Hamilton, and Newcastle, Charles's old governor and perhaps the most celebrated equestrian in Europe, but no politician.[37] These recruits reinforced the case against being over-scrupulous, of persisting with the disastrous axiom of 'never allowing any expedient conducing to our recovery lawful until it be ineffective'.[38]

The leading advocate of a deal with the Scots, and in 1649–50 the most potent influence on Charles, was his hospitable brother-in-law William II, a tough, aggressive and unscrupulous prince who had great ambitions of his own. William made particular use of the example of Charles's grandfather, Henri IV, who had gained his throne by skilful manœuvring, large-scale concessions and a politic religious conversion, but had then been able to rule as absolute sovereign. Moreover there was a basic compatibility, indeed complementarity, between William's own ambitions and Charles's plans to recover his kingdoms.[39] William aimed to free himself from the constraints of the Dutch federal constitution in order to establish a hereditary monarchy. In the immediate future he intended to re-establish the alliance with France which his republican opponents had broken by forcing a separate peace with Spain at Munster in 1648. Allied to France he would renew an aggressive war against Spain so as to conquer and partition the southern provinces with a greatly enlarged army, which he would also use as an instrument in domestic politics to coerce the principal cities in Holland. Consequently, if Charles could hold out in Scotland – and that kingdom had never been conquered by the English since Edward I's reign – he could expect aid from both William and France.

The character of the Orangist party enhanced William's value as an intermediary between Charles and the Scots. The clergy of the Dutch Reformed Church, who acted as the party's spokesmen in the cities, thoroughly approved of an agreement between Charles and their fellow Calvinists of the Scottish kirk.[40] The Scottish commissioners at Breda (wrongly) trusted William as their champion, not suspecting that he was giving Charles brutally machiavellian advice throughout the negotiations. William urged Charles to make all the concessions required of him in return for Scottish assistance to recover England, but, by slipping in a condition that religious changes in England would need the consent of an English parliament, to preserve his future freedom of action. On occasions William went further, advising Charles to concede whatever was demanded of him, since he could repudiate promises made under duress once he regained his throne.[41] Wisely Charles realized that such a course of action would give the impression of abject weakness: during the negotiations he refused to repudiate Ormonde's treaties with the Catholic Irish, and he declined to subscribe to the Covenant personally. The commissioners did not insist, but the Scottish parliament expressed extreme dissatisfaction. After Charles sailed for Scotland he was met by emissaries, off Heligoland, with new demands which he had little option but to accept (11/21 June), and when his ship arrived off the Spey, in the Moray firth, he had to sign the National Covenant and the Solemn League and Covenant.[42]

Soon after his arrival in Scotland Charles had to discard all the Scots who accompanied him, and his English entourage with the exception of Wilmot and Buckingham. For his first few weeks the king was kept isolated and allowed no independent or active part in public affairs. Secluded in a miniature Court at the palace of Falkland, in rural Fife, with Argyll's son Lorne as captain of his bodyguard and virtually his custodian, Charles was not permitted to attend the governing council.[43] When on 29 July he went unexpectedly to Leith, where he received an enthusiastic reception from much of the army and many people from the capital, the committee of estates ordered him to leave for Dunfermline.[44] These early experiences left a lasting mark. Later in life Charles often declared in consistently forceful terms that he would never consent to become a Doge of Venice, a nominal or figurehead ruler, which was what he had been during his first months in Scotland in 1650.

Charles's Scottish masters quickly found themselves in critical difficulties. The Rump reacted with phenomenal speed to their treaty with Charles, Cromwell leading an army into Scotland on 22 July. The extreme Covenanters, who were numerous in the west of Scotland and influential on the committee of estates, remained suspicious of Charles's sincerity and had no wish to find themselves involved in a war against the English republic.[45] To guard against the very real danger of its party disintegrating, the committee had to take drastic action. It purged the army of all suspected Engagers and Cavaliers, which did not improve its military efficiency. On 16 August it forced Charles to authenticate a declaration, issued at Dunfermline. In this extraordinary humiliating statement Charles humbled himself for his father's perverse opposition to the Solemn League and Covenant, and the bloodshed he had caused, and for his mother's papist idolatry. Charles expressed sorrow for his own sins, stated his abhorrence of popery, prelacy and superstition, and undertook to employ only orthodox Covenanters.[46] Again this enforced public confession revealed his abjectly weak position. It marked Charles for life. He developed an enduring hatred of presbyterianism, and especially for the moral tyranny exercised by the Presbyterian clergy. More generally these early experiences bred in Charles a lasting aversion to Scotland. He never revisited it after 1651. After his restoration Charles was to give full and unquestioning support to any individual minister or soldier who showed the necessary qualities of determination, ruthlessness and indifference to popular sentiment in tackling the problems involved in ruling Scotland. Charles as king ignored protests against the personal corruption or the cruelty that his ministers displayed. He endorsed the methods employed by brutal soldiers like Dalziel and Claverhouse, and by Lauderdale and his brother James, because they worked, and because those who suffered at their hands were the same kind of people as his tormentors of 1650.

Cromwell's defeat of the Scottish army at Dunbar (3 September 1650) promised some relief from Covenanting domination, but Charles had not yet learnt the value of patience. A premature attempt to escape from the Covenanters' control and to rally the Cavaliers (4–6 October, an episode known as the 'Start') ended in his recapture.[47] Charles remained in a peculiarly lonely and isolated situation. His two English companions gave him no real relief: Buckingham behaved irresponsibly, trying to ingratiate himself with the various Scottish factions; Wilmot lacked political ability.[48] As a result Charles during his time in Scotland did not possess ministers or a council whom he could trust. After dominating the king in 1650, Argyll began to detach himself as his position weakened in relation to the English invaders. The committee of estates continued to act as a basically suspicious, and at times hostile, body. Charles had only one, chance, confidant to whom he could unburden himself, John King, the Anglican Dean of Tuam: otherwise he had to be on guard the whole time with all those who stood closest to him.[49]

However unpleasant at the time, these experiences gave Charles an unsurpassable education in what seventeenth-century men regarded as the most useful of all practical political arts – the ability to dissimulate, to conceal true feelings, opinions and intentions. Charles treated the murderers of Montrose as men worthy of his trust – because he was at first entirely dependent on them. He controlled his emotions when, on his initial journey south, his hosts entertained him in a house in Aberdeen which overlooked one of Montrose's severed limbs. He impassively listened to long denunciatory sermons from Covenanting clergy and followed a lifestyle acceptable to them: this bred in him a lasting desire to remain free from the control of any variety of clergy, and inoculated him against all clerical condemnation of his casual and promiscuous sexual behaviour. Above all Charles's Scottish experiences sharpened and hardened his youthful cynicism which was to become perhaps the most valuable item in his survival kit as sovereign. They confirmed his low view of human nature. He came to suspect hypocrisy and concealed self-interest in virtually all those with whom he came into regular contact. He saw that most men would keep their promises only so long as this would serve or further their interests.

After routing the Scottish army at Dunbar, Cromwell occupied Edinburgh. Although Charles and the Covenanters retained Stirling and the whole country to the north of the Forth, they were now put on the defensive, both militarily and politically. Charles's overall strategy, which had depended on his being able to consolidate his control over Scotland so as to build up forces for an invasion of England, now collapsed. He had never expected Cromwell to invade so quickly and in such force. Furthermore he could not now expect significant aid from Europe. In September William II failed in an attempted coup against the Regent stronghold of Amsterdam. On 27 October/6 November he died suddenly: although a son was born posthumously, the Orangist party collapsed in Holland. The Regent party, for whom commercial interests were paramount, took over control of Dutch policy until 1672. For the immediate future this put an end to all hopes of an alliance between Charles, the United Provinces and France, the only combination which could have effected a restoration by armed force.

Although the defeat of the Scottish army at Dunbar discredited those Covenanters (including some clergy) who had interfered in military affairs, Charles did not benefit politically. Engagers and Cavaliers had to be allowed to take up commissions in the army in order to replace casualties, but at the cost of increasing the intransigence of the Covenanting faction that controlled the committee of estates. Many of the militant clergy began to retreat into a defensive shell, concerned only to defend the particular interests of the kirk.[50] Recriminations and mistrust worsened, and the coronation of Charles at Scone (1 January 1651), which saw Argyll personally placing the crown on the king's head, increased the confusion. During the previous summer the Covenanters had intended to accompany the coronation with a constitutional declaration that would bind Charles to their service and that of the kirk. But by this stage most of the militants had come to believe that Charles was going back on all the undertakings which he had made the previous year, and that his bad faith was such that there was no point in trying to impose new conditions.[51]

As Charles succeeded in installing men whom he could trust in positions of importance the previously dominant Covenanters tended to become sullenly inactive. Their suspicions received confirmation when the Scottish Parliament rescinded the Acts of Classes, which barred all non-subscribers to the Covenants from civil offices (30 May).[52] This was accompanied by guarantees for the kirk, but an overwhelming majority of the clergy rejected these as inadequate. Quite apart from his increasingly precarious military position, Charles faced an impossible task in trying to unite the Scottish nation. Effective royal authority had not existed since 1637. The differences between the various parties and factions were too wide for him to reconcile. He faced a kirk accustomed to independence. Unlike the turbulent feudal aristocracy whom his grandfather James VI had eventually tamed, the politicians with whom Charles had to deal possessed little freedom of action. They were tied by their ideology and could not ignore the views and interests of their party followers and clerical associates. Unlike the Engagers, the chiefs of the dominant Covenanting party were not open to personal persuasion, and material inducements could not be used to ensure their co-operation.

During 1650–1 Charles encountered, in particularly acute forms, all the problems that were to make the government of Scotland difficult over the next century, and of all these the division of the country into irreconcilable parties was the most intractable. He could not achieve national unity against the English invaders or mobilize the country's sparse resources. The admission of Engagers and Cavaliers to the army, and to the committee for managing its affairs, led many Covenanters to lapse into neutrality and some to approach Cromwell, despite his association with the detestable principle and practice of religious toleration. Charles's military position steadily worsened. He could not expand the army at Stirling to the strength needed to challenge Cromwell because he lacked the food supplies and arms.[53] Standing on the defensive, he had to wait for his enemies to take an initiative. In July Lambert crossed the Forth into Fife, literally hacked to pieces a detached force that obstructed him at Inverkeithing (20 July) and enabled Cromwell to advance on Perth. This move northwards, which contemptuously ignored Charles's army at Stirling, on Cromwell's left flank, forced the king and his generals into an irrevocable military and political decision.[54] The fall of Perth (which came on 2 August) would cut Charles's supply lines. He would not be able to subsist. Either he must split his forces and retreat into the Highlands, or he could stake everything on the supreme gamble of an invasion of England.

The only rational arguments in favour of an invasion of England consisted of the hope of gaining recruits and plentiful supplies. The march south began on 31 July, but was preceded by numerous desertions. The first English city, Carlisle, refused to admit Charles. Very few royalists joined the advancing army, but everywhere the county militias turned out against Charles. After he arrived at Worcester (22 August) appeals for aid evoked virtually no response.[55] The main reason was war weariness. The vast majority of the people had resented Charles I's relighting of the fires of civil war, with widespread disruption of ordinary life, in 1648 – a year in which the harvests largely failed – and now Charles II was repeating his father's inflammatory act, but with even less chance of success. The fact that he was heading a predominantly Scottish army and responsible for the third Scottish invasion in seven years gave an excuse to the majority (even of former royalists) who wanted to remain inactive.

With an army a third the size of Cromwell's, Charles was in a hopeless military position at Worcester. His outstanding personal bravery during the battle (3 September) which led to its annihilation was tinged with fatalism. He seemed almost eager to throw away his life. By contrast, during the following weeks' travels as a fugitive, until he escaped from England on 15 October, Charles saved his own life by unfailing ingenuity, resourcefulness and common sense. His adventures during this period were of some considerable importance. There developed after 1660 a royal myth about his resilience and courage. These extraordinary experiences left a lasting impact on his personality – complementary to the more searing impressions made by his unhappy time in Scotland. Charles gained what none of his predecessors (or successors) ever obtained, a worm's eye view of life in his kingdom, an insight into everyday life in the countryside. During his travels Charles literally put himself into the hands of humble strangers, many of them poor men and women who might be tempted to betray him by the cash rewards offered for his capture. The skill of which he was later so proud, in anatomizing characters, in penetrating men's and women's intentions, in knowing whom he could trust and how far, became a matter of life or death. In everyday contact with ordinary people – innkeepers, ostlers, servants, labourers – Charles behaved naturally and easily (in a way that neither his father nor his brother James ever could). In sharp contrast to the pressures exerted on him by petitioners and claimants after 1660, the humble people who served him (with a few exceptions) did not expect rewards for their practical loyalty. It is significant that Charles who, like all seventeenth-century kings, lived in public, under close and constant observation, took so readily to life in disguise, whereas his fellow fugitive, Wilmot, thought it demeaning and restrictive for an aristocrat to behave as an ordinary person, even though it was to save his life.[56]

Probably the most eye-opening part of Charles's experiences as a fugitive consisted of the devoted assistance he received from humble Catholics, especially in the most perilous early days.[57] They passed him on from one safe house to another. They concealed him in priests' holes. Their willingness to sacrifice their lives for him convinced Charles of the essential loyalty of the English Catholic laity, and of the simple priests who ministered to them in the provinces. At Moseley he met Father Hudleston, who was to receive him into the Catholic Church in 1685: what impression this modest man made in 1651 must be a matter of speculation.

In the dreary years of apparently hopeless exile, and again after 1660, Charles frequently relived his experiences as a fugitive, telling captive audiences of bored courtiers stories about these weeks. This escape from enemies who would certainly have put him to death if they had caught him marked Charles off from his contemporaries: curiously Buckingham also escaped after Worcester, but his adventure seems to have left him unaffected, although he may have been assisted by the Leveller underground network with whom he associated later in his life. After 1660 Charles briefly considered institutionalizing one aspect of his escape, by establishing a new Order, of Knights of the Royal Oak, as recognition of flawless loyalty, but this noble project foundered amid the welter of cynicism created by the frenzied competition for places and honours.[58] All that actually survived was the ceremonial wearing of oak leaves and oak-apples on Charles's birthday, a curious piece of symbolism since the latter are not the fruit of the oak but the product of parasites.

After reaching France in October 1651 Charles found himself virtually a refugee, living from hand to mouth, with few resources and limited expectations. France was still convulsed by civil war, the Fronde of the Princes: Louis and the Court did not reoccupy Paris until October 1652. Many royalist exiles (including James) fought in Louis' army. Charles's time in France (to July 1654) marked the nadir of his fortunes, and it ended by his being politely but unmistakably expected to leave the country when Mazarin decided to explore the possibility of an understanding with the Commonwealth.[59] Charles had to move his Court to Spa, then to Köln (October), which had few advantages on account of its remoteness from England but provided a pleasant place in which to live. There he existed on whatever money he could obtain from German princes and his adherents in England. In March 1655 he moved to Middleburg in Zeeland, ready to cross to England (without any army, with few arms and little money) if the royalist underground's plans for a nationwide rising came to anything.[60] They did not. Only after Cromwell's Western Design antagonized Spain could Charles obtain significant foreign support. After negotiations in Brussels (March 1656) Charles finally established his Court at nearby Bruges, which served as his base for the next four years.

During these years of exile, 1651–8, Charles found himself an observer of events in Britain, of changes to which he and the royalists contributed little or nothing, which he usually failed to foresee and consequently had little opportunity to exploit – the expulsion of the Rump, the short-lived Nominated or Barebones Parliament and the establishment of the Protectorate. This last development operated very much to Charles's disadvantage, although royalist propagandists pretended otherwise. Cromwell provided four years of relative stability, the first since 1642. He called parliaments and tried to secure the co-operation of the gentry in local administration. European attitudes towards Cromwell, reflecting his power and prestige, cast a shadow over the king's prospects. Charles faced intractable problems during the years that Cromwell ruled. His basic need for asylum and subsistence made it necessary to solicit princes for money, and a few, notably the Duke of Neuburg, were generous within the limits of their resources.[61] But support on the scale necessary to help him recover his kingdoms could only be expected if and when he established his credibility with those who made decisions in the major states.

Charles's early failure in negotiations with the republicans who now controlled the United Provinces demonstrated the weakness of his position. His earlier friendship with William made them suspicious, and when during the war of 1652–4 the Dutch found themselves in a desperate losing situation, they rejected Charles's offers of co-operation. As a long-term inducement he offered them the Orkneys and Scillies. He asked to be permitted to establish an admiralty to co-ordinate royalist privateers, and suggested his accompanying the Dutch fleet, promising that his presence would lead English ships to repeat their defection of 1648. Charles also put (greatly exaggerated) emphasis on the likely effects of Glencairn's rising in the Highlands.[62] De Witt, the *de facto* head of the Dutch government, realized that close association with Charles would make the Commonwealth an irreconcilable enemy. War disasters exposed him to violent demagogic opposition by the Orangists (whose extremists were to lynch him in 1672), but he saw that he could not obtain peace until he guaranteed Cromwell that the Dutch would not aid the Stuarts. De Witt could not get the landward, Orangist, provinces to agree, but (with difficulty) he persuaded the states of the province of Holland to pass the Act of Seclusion (May 1654) as a complement to the peace. This excluded the house of Orange from office in the province, and so indirectly ensured that Charles would receive no aid.[63] Subsequently Charles suffered the humiliation of being banned from entering the United Provinces, even for private visits to his sister Mary, who had to cross the frontier to meet him.[64] The Dutch government continued to treat Charles coldly, despite continuing friction with England, particularly with the Rump in 1659. Only when Charles's restoration became a certainty did the States General extend hospitality to him. In May 1660 they staged magnificent feasts for his Court, and characteristically gave him handsome presents of money.[65] Charles naturally pocketed these, but showed no gratitude.

Charles had much greater reason to expect the French government to give him aid and support, so that its failure to do so came as a great disappointment. He vainly relied on the close dynastic link through his mother, a daughter of France, and on the enmity which the Rump displayed towards France. The Commonwealth navy seized French ships, and in May 1652 destroyed a French fleet carrying reinforcements to Dunkirk, which capitulated immediately afterwards to the Spaniards.[66] This disaster emphasized one major disadvantage of possible French support. Unlike the Dutch they had no fleet in the narrow seas, and no major fortified port on the Channel coast. Single ships or small squadrons might be used to carry men or arms to England, but no major invasion could be launched.

Mazarin had no intention of committing substantial resources to the royalist cause. He discovered that Spain was offering the Commonwealth an alliance that would certainly cause the collapse of the Portuguese fight for independence, and more generally tilt the balance of power to the disadvantage of France. To avert this danger he sent Antoine Bordeaux to London as his personal representative. The immediate objective was to prevent the Commonwealth intervening in the Fronde to support Condé and the rebel city of Bordeaux.[67] However, Bordeaux was to continue in England until 1660, helping to negotiate an end to hostilities, and then as an accredited diplomat to reach an understanding and finally to negotiate an alliance with Cromwell.

This remarkable demonstration of machiavellian diplomacy compelled the rejected parties, Spain and Charles, to come together in a combination of weakness. The French agreement with the Commonwealth was reached in October 1655, although it was not until March 1657 that a full offensive and defensive alliance was signed.[68] Charles had to take the initiative in negotiating with Spain, whose government tried to delay a breach with Cromwell in Europe as long as possible. Even after they got instructions from Madrid, the ministers in Brussels showed no eagerness to commit themselves to Charles, and he had to force the issue by travelling there himself, without an invitation. Two treaties were agreed in April 1656, although a formal ratification by the Madrid government did not come until 1658.[69] In return for aid to form an army in the Spanish Netherlands, and the promise of an invasion of Britain by a 6,000-strong force of Spanish troops (provided that the royalists seized and secured a port for its disembarkation), Charles undertook to assist Spain recover Portugal after his restoration, to relinquish West Indian territories occupied since 1630 and to return any conquests made by the Commonwealth.

This alliance, one of necessity not choice on both sides, had to operate under adverse circumstances. Charles encountered continuous difficulties which prejudiced him for life against Spain. The slowness and indecision of the Brussels ministers, the need for them to refer to the junto in Madrid with whom final authority rested, the exhaustion of Spanish resources, and the growing predominance of French military power meant that Spanish undertakings were belatedly and partially honoured. Among Charles's ministers only Bristol could ensure harmonious co-operation with the Spanish ministers at Brussels, but by March 1658 Charles's frustrations mounted to the point where he resolved to travel direct to Madrid to deal directly with Philip IV and Don Luis de Haro. Humiliatingly he failed to raise enough money to finance the journey.[70]

In an additional treaty Charles promised to suspend the penal laws against the Catholics until he could have them repealed. But although Spain, or even France, might use the opportunity of a treaty to further Catholic interests, Charles knew that religious considerations played a secondary role. Their attitude would be determined by interests of state, and so must his. Charles therefore gave first priority to preserving his reputation as a Protestant, because any association with Catholicism would make him unacceptable to his English and Scottish subjects. In January 1650 he remonstrated unsuccessfully with his mother against her passionate determination to bring up her youngest daughter, Henrietta, as a Catholic.[71] In 1653–4 he became anxious as she turned her attention to her youngest son, the Duke of Gloucester. With James and Ormonde he foiled her attempts (in November 1654) to have Gloucester removed to a Jesuit college so as to convert him, with the promise of an early bishopric and ultimately a cardinal's hat.[72] This was not an easy decision to take. It inevitably alienated the Pope and angered many Catholic princes, but Charles preferred to consider the favourable effect it would have on his English subjects. However he could not prevent his mother doing him considerable harm by her consistent partiality – using pensions to purchase conversions, prohibiting Anglican services in her Court and depriving Anglicans of subsistence.[73]

Nevertheless Charles needed aid wherever he could find it. The election of a new Pope (Alexander VII, April 1655) encouraged him to open somewhat delicate negotiations with the Vatican.[74] His immediate objective was money. More generally Charles hoped that the Pope would use his influence to encourage Catholic sovereigns to assist him. The negotiations proved lengthily inconclusive, but at least they did not become known publicly. The Pope refused to negotiate directly with a heretic prince and expressed his resentment at Charles's action in preventing Gloucester's conversion. He told Charles's intermediaries that support would be forthcoming only if the king fixed a date for his own conversion. In a renewed negotiation (1658) Charles unwisely employed Cardinal de Retz to approach the Vatican.[75] De Retz proposed telling Cardinal Barberini that unless the Pope gave Charles assistance the Catholics would gain nothing, but that in return for aid the king would grant them liberty, or even re-establish the Catholic religion. Charles amended the document so that it said that he had the power to suspend, but not repeal, penal laws without parliament. He added that he expected a future parliament to consent to what he proposed, provided that the Catholics had aided his restoration – a clear inducement to the Pope. This was a much more subtle form of chicanery than de Retz's. It foreshadowed the 1662 and 1672 Declarations of Indulgence, but it failed to produce papal aid, and by employing de Retz Charles confirmed Mazarin's poor opinion of his judgement. Nevertheless Charles continued to regard himself as bound in honour to fulfil the private promises which he had made to his Catholic adherents. However in public he maintained a Protestant appearance: when Bristol publicly became a Catholic, Charles dismissed him as secretary of state.[76]

After leaving France in July 1654 Charles detached himself from the policies of his mother and the Louvre party. For the next six years he relied primarily on his Anglican and constitutionalist ministers, Hyde, Ormonde and Nicholas. He accepted their argument that it would be preferable to owe his restoration to his own subjects, rather than to rely on foreign intervention or conquest. But this line involved a mass of correspondence and negotiation with both committed royalists and potential converts from the parliamentarian and Cromwellian parties. At times, discouraged by continual reverses, Hyde and his associates complained that Charles did not impose on himself an equal burden of work.[77] Hyde recognized Charles's intelligence and sharpness, but deplored his addiction to pleasure and his refusal to use his powers of judgement. In the years of hopelessness in Paris (1652–4) even the censorious Hyde realized that the forlorn Court could hardly be a centre of virtue, but after the move to Bruges (1656) he rightly protested that its reputation for immorality and irreligion were damaging the king's cause.

The Court faced virtually insuperable difficulties in animating, organizing and directing the royalist party in England.[78] The Commonwealth authorities kept all Cavaliers under close surveillance, using house searches, preventive arrests and limitations on travel and assembly. Informers infiltrated the royalist organizations. Inevitably royalist agents faced insuperable difficulties in trying to ensure nationwide risings and simultaneous timing so as to baffle the authorities. The king encountered exceptional difficulties in organizing a reliable and reasonably speedy network through which he could communicate with his agents and give them relevant and intelligible directives. From overseas he could not reconcile the frequent disputes and recriminations, distrusts and jealousies, among his agents that accompanied and contributed to their frequent reverses. He had no option but to delegate authority to the handful of leaders who volunteered to serve him. The first organized group, the Sealed Knot, came into existence in late 1653 or early 1654.

Over the next six years its leaders achieved very little; plans for nationwide risings came to nothing – apart from the one-day occupation of Salisbury in March 1655, the Knot failed to stage an open appearance by royalists under arms. Nevertheless Charles had to allow the Knot to make use of his name since its leaders had extensive family and social connections with the Cavalier aristocracy and gentry. Its avoidance of rash adventures likely to end disastrously and provoke repression also recommended its cautious leadership to the wealthy and established. Charles, however, did not honour his promise to seek the Knot's approval before authorizing action by other agents, and the Knot did little to follow his suggestion that it should try to enlist Presbyterian as well as Cavalier support.[79]

The alternative group of royalist activists (institutionalized by Charles in 1659 as the Great Trust) differed in composition and characteristics from the Knot, so widely indeed that the two proved to be incompatible, even mutually hostile.[80] Its leader John Mordaunt, significantly a younger son of a peer, can be described as an adventurer who despised the Knot for its exclusivity and inactivity. In turn the latter deplored Mordaunt's impetuosity and criticized his political judgement. These differences frequently put Charles in impossible positions. For example in February 1655 the information and advice which he received from Mordaunt flatly contradicted the warnings sent by the Knot to call off plans for a national rising because of discoveries made by the authorities. Charles had no way of knowing which was right. He had to leave the decision to the leaders in England, although they disagreed fundamentally. He refused to restrain those who were eager and prepared to rise, and he told the Knot, lamely, that success would not be likely if its members sat still and discountenanced the activists, yet he ended by saying that he was not prepared to order them into action against their own judgement.[81] This was to get the worst possible result, a miserable fiasco followed by furious recriminations.

Charles's overall political strategy made him countenance Mordaunt's attempts to stage a general rising, since the Spanish ministers would not commit themselves to an invasion unless they could be provided with evidence that the king had substantial support in England – ideally they wanted the royalists to seize a port beforehand. During the winter of 1657–8 serious plans were made for an invasion, but the Commonwealth blockade of Ostend prevented the concentration of transports, and thereafter French military pressure ruled out any diversion of Spanish troops.[82] The king also approved of Mordaunt's willingness to reach agreement with the Presbyterians in England, whereas the Knot showed themselves reluctant to forget old differences. Like Mordaunt, Charles knew that there were risks involved, particularly the possibility that the Presbyterians would demand limits on royal powers as the price of aiding his restoration.

Charles opportunistically authorized negotiations with a far more radical group – the surviving Leveller leaders. He approved discussions with Sexby and Wildman in 1655–6, with the latter and William Howard in 1656–7.[83] Although now only a fraction of their former party, the Levellers claimed to be able to bring about mutinies in the army, Cromwell's power base, and they organized a determined conspiracy to assassinate the Protector.[84] Charles probably knew nothing specific about the murder plot, although he must have known that one existed (like James II in 1696), and he would have welcomed Cromwell's violent removal. But Charles revealed his scepticism about the Levellers in general by refusing to give them the £2,000 they demanded. Nor did he take seriously the Levellers' proposals for reforms – religious toleration, abolition of tithes, limits on the king's powers. Hyde replied for him that such matters would have to be decided by a 'free' parliament – elected on the old franchises and by the old constituencies, although this was not spelt out. Privately Charles committed himself against making any reforms of a fundamental character, 'as lessening the power of the Crown and devolving an absurd power to the people'.[85]

At the other end of the political spectrum a relatively small number of Anglican clergy gave Charles devoted service as organizers, couriers and collectors of intelligence. However they did so as isolated individuals. Surprisingly those bishops who survived from before the Civil War made no real effort either to serve the king's cause or to keep some kind of church organization working. Most failed to perform such episcopal functions as examining and ordaining men who presented themselves. Their lack of concern about the danger of the episcopal succession dying out earned Hyde's displeasure.[86] For Charles the Anglican failure to organize effectively underground must have appeared in sharp contrast to the Catholic maintenance of an effective clandestine system in England since the 1570s. It is not surprising that in the years before he returned to England Charles consistently underestimated the strength and appeal of episcopal Anglicanism, and overestimated the importance of both Presbyterians and Catholics. But Hyde saved him from sharing the dismissive view of the queen and her protégés that Anglicanism had died with Charles I, and as a false church would never experience a resurrection.

Between 1656 and 1658 Charles established a government in exile in the Spanish Netherlands – a small Court with a council at Bruges, and a miniature army sponsored by Spain. In England and Scotland generally ineffective royalist networks plotted insurrection. Charles occupied a position very similar to that of James II after 1688, but with one major difference. James at St-Germain received large-scale assistance from Louis XIV, while William III fought a difficult war of attrition that placed unprecedented and almost intolerable strains on government and economy. By contrast Charles was yoked to the dwindling power of Spain, while Cromwell possessed greater prestige and wielded more power in European affairs than any previous modern ruler of Britain. Yet of course Charles was restored, whereas James was not.

Charles owed his success not to his own strength but to the mounting weakness of his opponents, the ephemeral regimes of 1658–60. While Oliver ruled and kept his army under control, all Charles's efforts to dislodge him were as ineffective and puny as the efforts of the republicans after 1660 and the Jacobites after 1688. For all his unpopularity Oliver embodied authority and stability: he could be overthrown only by civil war or foreign conquest, alternatives that were equally unacceptable to all but a few Cavalier enthusiasts. But after his death the country experienced a descent into confusion and near-anarchy. Only then could Charles expect his case and cause to be taken seriously. The preservation of his credibility as the lawful sovereign represents Charles's crucial achievement during the apparently fruitless and demoralizing years of exile before September 1658. When after Oliver's death and Richard's eclipse his subjects began very generally to turn in Charles's direction, they saw a future ruler who was Protestant not papist, who promised to govern by legal and constitutional methods, and who showed that he wanted to reunite a divided nation by undertaking to pardon all except the regicides.

3   The Restoration

It is quite remarkable how little influence Charles and his ministers had on the course of events in Britain between Oliver's death (3 September 1658) and Monck's readmission of the secluded members to the Long Parliament (21 February 1660). The king and his advisers remained spectators of a distant scene which they did not comprehend. At first they were disappointed by the ease with which Richard assumed the government, and by the months of stability that followed until April. They were then taken by surprise and baffled by the sequence of fundamental and drastic changes that occurred – Richard's eclipse, the re-establishment of the Rump (7 May), its dispersal by the army (13 October), the collapse of 'sword government' and the second return of the Rump (26 December) – and not least by the reasons for Monck's subsequent march on London. Neither the exiled king nor the royalists in England played any part in these changes. Charles constantly made new policy decisions, only to have to change them and his directives to royalists in England. He wrote appealingly to many of the men who emerged during these months with influence and potential power, promising rewards if they would serve his interests – but with no visible effect. Charles committed himself in quick succession to two alternative (and essentially contradictory) lines of policy and personal action. Sick of idleness in Bruges, he set out in July 1659 to join Booth's rising in Cheshire. Fortunately he heard of its failure just before he was to embark at Brest: he then switched both itinerary and policy, travelling to the Pyrenees, where the French and Spanish ministers were concluding peace, in an unsuccessful attempt to persuade them to intervene on his behalf.

It was not only distance, with the consequent time lag before news of developments reached Charles and his ministers, but lack of understanding of the nature of these developments that prevented Charles from exploiting changes successfully. The politics of the Rump and the army were largely unintelligible to outsiders, who consistently misunderstood the principles, motives and intentions of the men and parties who dominated the political scene in 1659–60. This applied not only to the royalist exiles but even to their agents and informants in England, whose reports often misinformed Charles so that he based policy on such mistaken beliefs as that the 1659 parliament could be used to unseat Richard;[1] that

Lambert could be bought with money and a promise that James, or even Charles, would marry his daughter;[2] that Lambert and Monck were equally matched and would engage in a bloody fight to the finish.[3] When to Charles's surprise Monck emerged as the arbiter of events, the king had no idea of what he intended, and it took a tantalizingly long time to establish direct contact with him. Nor had Charles and his agents (except the perceptive Barwick) any understanding of the critical difficulties which Monck had to surmount before he could do anything for the king.[4]

Charles's remoteness from political developments, and his misreading of their character, did not in the long term damage his cause. Like him, the overwhelming majority of the nation were equally bewildered by the puzzling and unpredictable succession of developments, in which they too had absolutely no part, and which by December 1659 threatened the country with confusion and economic depression. Ordinary people could not understand the pretensions and proclaimed principles of the small groups of political activists who competed for power and used it, when they had it, in selfish and short-sighted ways. These groups earned the well-merited contempt of an overwhelming majority in all classes and sections of society: the sour Haselrig, corrupt Scott and doctrinaire Ludlow among the Rumpers; the blatantly ambitious generals – Lambert, Fleetwood and Desborough; the radical activists among the soldiers who repeated the slogans of 1647–9 about the people's rights but lived at free quarter, looting shops and houses; visionaries, notably Vane and Milton, who argued for rule by the godly, meaning the small segments among the sects who agreed with them. The collapse of the Commonwealth was to prove to be total and irrevocable, because each one of the principal competing groups and parties in turn had the chance in 1659–60 to put its ideas and principles into practice, but in doing so failed so abysmally that each covered itself in lasting discredit. Richard's position as Protector crumbled so ignominiously that the army and the Rump did not bother to depose him: he was left to slink away from Whitehall. The doctrinaires who led the Rump ignored the lessons of 1647, 1648 and 1653, making no real attempt to establish mutual understanding with the army that restored them. The generals who seized power in October failed either to establish a civil government or to agree among themselves. In its last phase the Rump totally antagonized the governors and people of London, and by clumsily machiavellian moves tried to undermine Monck's authority over his army.

Knowing that information often reached him too late for action to be initiated, Charles wisely adopted a critical attitude to his chief agents in England. He gave support to John Mordaunt, the bravest, most active and adventurous, but appreciated the scepticism of many royalists about a 'young man transported with his trust', impatient, abrasive and self-important.[5] For Charles also had to work with the older royalist group, the Knot, even though most of its members showed themselves lethargic and defeatist, because they represented the substantial gentry.[6] Anglican clergy made more reliable informants, but some of them did the king's cause great harm by their indiscreet talk of the revenge that royalists would have on all their enemies once Charles recovered his kingdoms. Charles appreciated the vital necessity of not appearing set on revenge or political proscription of former enemies.[7] Similarly he had to disown any intention of ruling arbitrarily or of favouring the Catholics. Charles's direct personal contribution to his restoration can be described as primarily negative: by avoiding major errors he was able to emerge in 1660 as the only credible alternative to the discredited republican regimes. Yet this achievement was partly inadvertent. By the end of 1659 Charles had exhausted his repertoire of largely opportunistic tactics. His royalist partisans had never managed to stage a serious insurrection in England. The 'Presbyterians' who had done so in 1659 became understandably cautious after Booth's defeat. Charles had failed to persuade France or Spain to give him assistance on the scale needed. The small army that Charles had formed in the Spanish Netherlands since 1655 would soon have to be disbanded for lack of resources to subsist. His adherents in Scotland and Ireland had been bludgeoned into submission.

Paradoxically Charles's weakness on the eve of the Restoration contributed significantly to his return. It made him visibly dependent on the goodwill of his subjects, and initially on the combination of Monck and the Presbyterian magnates. His restoration by invitation assured Charles's subjects that they would at last return to government by a constitutional sovereign – although the king was easily able to avoid being specifically limited by constitutional restrictions as the price of restoration. In 1658–9, as in preceding years, weakness forced Charles into endless and often discreditable as well as unsuccessful opportunistic expedients. But from January to April 1660 Charles's awareness of his political weakness led him to behave very differently. He almost matched Monck in the skill with which he dissimulated and reserved his position. Disregarding the impatient advice of his agents in England to intervene directly as the Commonwealth crumbled, keeping himself out of the traps posed by belated French and Spanish offers of assistance, Charles's prudent behaviour and tactical flair during the first months of 1660 brought about his unconditional restoration. They made Monck realize that he had no alternative to recalling the king, and it ensured an almost frantic welcome for Charles from virtually every section of society.

The rising which Booth led in north-western England in July 1659 posed the first serious military threat to the Commonwealth since 1651.[8] Unlike Penruddock's futile attempt in 1655, Booth's rising received a great deal of popular support, mainly from former parliamentarians but also from former Cavaliers. For a month he controlled an extensive area, but had to remain on the defensive. Mordaunt, the principal royal agent, had prepared a nationwide rising so as to keep the council of state guessing, and prevent the army concentrating. He planned to seize a port through which men and supplies from France and the Spanish Netherlands could enter. Charles gave Mordaunt his full backing, and had no choice but to empower him to decide the timing of the insurrection. In turn Mordaunt had to go ahead once his preparations had reached an advanced stage: any delay would mean that they would become known to the council, which would order preventive arrests and searches. However Charles failed to ensure that all royalists would follow Mordaunt. The Knot leadership regarded Mordaunt's plans as rash and likely to produce disaster. Their refusal to move meant that scattered attempts at assembling forces came to nothing, leaving Booth to await Lambert's offensive.[9]

Mordaunt seriously mistimed the rising, but he was inevitably absorbed by the technical problems of organizing and co-ordinating partisans scattered over the whole country, and ignored the general political context. By July relations between the Rump and the army were rapidly deteriorating. Booth's rising had the effect of forcing them into a temporary reunion. The ease with which Lambert suppressed the rising effectively ruled out another early attempt; although Mordaunt continued to make optimistic forecasts in his letters to Charles, they carried no conviction.[10] Booth's abject failure also devalued the king's claims, to the French and Spanish ministers, that all but a wicked minority of his subjects wanted his restoration.[11]

Charles narrowly avoided becoming personally involved in the disastrous defeat of Booth. He had no direct contact with him before the rising, and Booth very carefully and deliberately refrained from mentioning the king, or the possibility of restoring him, in the declaration which he issued. His proclaimed aim anticipated that of Monck's associates in 1660, a free parliament. Booth knew that many of his Presbyterian supporters, especially the clergy, would not favour an unconditional restoration, whereas the Cavaliers, whom he also hoped to attract, would object to conditions yet could read into the demand for a free parliament the certainty that it would lead to a restoration. Charles's unexpected arrival in Cheshire would have provoked divisions, but he decided to risk his life by attempting to join Booth when he heard of his initial successes at Calais on 10/20 August.[12]

The basic reason for this impetuous decision was Charles's increasing frustration. Since May a truce had existed between the French and Spanish armies. Money was no longer forthcoming to pay the royalist regiments and unpaid soldiers were drifting away to find employment elsewhere, while the Spaniards were considering the appointment of James to command their fleet against Portugal.[13] Charles was receiving only meagre information about the progress of Mordaunt's plans. But both he and James were sick of inaction, and ready to take risks. Throughout July the king wavered between two alternative and mutually exclusive strategies: to travel to the Franco-Spanish treaty negotiations in the Pyrenees (although Louis XIV had forbidden him to do so),[14] or to cross into England and put himself at the head of his adherents wherever they seemed to be establishing themselves. The good news from Cheshire made him decide to sail from Brittany, across seas controlled by the Commonwealth navy and without having been invited. He would embark with a small personal retinue, bringing Booth neither soldiers nor arms nor money. Nevertheless he assumed that he would be welcome. James was to attempt a diversionary invasion of Kent, with whatever forces he could collect: royalist soldiers, men lent by Spain, and some provided by Turenne and Schomberg, the governor of Calais, on an unofficial basis.[15]

News of Booth's defeat arrived two days before Charles was to embark. He immediately switched to the other strategy, of seeking foreign aid. In the past Charles had consistently shared Hyde's opinion that it would be better for a restoration to be carried out by the king's own subjects than by foreign intervention. Now Booth's failure left Charles with no alternative, and difficulties encountered during the attempt to organize a diversionary invasion had shown him that the only way to obtain adequate military assistance was to negotiate directly and personally with the chief ministers who controlled French and Spanish policy, Mazarin and Don Luis de Haro.[16] James had thought that he had Turenne's agreement to lend him soldiers, but when it came to the point the latter had refused to provide them without Mazarin's sanction.[17] Condé's refusal to help what he obviously considered a dubious adventure had been even more ominous. He was concentrating everything on ensuring his inclusion in the forthcoming peace treaty between France and Spain, so as to get a pardon from Louis that would enable him to return to France – and in the event he succeeded, whereas Charles's diplomatic efforts were to fail. Charles had no chance of achieving his maximum objectives, of getting the kings of France and Spain to commit themselves formally to a recognition of his right, or even to giving him joint aid in recovering it. At the least Charles wanted personal access to Don Luis and Mazarin, who were conducting the last stages of the peace negotiations. All his past negotiations had been indirect and unsatisfactory – with the junior ministers at Brussels or through the queen mother and the Louvre party of her dependants, whom he did not trust.[18]

Charles made personal mistakes that contributed to the failure of his lengthy diplomatic tour. Unwisely he chose Bristol, his former secretary of state, whom Mazarin detested, as his chief accompanying adviser.[19] He left too much to the discretion of Bennet, his representative in the

Pyrenees, who was hopelessly outmatched by the Rump's ambassador, William Lockhart. Bennet foolishly tried to force himself on to Mazarin, who repulsed him and refused an interview. This was on 5/15 August: Charles did not arrive at Fuenterrabia until 18/28 October, by when the peace treaty had been virtually agreed. This extraordinary delay was the result of a leisurely and unnecessarily circuitous journey, via Zaragoza.[20] Consequently Charles made no impact on the deliberations of Mazarin and Don Luis. Mazarin thought Charles was totally dependent on Spain, but Charles's attempts to arrange an interview with Mazarin aroused Spanish suspicions that he was trying to change sponsor, and indeed Charles would have preferred French support.[21]

News on 25 October/4 November of the army's expulsion of the Rump modified Mazarin's attitude. He now thought that there might be advantages in establishing contact with Charles, and agreed to see him, but no meeting actually occurred. Believing that Charles was tied to the Spanish ministers, and relying on inaccurate information and predictions from Bordeaux, his representative in London, Mazarin dismissed Charles's chances of being restored by his own subjects. He calculated that eventually Charles would recognize the need for French aid, but he saw no urgency in opening negotiations. The French Court spent the winter of 1659–60 in the south of France, largely out of touch with the rapidly changing situation. Only when Charles no longer needed aid, in March, did Mazarin invite him to Paris and offer him (interested) assistance in negotiating with his subjects.[22]

Charles returned empty-handed to Brussels from his diplomatic tour on 26 December 1659. A few days later he received encouraging reports of the collapse of the army regime in London, following the disintegration of Lambert's forces, a coup at Portsmouth, a fleet mutiny and riots in the City, where elections had produced a crypto-royalist common council. Wisely Charles disregarded the optimistic advice of Mordaunt and other agents that he had only to show himself in England to be restored.[23] The king rightly suspected that fear of his unconditional return was the only thing that could unite his enemies. He also decided to wait until Monck's intentions became clear: crossing the Tweed on 1 January 1660 with most of the English army of occupation from Scotland, Monck moved slowly south, although not invited to intervene by the restored Rump, or any other body, official or private. Charles and his ministers had no direct contact with the general, who for them (and everyone else) represented an entirely new and totally unpredictable factor in English politics. Neither Charles, nor Haselrig and the Rump, nor even Monck's small group of advisers (Cloberry, Clarges and Redman) had any idea of Monck's ultimate intentions, and it is likely that at this stage he had no idea himself.

Monck listened to those who met and tried to influence him on the march south, notably Fairfax at York, but royalist agents failed to get through to him. Charles had long since identified Monck, a royalist in the early stages of the Civil War, as potentially a key figure in effecting a restoration of the monarchy.[24] In August 1659 Grenville, a prominent west-country royalist who had presented Monck's brother to a living, had sent the latter to Scotland on a political reconnaissance, but Monck had explicitly refused to receive a royal letter.[25] More ominously, Monck made only one public commitment before he reached London, that he did not favour readmitting the MPs secluded by Pride's purge in 1648; these MPs were generally thought to favour a restoration.[26] Royalist agents did manage to talk to Cloberry and Clarges, but learnt little. They reported to Charles that Monck was apparently walking in the dark, in which direction it was impossible to say. They expressed fears that either Monck would allow himself to be exploited by the Rump, or he would set up himself as a new Protector.[27]

Haselrig and the doctrinaires who controlled the Rump were as afraid of Monck in February 1660 as they had been of Lambert the previous May. With suicidal haste, immediately after Monck's arrival in London (3 February), they set out to undermine his authority over his officers and soldiers. By ordering him (8 February) to occupy and disarm the City (where royalist sentiments were being openly expressed) they tried to destroy his popularity. By obeying the Rump's orders Monck made most royalists write him off: Hyde wrote of his 'lewd carriage' and Charles concluded that now foreign assistance provided the only way to bring about the recovery of his kingdoms – although no progress had been made in obtaining it.[28] Even Monck's decisive action in organizing and protecting the return of the secluded MPs (21 February) did not remove the suspicions of Charles and his ministers. They expected that the Long Parliament would now revive the negotiations of 1648, the Newport treaty that Pride's purge terminated, accepting that this would entail Charles accepting limitations on his powers as the price of restoration. Instead Monck insisted that parliament must at last dissolve itself (16 March), so that a 'free' parliament could be elected. But although these elections were to be on the basis of the old constituencies and franchises, all former royalists were declared ineligible as candidates. This move made Charles and his ministers fear that Monck intended to become Protector.[29]

Neither Charles and the royalist exiles nor royalist agents in England appreciated the difficulties Monck encountered in keeping his army under control. Any hint that he intended to restore Charles would have provoked discontent and even threatened his authority. In February political activists canvassed support for a remonstrance against rule by a single person, king or Protector. As late as 15 March officers met at St James's Palace to express fears and suspicions about the likely attitude of a new parliament.[30] In fact by early March Charles was receiving more reasoned advice that took into account Monck's difficulties with his army as the explanation for his cautious and opaque behaviour. One agent commented shrewdly, 'Monck protests against, and acts for, the king'. The clearest sign of this came from Monck's appointment to key posts in the militia of men whom he knew were working for the king, notably alderman Robinson in London.[31]

It was not until the end of March that Charles could be entirely confident that Monck intended his restoration. Charles Howard, who as a former Cromwellian had a better understanding of current politics than former Cavaliers, assured Charles that Monck was no enemy, but that his army would not yet publicly hear the king named, although he was beginning to weed out the disaffected. He advised that it was entirely a matter of tactics whether to start negotiations immediately, or wait until the new parliament met. Howard concluded that since restoration by his own subjects was now assured, Charles should avoid making any agreement with a foreign state.[32] In the crucial letter (27 March/6 April) that got through to Monck, Charles explained that he had been trying for some time to enter into correspondence. He acknowledged that he depended on Monck's assistance to regain his right, and promised to let all the world see that he trusted Monck entirely.[33]

Although a restoration was now assured, a major uncertainty persisted: would Monck's new-found Presbyterian associates (Manchester, Northumberland, Pierrepoint) succeed in their design to impose conditions on the monarchy as the price of restoration? Charles learnt that these magnates were considering propositions that Parliament should permanently name all the great officers of state, and have control over the army and militia, or alternatively confer the latter power on Monck for life as captain-general. In ecclesiastical matters the church would be organized on a comprehensive, broadened basis with bishops retaining severely modified powers. Charles would have to contract a Protestant marriage. Purchasers of Crown and church lands would keep them. Soldiers would receive arrears of pay.[34] Charles had already decided on his response in 1659, when it seemed possible that he would owe his restoration to Booth. On instructions from Charles, Hyde wrote to Mordaunt:

> nor can it be imagined that a king who hath endured banishment so long will be persuaded to be no king, that he may have leave to live in England.[35]

Charles used two methods to conceal his rejection of limitations on the Crown, such as the Presbyterian grandees were discussing. First he made profuse general promises on matters of great, but essentially short-term, importance. From the beginning Charles promised an almost universal indemnity, with the regicides as the only specified exceptions. He was genuinely concerned to consign the past to oblivion, erasing all its divisions, illegalities and recriminations, and sternly discouraged vindictive royalist talk of revenge. He also held out the prospect of continuing religious toleration, and of negotiations for some form of ecclesiastical comprehension.[36] Comprehension, that is the broadening of the basis of the church so as to include or 'comprehend' the maximum number of protestants, can be seen as the conservative alternative to toleration, but it was essentially impractical for political reasons as well as theological. It had a narrow appeal, almost entirely restricted to moderate presbyterians; the more dogmatic presbyterians and almost all the sects did not want to be comprehended. Similarly most of the anglican clergy, and certainly those with influence in 1660–2, rejected it as weakening the authority of the church. Furthermore the introduction of comprehension would have required a long, complex and difficult legislative act. Nevertheless the royal offer to consider comprehension brought tactical advantages; it helped to gain time for Charles to re-establish himself as king de facto as well as de jure. Secondly, he cleverly referred all the most complex and difficult issues to a free parliament for decision – problems relating to land, including purchases of property confiscated and sold during the interregnum, confirmation of judicial proceedings, the situation created by the abolition of the Court of Wards. However, the danger of Charles having to accept serious and permanent limitations was never as great as his ministers feared. From overseas the Presbyterian party looked stronger and more united than it was: after returning, Charles found it easy to detach the leaders by giving offices to Manchester, Northumberland, Annesley and others. He exploited the lack of understanding and sympathy between this small group and the very numerous Presbyterian clergy (who were also split into factions). Presbyterian weaknesses also became evident in the elections to the Convention Parliament, and even more so when it met. The faction's spokesmen failed to give effective leadership in the crucial weeks before the king's return.[37]

Formidable technical and constitutional obstacles would have had to be overcome for the Presbyterians to have enforced conditions. Their enactment in statutory form would have been a complicated and time-consuming Parliamentary task, quite beyond the tactical skill of their managers in the Convention. Charles could hardly have been kept waiting overseas for weeks or even months while this was being done, not least because Monck would have had difficulties in controlling even his own remodelled army as well as other regiments. More fundamentally, the Convention was elected in a doubly irregular fashion: writs for the elections were issued by the Council of State, a constitutionally illegal (Commonwealth) body, and known royalists had been arbitrarily disabled from membership. Even if the Convention had passed a statute imposing restrictions on the king, and Charles had assented as the price of restoration, such a statute would have had to be legalized retrospectively by the next parliament, elected on writs issued by the king in proper form. This would have been unlikely.

Furthermore the advocates of imposing conditions seem to have forgotten what Charles had done in Scotland, after severe and indeed humiliating restrictions had been imposed on him in 1650. He had never regarded his acceptance of these, out of necessity, as binding but had manœuvred to free himself from them. In 1660 he treated the Spanish government in a similar fashion. By the 1656 treaty and subsequent undertakings, Charles had promised to return all conquests made by the Commonwealth, in return for aid that had never been provided in full. This meant giving up Dunkirk, Maardijk and Jamaica, and Charles had also agreed to give Spain support against rebel Portugal, relax the laws against Catholics and, by implication, select a Spanish nominee as his wife. Spanish support had invariably proved to be slow and incomplete, and virtually ceased when actual hostilities between France and Spain ceased in May 1659. But when the Spanish ministers in Brussels realized that a restoration was increasingly likely they began to take steps to ensure that Charles would fulfil his undertakings, even if they had not fulfilled theirs. Learning that he was about to be placed under polite house arrest, Charles did a moonlight flit early on 4 April, crossing the frontier to Breda in the United Provinces.[38] From there he could communicate freely with Monck, the Convention and his subjects, and he ignored the extraordinarily belated French offer of hospitality in Paris, with what would now be totally unnecessary aid.

Monck had moved slowly, cautiously and, for a time, invisibly in the direction of a restoration. He had the wisdom to realize that no alternative existed. Clarges expressed his principal argument in telling army officers on Monck's behalf that no government based on the army would now be willingly accepted by the nation. His personal experiences showed Monck how little the Rump could be trusted, and he does not seem at any time to have considered setting himself up as Protector. However, Monck developed unfavourable impressions of many of the king's agents, whose numbers and self-importance increased as a restoration became more probable. He took precautions to safeguard himself from any indiscretions on their part. For example, he tested Grenville's ability to keep secrets before agreeing to see him. Even then he declined to write to Charles, for fear that a letter might be intercepted, or even maliciously published in order to commit him publicly – which would probably cause a mutiny in his army. Grenville was obliged to memorize Monck's message, for oral transmission to Charles.[39]

Monck's prudence and caution paid off significantly when Lambert escaped from the Tower on 10 April and issued a rallying call to all Commonwealth partisans, especially disaffected soldiers and those who had been disbanded, to rendezvous at Edgehill, site of the first major battle in 1642 – a really cyclical piece of symbolism. His stated objective was to prevent the return of Charles Stuart, but he deliberately refrained from stating explicitly the form of government which he intended to restore – whether the Rump or Richard Cromwell. Some cavalry assembled at Edgehill, and many disbanded officers and men tried to reach the rendez-vous, but a momentarily dangerous crisis ended with the interception of Lambert and his main band of supporters, near Daventry (22 April) by Richard Ingoldsby, a regicide ex-Cromwellian, whom Charles later rewarded and made a baronet. None of Lambert's men resisted. As in the other confrontations of these confused months, officers and soldiers were not ready to fight and kill each other – to prevent Richard Cromwell being put out (April 1659), to defend the Rump (October), to prevent the Rump being restored or to attack Monck's army (December). Charles's enemies made themselves contemptible by using threats of force in order to seize power, but then failing to fight in order to retain it.[40]

But however despicable the conduct of the army, which made it gen-erally despised as well as loathed, Charles realized the necessity of appeasing both officers and men. In his letters and publicly in the Declar-ation of Breda he undertook to pay arrears of pay and grant an indemnity. He avoided repeating the mistakes of earlier administrations. Parliament had alienated the army in 1647–8 by failing to meet its demands on arrears of pay and indemnity. In April 1659 radical agitators used grievances over pay to create disaffection, forcing the General Council to take up their case; this proved to be the first stage in the army's desertion of Richard Cromwell. The following December Lambert's army disintegrated because he could not pay it. Knowing that at heart most of the officers and soldiers were at best suspicious of the monarchy, Charles laid great emphasis on the issue of pay, and also offered a full indemnity. This was not an obvious or easy decision, since full payment of arrears would necessitate imposing heavy taxes on a nation that absolutely detested all soldiers. Of course Charles intended to disband the army as quickly as possible, since he could never feel secure until this was done, but he had to conceal this intention. In the Declaration of Breda he misled the army, by promising to take it into his service although he planned to disband it once arrears had been paid.[41]

The Breda declaration (4/14 April) preceded the first meeting of the Convention (25 April). In this declaration Charles addressed the nation, skilfully contrasting the 'general distraction and confusion' of the interreg-num with the legality and stability that everyone desired but that only a restoration of the monarchy could bring. Charles equated the restoration of his own right as monarch with that of the lawful rights of the nation, and disclaimed all intentions of trying to extend his own power. He placed great emphasis on his offer of a general pardon, adding in a particularly shrewd tactical move that the only exceptions were to be decided by parliament. He also brought parliament into the decision-making on the central, complex and controversial issue of religion. This gained him time, and also freed him from what promised to be strongly contradictory pressures.

In the last days of the Long Parliament the majority tried to present Charles with a *fait accompli* by establishing a Presbyterian system of church government. This was inevitably a futile move, since there were insufficient clergy and patrons ready to operate a classis system. But the project would certainly have infuriated Charles, with his bitter memories of clerical tyranny in Scotland. He does not seem to have doubted the need to restore episcopal government in some form. He accepted Hyde's advice that the filling of vacant bishoprics should be treated as a matter of urgency, because those bishops who had survived the interregnum had done little to keep the Anglican church alive. Charles carefully refrained from mentioning the subject of church government in the Breda declaration; instead he concentrated on the entirely separate question of toleration. His statement deserves careful analysis since it raises fundamental issues. Charles announced,

> we do declare a liberty to tender consciences, and that no man shall be disquieted or called in question for differences of opinion in matter of religion which do not disturb the peace of the kingdom; and that we shall be ready to consent to such an Act of Parliament as . . . shall be offered to us for the full granting that indulgence.

Was this a sincere or a devious or even a deceitful pronouncement? Down to 1673 Charles was consistently to favour toleration, but he prevented the Convention from enacting a religious settlement in 1660, and of course no toleration Bill was ever to be presented to him for his assent. However the Convention's Bill concerned comprehension, not toleration, and by November 1660, when it was introduced, the current in the political nation was running strongly in an Anglican direction: even if the Bill had passed, the next parliament would almost certainly have amended or repealed it.

The most likely explanation, that Charles was playing for time in religious matters, as with the army, is borne out by developments after his return. He quickly discovered that he had greatly overestimated the influence and unity of the Presbyterians. He was surprised by the vigorous and spontaneous revival of militant, episcopalian Anglicanism, led by a group of energetic and determined clergy who resisted both comprehension and toleration. On the other hand Charles discovered that, although he owed his restoration entirely to Monck, he stood in no danger of being permanently overshadowed by the general. While at Breda Charles treated Monck as if he would continue to wield predominant influence. For example he accompanied the declaration with two skilfully composed letters, one addressed to the Commons, the other to Monck.[42] Egged on by the opportunists who rallied to him after the restoration of the secluded members, Monck presented the king, on his first day in England, with a list of nominees for most major and many minor offices. This staggered Charles, but Monck failed to persist in his demands. Nor did he press the stratagem which his associates suggested, that Monck should tell Charles that Hyde was unacceptable as a minister and should therefore be left behind in exile.[43] Monck also made no serious effort to prevent the disbanding of the regiments which he had commanded and which were officered by his associates (the retention of the Coldstreamers was an exception, the result of Venner's rising). Consequently Monck's political interest simply disappeared when his dependants found that he would not try to perpetuate his temporary predominance, or even allow them to do so in his name.

In writing to the Convention Charles expressed his belief in the necessity of trust and co-operation between king and parliament, and his confidence in the peers and MPs as 'wise and dispassionate men and good patriots'.[44] Some of his ministers and most former Cavaliers expected him to dissolve the Convention almost immediately after his return, but in an early decision (June 1660) he preferred to prolong it until the end of the year so as to enact urgently needed legislation, settle his revenue and vote extraordinary supply for disbanding. This heavy programme of business required men with parliamentary, administrative and especially fiscal experience, who enjoyed good connections with financial interests in the City. Charles faced the difficulty that MPs who had served the Long Parliament and Cromwell possessed these necessary qualifications: former royalists who had been excluded from all official business for nearly twenty years did not. For the same reason, as well as to conciliate former opponents, Charles had to give former parliamentarians a share of offices, although far fewer than Monck had demanded.[45]

In the intensely competitive circumstances of 1660, with every office for disposal and many more claimants than places, when former royalists constantly reminded Charles of his and his father's promises, and itemized their sufferings and losses, nothing could have caused so much bitter resentment. The intensity of pressure surprised the king, but his understandable responses were to provoke lasting disillusionment. Charles refused to withdraw behind a screen of servants or to adopt an attitude of personal reserve, like his father, or to institute elaborate protocol at Court to protect himself. Open access and informality which suited his personality meant constant exposure to petitioners, claimants and beggars. In the Mall or the Park he used his long stride to outpace them, but when cornered at Court he readily promised whatever he was asked, without any intention of fulfilling his word, a short-term tactic that quickly damaged his reputation.[46]

At the highest level Charles set a pattern that continued throughout the reign, by not establishing a homogeneous administration. At this stage he did not want to be restricted by an over-enthusiastic ministry of inexperienced former Cavaliers, only one of whom now assumed high office. Southampton, who had stayed in England living privately, became lord treasurer – certainly the worst and most damaging appointment ever made by Charles. Southampton was honest, loyal and entirely incapable of initiating the changes needed to put royal finances on a business-like basis. Increasingly ill as well as inefficient, he clung to office on the bad advice of his friend Hyde, delegating his administrative work to a mediocre subordinate, Sir Philip Warwick.[47] When Southampton died in office (May 1667) the king's finances required drastic reorganization, which Charles tried to secure by appointing a reforming treasury commission. Hyde, Ormonde and Nicholas continued in the offices which they had held in exile – chancellor, steward and secretary of state. Bristol remained in the privy council, as a lone member of the Louvre faction. By appointing Manchester, Northumberland and Annesley,[48] Charles effectively deprived the Presbyterians, lay and clerical, of their nominal leaders. Anthony Ashley Cooper and Morrice gained office (chancellor of the exchequer, secretary of state) through Monck's influence.

Most former Cavaliers resented the appointment of former parliamentarians. As late as 1662 Charles heard the outspoken Dr Creighton, whose denunciatory sermons he always greatly enjoyed (among them a fulmination against adultery) preach a violent polemic, saying that the heads of several ministers ought by rights to be stuck on spikes on Westminster Hall and the Bridge, alongside those of the regicides.[49] However Charles was to continue, as he began, making appointments on the basis of 'policy', that is, of a deliberate calculation of the advantages to be obtained, and not out of gratitude for past services, or in recognition of loyalty. His distribution of offices and council membership to men who were associated with different and competing groups, left him in the position of ultimate arbiter. Clarendon's refusal to act as chief or, to use an opprobrious word, prime minister, directing policies and co-ordinating other ministers, is often derided as an example of his obstinate attachment to anachronistic concepts of government. However, it can be seen as an acknowledgement that this role was reserved for the king alone, although once he had consolidated his position Charles assumed it only on intermittent occasions.

Charles and his ministers skilfully overcame what could have been troublesome political and technical difficulties in getting the Convention to pass necessary legislation. It raised money to pay off most of the army, and to discharge navy debts. It passed a Navigation Act, continuing but strengthening the 1651 ordinance. Charles established a council for trade and the plantations. A statute declared that control over the militia rested exclusively with the Crown. Another retrospectively legalized the Long Parliament's abolition of the Court of Wards, military tenures and purveyance. The Act of Indemnity and Oblivion required frequent royal interventions. Charles had to warn peers that private Bills restoring the estates of some of their own number imperilled the general principle of indemnity, and he exercized his power of veto to prevent some passing into law. He warned MPs that their growing zeal to except an increasing number of individuals from pardon was perpetuating uncertainties. There was more political realism than personal mercifulness in Charles's insistence that the widest possible pardon should be granted.[50]

Charles was not himself involved in the crucial mistakes that the Convention made in calculating his settled revenue. Its committee estimated likely expenditure at £1,200,000 per annum, an approximate but not wildly inaccurate figure. The mistake, caused largely by rush of business, was greatly to overestimate the product of the specific revenues voted to Charles for life to cover this level of expenditure. It was not until 1661 that Charles and his ministers became aware of the serious deficiencies in the settled revenue, and it is unlikely that MPs in the Convention deliberately set out to ensure that the king would be financially dependent on votes of extraordinary taxation by parliament. Rather it was the 'loyal' but traditionalist Cavalier Parliament of 1661–79 that failed to rectify these financial miscalculations, when it was made aware of them, because MPs of various political outlooks realized that the king's need for votes of supply gave them unprecedented power.[51]

From the very beginning of his reign Charles was also made aware of the independent attitudes and considerable influence possessed by another group of his subjects, the militant Anglican clergy, who in practice were to restrict and curb the king's decisions and policies even more effectively than parliament succeeded in doing. Religion provided the most controversial of all issues in 1660.[52] The eventual ecclesiastical settlement of 1661–2 was to divide the nation, and cause a deep and lasting rift in society as well as politics between conformists and dissenters. It was also the first major issue on which Charles chose to dissemble. Keeping his real intentions secret, he apparently followed a policy which was not just at variance with, but in fact diametrically opposite to, the one he privately favoured. In the Breda declaration Charles granted what amounted to an interim 'liberty to tender consciences', and promised his assent to an Act of Indulgence. However from his first discussions with peers, MPs and both Anglican and Presbyterian clergy he quickly discovered that a toleration Bill was unlikely to pass the Convention, and that there would be formidable opposition to any suggestion of giving any form of toleration to

Roman Catholics, as he desired and had privately promised. He also realized that no broad and permanent compromise could be expected to emerge from discussions carried on by the various clerical factions.

The Presbyterian clergy with whom Charles had to deal were themselves divided into three factions. A relatively small number were attracted by the offers of chaplaincies, bishoprics and deaneries that Charles made them – for the same tactical purpose as his appointment of Presbyterian magnates to honorific state offices – their detachment from the rest of the party. In fact only Reynolds accepted a bishopric (a move which Presbyterian colleagues blamed on the ambition of his wife). 'Moderate' Presbyterian clergy declined the offers, but were very willing to consider comprehension, the modification of ritual and doctrinal requirements by the church so as to broaden its base, enabling most Presbyterians to continue within it. But a fiery minority regarded Charles as a renegade for going back on his 1650 treaty with the Scots and repudiating by his practice the subscription to the Covenant which had been imposed on him.[53]

The intransigence of the Presbyterian zealots was matched by that of a much more vocal, determined and, above all, numerous section of the Anglican clergy. They enjoyed one decisive advantage over those whom they regarded as their opponents: the rights that the Anglican militants contended for were theirs by law. On 28 May, the day before Charles's return, the Commons received reports about riots and forcible entries caused by incumbents who had been dispossessed of their livings during the interregnum, mostly by commissioners appointed by the Long Parliament or the Rump, but occasionally by mob action. It was unwise, because unnecessary, for these dispossessed clergy to take direct action, which could provoke disorders (and which the Convention prohibited in a proclamation on 29 May).[54] Once Charles returned, the rule of law was restored and the courts were available for patrons and clergy whose rights had been arbitrarily infringed. By legal action intruders could be evicted, but the number of cases during the summer alarmed the Presbyterians. In addition some militant Anglicans who were already active as JPs began to threaten to enforce the law against any minister who did not use the Anglican Book of Common Prayer – long since, but illegally, prohibited by the Long Parliament. In another area of the law, surviving bishops, deans and members of cathedral chapters quickly resumed their rights, totally disregarding the possibility of the Convention passing a statute to give purchasers of church property either rights and titles or compensation, and began to issue new leases, collect renewal fines and eject those who refused to accept their authority as landlords.[55]

The anglican militants acted entirely on their own initiative in reaching out to regain what was theirs by right, and did not consider Charles's consequential difficulties. Charles had to assent to a Bill for settling ministers, which gave security to existing incumbents with some exceptions where patrons' rights had been infringed. He also convened a series of meetings in which a small number of Anglican and Presbyterian clergy drafted an interim agreement that went a long way towards comprehension – although of course this would need statutory embodiment if it was to be permanent, something the Anglican participants had no intention of allowing. This was published on 25 October as the Worcester House Declaration.[56] By then Charles had already clearly signalled his own preferred solution to religious problems. Speaking for the king, Clarendon told the Convention that the king had never refused confirmation in his living to any minister who had petitioned for it: this represents the relationship that Charles consistently wished to establish with 'moderate' religious dissenters. They should apply to the king for protection. He would grant it on his own authority, but only after satisfying himself that the petitioners were peaceable, and seditious preaching or activities would result in the withdrawal of concessions. In other words toleration would be extended to those willing to enlist as royal dependants.[57]

Few Presbyterians trusted Charles after his behaviour in Scotland. Their partisans in the Convention, who were nominally in a majority in the Commons, introduced a Bill to convert the Worcester House Declaration into a statute.[58] The king had never intended it to form the basis of a permanent settlement. For him the declaration was part of a series of moves designed to prevent the ecclesiastical settlement being dictated by a single, predominant party. He needed the 'moderate' Presbyterians to act as a counterweight to the fanatical Anglicans, and he had to detach them sharply and permanently from the minority of Presbyterian zealots. His offers of bishoprics and deaneries had failed to enlist such leaders as Baxter and Calamy. Consequently the declaration contained religious concessions in the attempt to activate the surprisingly inert 'moderates'. He also used the declaration to vindicate his own Protestantism, by saying that the concessions it contained were based on his experiences during his exile, when he had (very occasionally, and always against his ministers' advice) attended Dutch Reformed and French Huguenot services.[59] In addition the Worcester House Declaration represented the exercise of the royal prerogative in ecclesiastical affairs, although Charles did not draw attention to this aspect explicitly, as he was to do in the 1662 and 1672 Declarations of Indulgence. He cited the 'over-passionate' climate of opinion, the rancour with which religion was being debated, as reasons for the declaration, justifying intervention 'to give some determination ourself to the matters in difference'. Obliquely he emphasized the central role to be played by himself; he would later call a synod as an auxiliary, 'to give us such further assistance towards a perfect union of affections'.[60]

Charles did not intend the declaration to be turned into a statute, because this would imply that his prerogative was insufficient, and he planned to use prerogative powers later to grant toleration to the Catholics, something that no parliament would ever include in a statute. In any case he soon saw that the Bill to embody the Declaration antagonized moderate as well as intransigent Anglicans, and would not pass unless he came out in its support and extended the length of the session, something that did not suit his plans. Charles therefore quietly encouraged the Court interest to organize the defeat of the Bill (28 November, by 183 to 157).[61] Furthermore he was disappointed by the insignificant impact made by the declaration: few of the Presbyterian clergy it was intended to attract actually approached the king.

In contrast Charles's other major move during the autumn had momentous and lasting effects. Between 28 August and 29 November Charles filled the vacant bishoprics. He could not delay doing so further, for fear of intensifying the growing doubts about his intentions in religious matters. Charles's appointments have provoked historical controversy, raising the question of whether they were Laudian in character, and disagreement on the influence exerted by Sheldon, the leading Anglican militant.[62] When so many appointments were made in a short period, it is not surprising that several influences can be detected. Juxon, Laud's old friend who had attended Charles I on the scaffold, symbolized continuity as Archbishop of Canterbury. Key bishoprics went to Sheldon (London), who acted as *de facto* head of the church, Henchman (Salisbury), as his understudy, and Frewen (York). Because of their past associations they could be described as Laudians, but Sheldon already saw how unrealizable Laud's ideals now were, under a different king and in drastically changed circumstances. Hyde's influence was reflected in the contemptuous passing-over of all but one of the bishops who survived from before 1642, whom he had bitterly criticized for inactivity.[63] Charles's personal preferences played a part: he nominated Gauden (who had 'ghosted' *Eikon Basilike* which Charles I was supposed to have written) to Exeter (earning Sheldon's dipleasure), and the Commonwealth conformist Reynolds to Norwich.[64] He also consigned the scholarly and saintly Jeremy Taylor to an obscure Irish see, perhaps because the presence in England of a bishop married to an illegitimate daughter of Charles I would have damaged the growing cult of the Royal Saint and Martyr.

Overall Charles seems to have tried to establish an episcopate in which no single group predominated, as he had done with his council. In the next few months it quickly became apparent that the militants were in control. Charles underestimated the energy, determination and political courage and skill of Sheldon, who became the architect of the 1661–2 religious settlement, and who subsequently obstructed, restricted and outmanœuvred the king until he was forced to change his policies in 1673–4. Indeed Sheldon proved to be the only politician whom Charles never got the better of, his only superior as a tactician, who consistently defied him and defeated his toleration policies. It is not surprising that when Sheldon died he was replaced by a colourless and apolitical scholar, Sancroft (1678).

Charles was also taken by surprise by the strength of the Anglican revival after his restoration. During June and July 1660 large numbers of gentry subscribed to county addresses calling on Charles to resume enforcement of the law in religious matters, and especially to require use of the Book of Common Prayer.[65] This was the first sign of what was to emerge as the dominant political combination of the reign. Before 1640 most of the country gentry and parochial clergy resented Laud's innovations: after 1662 clerical dissidents within the church were few, and in most parts of the country a majority of the gentry rallied to support the bishops and clergy, whom, in sharp contrast to the position before 1640, they saw as defenders of the law as well as of the social order. They associated toleration with the political and social flux and instability of the interregnum. By consciously and vociferously taking their stand on the rights that were theirs by law, in virtue of their property qualification, the clergy effectively absolved themselves of the charge of favouring arbitrary methods of government that had proved fatal to Laud. Sheldon paid particular attention to building the closest possible alliance with the aristocracy and gentry.[66] Not until the crisis of 1679–80 did Charles finally and fully come to terms with this, accepting the fact that in practical political terms he was dependent on the Anglican interest, which formed the essential basis of popular Toryism.

The complete restoration of the church in 1661–2 was due more to this groundswell of opinion – within the political nation certainly, although there is much evidence of wider popular support – than to the clever political tactics of Sheldon and his associates. Charles was also surprised by another strong current of mass opinion – continuing fear and hatred of Catholicism. During his exile Charles had always taken great care to maintain his public reputation as a staunch Protestant, but he had made private promises to Catholics of relief from the penal laws. These promises were not just tactical or opportunist but sincerely indicated his own personal sympathies, both for the Catholics who were displaying such conspicuous loyalty and for their faith.[67] After his restoration it was some time before Charles appreciated the prevailing fear of popery. The new bishops, in contrast, felt great hostility to the Catholic clergy who had harassed the Anglicans in exile and prematurely gloried in the apparent collapse of the Anglican Church.

In its essential features the Restoration significantly resembled the Revolution of 1688. A change of regime was effected so quickly that there was no opportunity for a prolonged debate on political fundamentals, and consequently the conservative solution of reinstituting the old order was not seriously questioned. The instability and failures of the recent past discredited all concepts of reform, innovation and religious freedom. Few contemporaries would have asked whether the Restoration was 'popular'; acquiescence is the word which most accurately describes the general mood of the nation in 1660. Inevitably the euphoria of 29 May and the succeeding weeks evaporated. Harsh political realities asserted themselves, especially in the frenzied competition for places, favours and compensation that left a host of disappointed and embittered unsuccessful contenders. Among members of the political nation, frustration provoked an early revival of Country attitudes, of the old suspicion of the Court and hostility to ministers, but these now found a new form of expression in a devotion to the Anglican Church. Popular dissatisfaction with the restored monarchy, that is, on the part of the vast majority who were outside the ranks of the political nation, was not long in developing, caused by the actual faults and vices that Milton predicted in his 1660 pamphlet, The Ready and Easy Way, would follow a Restoration – flagrant immorality at Court, corruption among ministers and officers, petty tyrannies practised by JPs and Anglican clergy. But radicals, those whom Milton described as Patriots – 'the best affected . . . and best principled of the people', had been fatally discredited by their participation in the far more actively tyrannical governments of the recent past.[68] Consequently when the former rulers – the sectaries and disbanded officers and soldiers – discovered how Charles had deceived them with the promises in the Breda declaration, their plight did not win them any sympathy among a people who had at all levels of society suffered under their arbitrary rule. The skilfully composed and widely circulated 'dying speeches' of the thirteen executed regicides evoked virtually no response.[69] Not only did their association with the failed regimes of the past isolate Rumpers, Cromwellians and sectaries in 1660, but it meant that when the restored monarchy became vulnerable to criticism these causes failed to revive. When discontent with Charles's government became a serious political factor it found expression in support first for the Country opposition in parliament and then for the first Whigs. Charles, his ministers, lord-lieutenants and JPs could never ignore the existence, and intermittent activities, of underground radical groups, but these never posed an acute threat to the monarchical order.[70] Not until 1670, at the time of the enforcement of the second Conventicle Act, did mass disturbances and protests occur, and then they were the work not of old radicals but of a new generation of proto-Whig activists in London.

The Anglican clergy, whose victory was to follow in 1661–2, saw the Restoration as a literally miraculous event, the result of God's direct intervention on behalf of His rightful ecclesiastical and political order. For the cynical Charles, with his superficial scepticism, it certainly represented a dramatic change of fortune. Fortune, however, had some mortal blows to strike at the royal family during this eventful year. In September the youngest brother, Henry Duke of Gloucester, fell victim to smallpox – which Charles had survived in 1648. Henry died too young for it to be known whether this was a major loss, but he had gained a reputation by resisting his mother's brutal attempts to convert him to Roman Catholicism. The queen mother paid an unwelcome (and expensive) visit during the autumn, to find herself involved in James's tragi-comical difficulties over his marriage to Anne Hyde, daughter of the lord chancellor. Finding that he had made her pregnant after a promise of marriage, James was strongly urged by Charles not to keep his promise. Ignoring this advice James married Anne secretly (3 September). The royal brothers then reversed attitudes. James tried to get out of the marriage, encouraged by his personal friends, several of whom claimed that they too had sexual intercourse with Anne. The queen mother, beside herself at such a *mésalliance*, urged setting the marriage aside, but once he knew about the secret marriage Charles made it clear that this would not be done. The birth of a son to Anne in October reconciled James to his fate, but Henrietta Maria remained hostile.[71] In December the latter suffered a double blow. Her elder daughter Mary, dowager Princess of Orange, died at Whitehall, also of smallpox. The queen mother's attempt to storm her daughter's sickroom, in an attempt at a death-bed conversion, failed and she soon left for France.[72]

In partial compensation for these losses a splendid marriage was arranged for Charles's surviving sister, Henrietta (a Catholic from birth), to Louis XIV's younger brother, the bisexual Duke of Orléans. Although the marriage (solemnized in 1661) proved to be one of miserable unhappiness, Charles gained considerable advantages from it. Apart from the prestige involved, it represented a vote of confidence by Louis in the stability and permanence of the newly restored Stuart dynasty. Charles soon began to employ his sister as confidential intermediary in negotiations with Louis, largely superseding the queen mother whose fanatical Catholicism and dubious political associates made her an object of general suspicion in England.[73]

4 *Charles and Clarendon*

By the spring of 1661 the restored monarchy had secured itself so effectively that there was no apparent danger of its being seriously challenged, let alone overthrown. A magnificent coronation (23 April) symbolized the self-assurance of the monarchy; for the last time it was preceded by the king riding ceremonially through his capital. The overwhelmingly loyal new parliament met for the first time on 8 May; Charles retained it until January 1679. At its opening an announcement was made of the decision to contract a Portuguese marriage for Charles, although it was not solemnized until May 1662.[1] To outward appearances Charles was now as much a sovereign ruler as any of his predecessors.

The surprising speed with which the king consolidated his position was due as much to his clear-minded resolution in carrying out precautionary moves as to the disrepute and divisions that made his fallen rivals totally ineffective. Charles and his ministers had taken as their first priority the rapid disbanding of the Commonwealth army, and the formation of a new force under reliable officers. The militia also received attention throughout the country. In consequence such republican plotting as did occur proved to be even less effective than royalist conspiracies in 1649–60.[2] Apart from Venner's suicidal rebellion in London in January 1661 (by all of sixty fanatics) the republicans never managed an actual rising. Only in Yorkshire in October 1663 did preparations become sufficiently advanced to compel the government to undertake mass arrests and widespread house searches. The divisions that had brought down the Commonwealth persisted after 1660. No credible leader survived or emerged: Ludlow and Richard Cromwell lived out of reach overseas, but the events of 1659 had discredited both of them. Charles held Lambert in lifelong custody, but personal animosity rather than political necessity explains his determination to carry out the judicial murder of Henry Vane.[3]

Once securely on the throne Charles undoubtedly gave a great deal of his time and energies to enjoyment of his position at the head of a young, pleasure-loving section of the Court. In 1661–7 the king behaved for much of the time in the ways that earned him the moral disapproval of Victorian historians, and the simplistic title of Merry Monarch. These were the years in which he delegated day to day control of routine business to Clarendon, while he shared the eagerness of his closest intimates, mostly returned exiles, to compensate for lost time and make hay while the sun shone. To the shocked Venetian ambassador, only Constantinople could match Whitehall for its corruption, and observers deplored its promiscuous immorality and irresponsible extravagance.[4] The restored Court did not in essentials differ greatly from that of any young or recently crowned monarch – for example Henry VIII, François I and Louis XIV. But special factors made life at Court a cause of political discontent. A population that had lived without a Court at Whitehall for eighteen years gave much prurient attention to the ways in which Charles and his courtiers lived and misbehaved. Charles's dislike of protocol made his Court the most relaxed, informal and open in Europe, so that its often scandalous doings quickly became public knowledge.

More fundamental still was the readiness of the public to believe ill of its superiors, to censure its betters. This tendency antedated the Restoration. Clarendon retrospectively expressed his dismay at the way in which negative attitudes of criticism and cynicism, which he regarded as natural and appropriate during the time of usurpation, continued after the return of the legitimate sovereign. In fact Mordaunt perceptively warned Charles before the Restoration that everyone, including royalists, had been infected by a new malaise – a loss of reverence and deference, a lack of any sense of duty and responsibility. Ambition and enrichment, the pursuit of individual interest, actuated most men, not loyalty and principle.[5] Most historians have assumed that the undeniably general public and private immorality of Charles's reign originated somehow with the return of the king, and it cannot be denied that he and his Court set a spectacularly bad example to the nation. But public corruption, often imperfectly cloaked by particularly repellent varieties of hypocrisy, had earned for the Rump and the military grandees of the 1650s the contempt of a cynical public. Charles had acted on Mordaunt's advice in attempting to engage support by appealing to the self-interest of prominent persons, to whom he made promises on an indiscriminate scale that he simply could not honour in 1660, when current influence and connection determined the bestowal of appointments and favours. Consequently Charles and Clarendon incurred resentful reproaches from loyal Cavaliers who lost out.[6]

Inevitably, if not altogether justifiably, Clarendon attracted the most hostility from the disappointed. However much Clarendon disavowed any intention of acting as a prime or chief minister who directed the administration, Charles gave him more authority than any other servant. In the years after 1651, operating within a small Court, Clarendon had usually been successful in preventing the exiled Charles from making wild and impracticable policy decisions. He had acted as a brake on the king's rasher and less responsible companions. This had contributed significantly to Charles's peaceful Restoration, but after 1660 Clarendon's persistence in offering predominantly negative advice began to irritate the king. Clarendon's obstinate rejection of innovations, and his obstruction of all reforms in areas where government was obviously functioning less than effectively, have to be related to the ideological concepts underlying the Restoration. In his view only a complete and comprehensive re-establishment of the old order in all spheres of life could permanently reunify the nation, bring back habits of obedience and respect, and secure religion, liberties and property. We can see that he was expecting to achieve things that were impossible, but he was right to fear that Charles's own inclinations, fortified by the advice which his younger and unofficial friends gave him, would lead to ill-considered projects and changes, provoking controversy, uncertainty or even confusion.

However, by failing to oppose, or even obstruct, the most important attempted innovation – Charles's personally sincere but politically provocative attempts to bring about major religious changes – Clarendon put himself in an ultimately false position. A combination of illness and political timidity rendered him inactive in December 1662, when the king attempted to inaugurate forms of religious toleration, although parliament had enacted the Uniformity Act only a few months before.[7] This created a disturbing rift between Charles and the church. The bishops successfully opposed this first Declaration of Indulgence, but at the cost of virtually severing relations with the king. Formal religious life continued at Court, with Charles attending or, as legend has it, snoring at services in the Chapel Royal, but he lost contact with the leading clergy. Bishops were not to be found in regular attendance at Court, as they were at Versailles and had been in Charles I's Whitehall. Mutual trust collapsed at the time that the Anglican clergy were fervently promoting the cult of Charles I, as the king who had sacrificed his life and crown to ensure the resurrection of the church. Consequently, in a reversal of attitudes that also testified to a shrewd appreciation of the new location of power and influence, Sheldon and the bishops consciously allied with the Commons to check royal policies and tendencies.

Charles worked the Cavalier Parliament hard in its long initial session (May–July 1661 and November 1661 to May 1662). He required from it the enactment of a heavy programme of legislation, intended to prevent a repetition of the techniques and tactics used by Pym to weaken royal authority. Parliament passed Militia Acts (giving the king exclusive powers, with parliament explicitly renouncing any right to control the militias); the Act against Tumultuous Petitioning; a strengthening of the treason laws; a Licensing Act to put the press under control. The dominant and triumphant majority who demonstrated their loyalty by passing these acts also displayed an independent attitude by wishing to go much further in securing the monarchy (and themselves) than Charles and Clarendon wished. Despite extremely strong and explicit instructions from the king at the start that the Act of Indemnity and Oblivion must remain intact, the Commons tried to amend it so that exceptions could be multiplied. A further attempt to undermine the Act by indirect means also failed because of Charles's firmness: he insisted that the validity of the Convention Parliament and its statutes should be specifically confirmed.[8] He also blocked another sweeping retrospective proposal – that all the statutes of the Long Parliament should be rescinded *en bloc*, with parliament re-enacting only those it thought fit, and in amended forms if it wished.[9] Fearing that occult influences and Charles's own desire for leniency were causing what they considered were unnecessary delays, fervently Anglican MPs actually brought in their own Bill on the most important and controversial of all issues – the religious settlement – although Charles managed to delay this Bill during the first part of the session.[10]

On his side Charles had to make a significant retreat on the main Bill that passed during 1661, the Corporation Act. The original draft would have greatly increased royal influence over the municipal corporations, with far-reaching consequences since they elected a majority of MPs. The draft gave the Crown the nomination of key officials and proposed a standard parliamentary franchise, confining the right to vote to members of the governing body of the corporation. It is not clear who initiated this attempt at fundamental reform, and there is no evidence to suggest that it was a conscious attempt by the king (like that of James in 1687–8) to establish royal mastery over the Commons. Charles quickly amended the Bill when MPs raised protests that it contained constitutionally dangerous provisions. The final Act represented a compromise. Charles named commissioners, who received wide powers to purge all corporations of known or potential dissidents, but they had to act within a limited time, and he chose mostly independent country gentlemen from the counties, not royal agents or officials. Each group of commissioners followed their own judgement of the local situation, so that wide variations in practice resulted, and it was the Cavalier gentry, not the king, who gained in influence within the corporations. The Bill did not produce constitutional changes: the franchise was not changed and those corporations with jurisdictional autonomy were not merged into the counties. The modification of the original draft, together with the absence of any serious attempt to revive the prerogative courts in 1660–2, show that Charles and Clarendon had no plan for centralization as a step towards an establishment of royal absolutism.[11]

The monopoly of corporation offices by reliable men proved to be temporary: by the 1670s many of those purged by the commissioners were recovering their positions. By contrast the Uniformity Act (1662) had effects that lasted for centuries. The restoration of strict religious uniformity in a church under tight episcopal control, armed with coercive powers against dissenters, produced in practice a permanent division of the nation. This religious settlement bore no resemblance to the one that Charles wanted and had envisaged. He continued to regard himself as bound by the Declaration of Breda, which he saw as a public commitment on his part, and emphatically not as a clever tactical manœuvre concealing an intention of restoring an exclusive, persecuting church when it became politically possible to do so. MPs in the Cavalier Parliament took a very different view, treating the Breda declaration as only an interim promise, pending a statutory settlement, and once Charles consented to the Uniformity Act they believed that the declaration had been nullified.[12]

Privately Charles adhered to the principles and arguments that underlay the Declaration of Breda, and was to embody them again in the 1662 and 1672 Declarations of Indulgence. He believed that attempts to establish religious uniformity by coercion would never succeed completely, but would, rather, perpetuate political disaffection and tension, with damaging social and economic effects. Charles accepted the necessity of establishing an episcopally governed church, but he did not think that such a church would ever regain the loyalty of the entire nation. Throughout his reign he was consistent in wanting toleration of those dissenters (including, of course, the Catholics) whom he judged to be politically innocuous, on condition that they pledged their loyalty to the king. The distinction that he drew between the reasonable and docile, who could be tolerated, and the fanatics, who required repression, cut across confessional groups. For example, at times Charles expressed real anger at the subversive intrigues of Jesuits, and although he negotiated amicably with moderate Presbyterian ministers, he remained intensely hostile to those whose clerical pretensions reminded him of his humiliating experiences in Scotland in 1650–1, and who denounced him as an ungodly ruler. Charles was ahead of most of his subjects in recognizing in the Quakers whom he met a quietism and sincerity that earned his respect.[13]

Charles's outlook could not have been more different from that of the Commons in 1661–5. Militant Anglicanism carried all before it, from the first symbolic vote (17 May 1661), which passed by 228 to 103 a resolution to have the Solemn League and Covenant ceremonially burnt by the hangman.[14] The Commons, not the king or the Lords, initiated the most important Bills – to restore bishops to the Lords, to re-establish ecclesiastical courts and, on 9 July, a Uniformity Bill drafted by independent MPs, not the royal officers, which went through all its stages there. The Commons ignored the continuing meetings of the Savoy Conference between bishops and Presbyterian clergy, which Charles had promised in the Breda declaration. Charles never took a real interest in such discussions of comprehension but on grounds of good faith he could not allow a Uniformity Bill to pass before the Savoy Conference failed, as inevitably it did. Acting through Clarendon, Charles persuaded the Lords to neglect the Bill during the summer part of the session, but in November he saw that the Commons' zeal for the bill, and the return of bishops to the Lords, made rejection politically impossible.[15] This enforced acceptance of the Bill is perhaps the most striking example of the way in which the king's position had weakened in relation to parliament. Nevertheless Charles tried to salvage something. To outward appearances, and in an attempt to induce the Commons to vote him an adequate settled revenue, he gave parliament the go-ahead to pass the Bill in a more stringent form, declaring that he was opting out of the ecclesiastical details because they were 'too hard for me'. These words had a hidden meaning. By saying that he left the detailed provisions to parliament's care, 'who can best provide for them', Charles superficially flattered peers and MPs, but he was also signalling to dissenters and their sympathizers the message that it was parliament, not himself, that carried responsibility for religious repression. Even though he gave parliament freedom to enact the Uniformity Bill, he still endeavoured by indirect means to secure amendments. Charles instigated in the Lords a proviso giving himself the right to dispense with requirements contained in the Bill, to benefit clerics of whose 'peaceable and pious disposition' he was convinced.[16] This disturbed many peers, and Bristol tried to exploit their misgivings in order to do Clarendon mischief. The proviso passed in the Lords, but it was rejected by the Commons.[17]

Charles gave his assent to the Uniformity Act on 19 May 1662. The Act gave the clergy until 24 August to satisfy its requirements, but Charles persisted in attempts to mitigate its effects. With his encouragement, some Presbyterian ministers petitioned him for protection. The council considered this on 27 August, only three days after the Act came into force, a piece of mistiming which gave Sheldon strong arguments against interference with a new and (from the first reactions) unexpectedly successful and unopposed measure. Sheldon also hinted at the explosively unfavourable reaction that such a move would provoke in parliament. The project was abandoned, but it had done immense damage in that Sheldon never again placed any confidence in Charles. Furthermore he blamed Clarendon for having failed to dissuade the king from taking such a subversive initiative.[18]

Contrary to expectations, enforcement of the Uniformity Act, which involved the ejection and replacement of nearly a thousand clergy, went off smoothly and peaceably. Sheldon had prepared preaching ministers to fill the key vacancies.[19] He had made sure that the magistrates were also ready, and over the next nine years he systematically encouraged them to enforce this and later, additional penal laws with energy and severity. Sheldon was not consciously encroaching on the governmental rights of the king, but he rightly suspected that Charles was reluctant to enforce laws of which he did not approve. As a bishop and privy counsellor it was his duty to see that the laws were obeyed, regardless of the king's wishes. He knew that if he did not act to ensure enforcement the laws could soon become dead letters.

Henry Bennet, who became secretary of state in October, had earlier suggested using the need to enforce the Uniformity Act as a pretext for expanding the army. Charles did not act on this foolish advice, but the proposal leaked and added to public alarm and uncertainty. Clarendon's prolonged illness, which became incapacitating in early December, produced rumours that Charles was about to dismiss him. Former royalists with obvious motives spread reports that Albemarle and his large interest group (of former parliamentarians) would soon be displaced from their positions in the army, navy, ordnance and royal stables. There were reports of republican plotting in the north. In this uncertain situation Charles recognized the need to reassure his subjects, and this was the purpose of the so-called Declaration of Indulgence which he issued on 26 December 1662.[20]

This declaration covered a far wider field than religion. It amounted to a general statement by Charles of the principles on which his administration was based, but the strong self-justificatory tone shows his awareness of the criticisms being directed against him. He disclaimed any intention of using the kind of machiavellian manœuvres that formed the basis of malicious speculation about royal designs to establish absolute government based on use of the army. With complete justification, he emphasized his continuing and irrevocable commitment to the Act of Indemnity. He categorically denied the disturbing allegations that he had promised and assented to this Act solely to regain and then consolidate his hold on the throne, and that now that it was safe to do so he would shortly revoke the protection which it gave to former parliamentarians. It was being rumoured that this would enable him to confiscate their property, in order to distribute land and money to former royalists – not as compensation for their former losses and to reward their loyalty, but to purchase their acquiescence in the introduction of 'a military way of government in this kingdom'.

Charles skilfully linked his denial of this preposterous story with his strenuous refutation of a similar but much more plausible allegation. He denied that the Declaration of Breda, like the Indemnity Act, had been intended as a trap, that he had never intended to fulfil its promises once they had served their purpose in reconciling the nation to his Restoration. Charles had to overcome the undeniable facts that no indulgence to tender consciences had been granted, and that he had assented to the Uniformity Act with its 'straiter fetters'. In this declaration of December 1662 Charles used his need to vindicate his integrity as justification for making yet another attempt to mitigate the severity of old and new laws against dissenters, to obtain legal exemptions for men of tender consciences and peaceable dispositions, and incidentally to convert sections of the dissenters into royal dependants. He also proposed doing something for the Catholics, creating a major sensation by openly avowing in the declaration his sense of obligation to them for past loyalty, and stating his intention of obtaining for them the same benefits as for Protestant dissenters.

Charles's defensively phrased assertions about his fidelity to the Protestant religion did not carry conviction. His repetition of warnings which he had made to parliament in May about the serious moral problems that faced the nation must have aroused derision, given the scandalous rumours being eagerly retailed about his private behaviour, and that of the Court.[21] Charles claimed credit for checking the licentiousness and impiety that he said he had inherited from the Commonwealth, promising to show an example of frugality so as to restrain extravagant spending by all sections of the nation. He drew attention to the start he had just made in retrenching government expenditure, claiming that it would be reduced below the level of his income from the settled revenue. This prospect would lead to a situation in which he would not again require extraordinary taxes. It is difficult to see how anyone could have been expected to believe a word of this, but Charles's nebulous promises that lower taxation and religious toleration would lead to general economic prosperity were symptomatic of the way in which secular and indeed materialistic values were advancing at the expense of religious principles.

The king's explicit statement of intent on religious policies monopolized public attention, virtually effacing the remainder of the declaration. Charles promised to try to get parliament to agree to his honouring the Breda undertaking on an indulgence. He would not invade parliament's freedom, but he wanted it to pass a statute. The purpose of this would be to enable him to exercise 'with a more universal satisfaction that power of dispensing which we conceive to be inherent in us'. Charles implied that he could institute an indulgence by using such purely prerogative powers. When parliament met (18 February 1663) he again carefully spelt out his intentions, knowing by then that peers and MPs would probably react strongly. Charles made great play of his declared belief that it had been essential to pass the Uniformity Act, because the security of the monarchy depended on the re-establishment of the church under episcopal government. However, he added, 'I am in my nature an enemy to all severity for religion and conscience how mistaken soever it be '. He made it clear that he would indulge dissenters, provided that they lived 'peaceably and modestly' under his government, but he wisely confined himself to generalities, and refrained from suggesting specific propositions.[22]

The Commons demanded withdrawal of the declaration. In 1673 MPs were to attack Charles's second declaration on constitutional grounds, denying his claim to a suspending power in ecclesiastical matters, by virtue of his prerogative. In 1663 this aspect received comparatively little

attention. The Commons was concerned to refute Charles's contention
that he was still bound by the Breda declaration. A majority of MPs
regarded this as dead, invalidated by the Uniformity Act to which Charles
had assented.[23] Although the king did not withdraw his 1662 declaration,
his attempt to introduce a measure of indulgence ended in abject failure.
Charles allowed one of his ministers, Robartes, to introduce a Bill in the
Lords authorizing the king to give exemption from the penal laws to those
dissenters of whose peaceableness he was convinced, although they were
not to be capable of holding office. The Bill divided the ministry. Bennet
and Ashley supported it, but Clarendon hotly opposed it.[24] As a consequence of his inactivity over the Declaration of Indulgence Clarendon had
received strong reproaches from the bishops, which stung him sufficiently
to lead him to criticize the bill in the Lords debates, although he knew that
it stood no chance of passing. Clarendon used gratuitously offensive
language, describing the bill as 'ship money in religion', because it gave
the king such wide discretionary powers. He argued that under the Bill
royal dispensations could be used to give Anglican bishoprics to papist
priests, and used Father Goffe as the example of such a possible beneficiary. Clarendon could not have chosen a more dangerous example, and it
speaks volumes for Charles's self-control that he did not react to this
extraordinarily revealing comment. Clarendon and the bishops had good
reasons for detesting Goffe and fearing his influence. After converting to
Catholicism in 1651, Goffe became chaplain to the queen mother, and an
active member of the Louvre party. With her encouragement he engaged
in an aggressive, ruthless and often productive campaign to convert
royalist exiles. But in his 1663 speech Clarendon was discussing the use
Charles might make of a discretionary power, and Goffe's name must
have come into his mind because he could never forget that a moment of
absolute intimacy linked Goffe with Charles. In February 1649, while
serving as Anglican chaplain, Goffe had been chosen to go alone into
Charles's chamber to tell him of his father's execution, the most traumatic
moment of his entire life, and he had done so with supreme tact. In
Clarendon's presumably impromptu citation of Goffe was contained the
implication that Charles secretly favoured Catholicism.[25]

Frustrated by the hostility provoked by the declaration, and obliged to
watch Robartes's Bill lapse, Charles showed resentment of Clarendon's
words. Courtiers alert to every change in the atmosphere at Whitehall
began to speculate on Clarendon's early dismissal, but he realized his
danger, arranging a (by now rare) private interview on 19 March. He
explained his conduct, apparently to Charles's satisfaction, and went out
of his way to please Charles by opposing a motion for the Lords to join
with the Commons in an address calling on the king to expel all papist
priests.[26] However, Clarendon's position was not as precarious as
courtiers assumed. Bennet and his associates certainly stood ready to

replace him, but they lacked credibility as an alternative ministry. They constituted a faction at Court, but the fiasco over the declaration and the Bill exposed their limited influence in parliament. This faction anticipated the ministries of 1670–3 in many characteristics. None of its members could be termed a committed Anglican. All favoured toleration, although for different reasons. Each aimed at advancement in office. Buckingham had by now recovered from his mistake in submitting to Cromwell in 1657. He relied too much on Charles's personal friendship, but he had shown himself effective as lord-lieutenant of Yorkshire.[27] Charles Berkeley had for long been an intimate friend of James: he was now engaged in winning Charles's confidence and saw himself as future chief minister.[28] Ashley had more limited aims, to become a member of the inner group of ministers, in the cabinet council.[29]

Henry Bennet was generally regarded by contemporary observers as the minister most likely to succeed Clarendon. Charles in October 1662 insisted on his appointment as secretary of state to replace the loyal but increasingly incapable Nicholas, and told Clarendon that he must work with him.[30] Clarendon failed conspicuously to do so, seeing in Bennet not only a personal rival but a minister whose working principle was to try to foresee the king's wishes so as to advocate policies that would please him, whether they were right or wrong. Clarendon also disapproved strongly of the start which Bennet and his man of business, the obscure Thomas Clifford, were making on constructing a working minority in both Houses. Charles had insisted that this should be done, over-riding Clarendon's protests.[31] As manager-in-chief Bennet made promises in the king's name, creating expectations and publicizing himself as the minister who could get things done, grievances rectified and petitions considered – all in contrast to Clarendon's neglect of business and lack of energy.

Throughout his career Bennet concentrated on acting as the king's confidential adviser. He seldom spoke in parliament, or even at council, but worked indefatigably in private. It was characteristic of his methods that when he took over Nicholas's Whitehall apartments he immediately had a door built to give him direct (and secret) access to a staircase leading to the king's private rooms. Bennet always behaved cautiously on public affairs of state. By 1663 he had got no further than laying the basis of an alternative ministry. He had drafted the text of the Declaration of Indulgence on Charles's orders, but its failure made him more wary. Seeing that Charles's reaction to the failure of his policies was to turn away from state business, and throw himself into the pursuit of private pleasures, Bennet prudently kept himself in the background. He also realized how suspicious MPs had become of Clarendon and the whole Court.[32]

Scenting danger, Bennet detached himself from the most flamboyant and impatient member of the anti-Clarendon faction, the Earl of Bristol. The latter, as George Digby, had been a constant source of bad advice to

Charles I, and the years of exile had not improved his judgement. He placed an unthinking reliance on Charles's personal favour and friendship. The model of an improvident magnate, he could not afford to wait until a fresh set of issues gave him pretexts to strike at Clarendon.[33] In July 1663 Bristol precipitated a trial of strength and caused his own downfall by prematurely revealing his ambition to become chief minister. This started when he passed on to the king a secret offer by his protégé, another maverick politician, Sir Richard Temple, to obtain an increase in the king's settled revenue. Temple made the offer conditional on being given full management of the king's affairs in the Commons, with all royal dependants being given instructions to follow his directions. This showed that he had no significant interest of his own, and Charles rightly showed himself sceptical of the project's success. But unscrupulously the king then decided to extract political advantage for himself by revealing Temple's confidential offer to the Commons (13 June).[34] Bristol's part came out later; when it did he moved quickly to vindicate himself. He outraged Charles by appearing at the bar of the Commons to explain his conduct without asking Charles's permission – which would have been refused. Bristol set out blatantly to ingratiate himself with MPs at the expense of the other ministers, with the aim ultimately of displacing them. He further infuriated Charles by breaking his oath as a councillor. He claimed credit for opposing in council the advice of others that Charles should try to obtain additional supply. He coupled this claim with advice to the Commons to call for a searching investigation into alleged official corruption – a field for endless mischief-making. He denied holding the subversive political theories generally attributed to Catholics, but in such terms as to suggest that an active bloc of his co-religionists at Court were basing their conduct on them.[35]

Charles reprimanded Bristol for this performance, his anger increased by its surprising success. MPs generally responded favourably to Bristol's maliciously clever speech. They not only cleared Temple of improper conduct, but gave him leave to ask the king for favour, meaning by this the grant of office, a direct rebuff to Charles's manoeuvre. Bristol sought to capitalize on his success with the Commons. Although the end of the session could not be more than three weeks away, on 10 July he launched charges against Clarendon, accusing him of treason. The reason for this move is most revealing. No one was more experienced than Bristol in the techniques of Court intrigue, but he realized that no move within the Court alone could bring him the certainty of ousting his ministerial rivals, because of what he termed Charles's fickleness – the king's ability to avoid being pinned down to a particular line of policy. If Bristol was to remove Clarendon it was necessary for him to enlist the support of parliament.[36] Bristol spoiled his chances by slovenly inattention to important detail. The badly formulated articles, even if they could be proved, did not constitute treason. They also reflected obliquely on Charles personally. Bristol woundingly depicted Charles as being treated by Clarendon as his puppet. Ironically he drew attention to Bennet's crypto-Catholicism. More dangerously Bristol laid trails of gunpowder which he intended the Commons to follow up, even if no formal impeachment occurred. These would have ignited devastating political explosions. Bristol made the first public mention of a project to legitimize Charles's eldest son, Monmouth. He referred to secret royal negotiations with the Pope, via Bellings and d'Aubigny, and to details concerning the sale of Dunkirk to France. Although in form Bristol was making accusations against Clarendon, in reality he was pillorying the king's conduct of government.[37]

Fortunately for Charles the articles had been hastily drafted and did not carry conviction, but he felt it necessary to intervene personally, telling the Lords that to his own knowledge several of the charges were untrue. He completely identified himself with Clarendon, saying that the charges reflected on himself, and constituted a libel against his person as well as against his government. On 14 July the Lords unanimously rejected the charges. Charles followed this up by bringing criminal charges against Bristol, who went into hiding rather than risk being tried by his peers. This ended his political career. Bristol was the first notable politician to be out-manœuvred and destroyed by Charles.[38]

The failure of Bristol's attempted impeachment of Clarendon had the effect of prolonging the latter's tenure of office. It also postponed any attempt at reorganization of the administration. The most serious effect was that Charles retained the incapable Southampton as lord treasurer, despite his increasing financial difficulties which created serious problems in 1663. Clarendon defended an old friend from motives of personal loyalty, but he vehemently opposed radical reforms, such as putting the treasury into commission, which he succeeded in delaying until 1667.[39] For him such an arrangement was more appropriate to a Commonwealth than to a monarchy, but he suspected that Charles – who had 'little reverence or esteem for antiquity' – was seriously attracted by the proposition. Similarly Clarendon retained notions about the constitutionally appropriate functions and attitudes of parliament that the unruly and disorganized session of 1663 exposed as anachronistic and unhelpful. By the time of this session Charles was coming to realize that his legislative as well as his financial needs would necessitate his making continuing use of parliament, probably in the form of annual sessions.[40]

A majority of old Cavalier MPs, men who were in no way dependent on the Court, increasingly adopted attitudes that resembled those of the Country faction of the 1620s. A Bill was introduced by private members in the Commons against the sale of offices. Another Bill concealed self-interest under the cloak of loyalty and, like a dog going back to its vomit, tried again to undo the 1660 Act of Indemnity. It provided for the incapacitation of all who had fought against Charles I, or acknowledged the Commonwealth, from holding office.[41] Neither Bill passed, but Charles went out of his way to appear conciliatory. At the end of the 1663 session he expressed surprise that parliament had not spent its time in legislating against both dissenters and papists (who had been the intended beneficiaries of his declaration), adding that he would spend the recess preparing Bills against conventicles and papists (27 July).[42] When parliament met in March 1664 he again emphasized his love for parliaments, and denied that he had intended to dissolve, or prorogue for an unusually long period.[43] Almost without realizing what he was doing, Charles was taking the Cavalier Parliament into permanent partnership.

Political attention (like that of modern historians of the period) was concentrated on parliament during its sessions. But although these were longer and more frequent than those of pre-1640 parliaments, political activity at Westminster did not have the continuity that was to be found only within the royal Court at Whitehall, presided over by Charles in person. Ministers had to try to control access to the king, and to satisfy the retinue of clients on whom they depended, if they were to maintain their influence. During 1663 the Court was convulsed by a violent retrenchment necessitated by the king's financial difficulties. Clarendon and his closest allies, Southampton the treasurer and Ormonde (lord steward), botched the operation. Although absent in Dublin as lord-lieutenant, Ormonde incurred the most odium because the retrenchment was carried out in his name. Clarendon disapproved of altering a Court restored in 1660 as a replica of Charles I's, and did not intervene to protect his clients. Albemarle did, to the fury of former royalists, and shielded his subordinates in the royal stables (one of the largest and most expensive departments of Whitehall) from the worst effects. Finally, thanks to Southampton's lack of attention and competence, the operation saved little money. Admittedly it affected menial servants rather than courtiers with ambitions, but it demoralized Whitehall, infecting servants in every category with feelings of insecurity.[44]

Charles very properly and wisely did not concern himself with the retrenchment, but he intervened very actively in what became the major issue within the Court during the first years of his reign – the prolonged attempts to modify the Irish land settlement for the benefit of a faction of leading Catholic landowners.[45] He did not share his English subjects' almost universal hostility to Catholics, and above all to those Irish who had taken part in the rebellion of 1641 and associated with the Confederation of Kilkenny. Charles and James almost alone saw no difference between Irish rebels and those who had supported the Long Parliament in its rebellion against Charles I. The king did not think that their Catholicism made them anti-monarchical: as he wrote to Clarendon, 'rebel for rebel, I had rather trust a papist rebel than a presbyterian one'.[46] Charles was swayed by the loyalty which Irish Catholics had demonstrated to him in the 1650s by rallying to join his regiments in the Spanish Netherlands, and they enjoyed the advocacy of an influential Court faction.

Initially Charles confined himself to intervening on behalf of individuals. He wrote to the commissioners who were (very corruptly) adjudicating claims, supporting the case of Antrim, a well-connected Irish Catholic with a deeply ambiguous past. Unfortunately his letter was leaked and published as a damaging pamphlet, *Murder Will Out*. The Court faction then pressed the king to intervene generally, arguing that, although approved by the English and Irish councils and enacted by the Dublin parliament, the Act of Settlement encroached on his prerogative. Charles was urged to authorize a general revision, which would ensure that every landowner concerned would have to lobby at Whitehall to protect his property rights. This would give courtiers and ministers handsome rewards in the form of bribes and presents and the possibility of gaining grants of land.[47]

James gave the project his strong support: it would certainly benefit the many Catholic Irish in his entourage, notably the ambitious Talbots. The queen mother and her avaricious crony, St Albans, also had long established links with prominent Irish claimants. Bennet naturally followed Charles's wishes, hoping to make money for himself, but his new rival Charles Berkeley had much wider ambitions. The rising figure among the younger generation at Court, he seized on the issue, as also did Lauderdale.[48] Within the council only the minor politicians Anglesey and Morrice tried to resist the projectors. Clarendon remained on the sidelines, commenting that Charles did not understand the business, which was true, and justified his inaction by asserting that nothing would come of the project. His inaction left Ormonde vulnerable, but the latter held on to the lord-lieutenancy and eventually a messy compromise resulted. Some individuals connected with the Court gained partial restitution, but the main framework of the settlement survived and Charles abandoned the claim that by using prerogative powers he could dispose of all forfeitures.[49]

During the intrigues and manœuvres, courtiers became increasingly aware of Berkeley's growing influence with the king. He showed that he was capable of leading and directing an interest composed of separate factions, and above all of ensuring harmonious relations between Charles and James. His creation first as Viscount Fitzharding and then as Earl of Falmouth demonstrated Charles's favour. The reign of a new *privado* (the Spanish word used in the seventeenth century to describe a favourite) seemed to be beginning.[50] Death in the battle off Lowestoft, in a Dutch War which he had done much to bring about, suddenly terminated this promising career. Clarendon again remained largely inactive while an aggressive and enlarged Court faction brought pressure to bear on Charles to undertake a new initiative in foreign policy, which resulted in the second Dutch War of 1665–7.

During the first three years of the reign foreign affairs were not of major importance. With two relatively insignificant secretaries (the aged Nicholas and the inexperienced Morrice), it fell to Clarendon to act as the king's principal adviser. He followed a general line of friendship with France that very much accorded with Charles's own preferences. Louis showed himself receptive, because he was concerned to isolate Spain. French diplomats facilitated Charles's Portuguese marriage. Louis subsidized English troops who helped repulse Spanish attacks aimed at reconquering Portugal.[51] In December 1662 Charles sold Dunkirk, Cromwell's conquest and strategic key to west Flanders, to Louis for 5,000,000 livres. From Charles's point of view this was an attractive bargain, at least in the short term. Dunkirk (unlike medieval Calais) never developed as a trading port, and so did not generate revenue from customs duties to offset the considerable cost of the necessarily large garrison. The sale did not hurt Charles's pride or prestige. The capture of Dunkirk had been the final achievement of the hated Cromwellian army; Charles and his army of royalist exiles had been defeated in attempting its defence. Only one man protested against the sale: George Downing, Charles's (and earlier Cromwell's) envoy at The Hague, appreciated its strategic value, both as the key to Flanders and as a privateering base, for use against Dutch shipping. However, Downing ignored the lack of military resources at Charles's disposal, which meant that Charles could not have defended Dunkirk successfully against any major French offensive. Charles was wise to sell it in 1662, when he would have lost it during the war against France in 1666–7.[52]

Downing valued Dunkirk as a means of putting pressure on the Dutch, so as to compel them to rectify English commercial grievances. Charles and Clarendon preferred to negotiate a settlement. The treaty of September 1662 proved to be Clarendon's last foreign policy assignment.[53] In October Charles appointed Bennet as secretary of state. He had considerable experience and undoubted skill as a diplomat, but his curious combination of ambition and timidity put him entirely at the king's disposal; unlike Danby a decade later he would never dare to develop any policy without having the king's approval. He was also influenced by the fear of antagonizing other and more assertive servants of the king. In 1662 he had the reputation of being pro-Spanish, but, knowing that Charles, James and their favourite Berkeley wanted a French alignment, Bennet set himself the task of fulfilling their wishes.

Although Bennet never pressed the king to follow a particular line of policy, there were plenty of other ministers and courtiers who did. In theory Charles believed that by virtue of his prerogative he possessed an exclusive power in matters of foreign policy. Indeed Clarendon acted on this belief, denying to parliament and public opinion any right of influencing royal policy. But in practice, during these first years after the Restoration, Charles showed himself far more responsive to mercantilist pressures than Charles I or Cromwell. Although some historical apologists for Charles have depicted him as the exponent of vigorous expansionist policies there is little evidence to suggest that he initiated or pressed policies aimed at naval predominance, at colonial imperialism on a large scale or at greatly increasing the commercial wealth of England.[54] But he did show himself susceptible to pressures, especially from organized interest groups. He could not afford to do less than the Commonwealth governments, although he studiously avoided acknowledging the precedents that they had set. He assented to the Navigation Act which the Convention passed, an improved and strengthened replacement for the Rump's (constitutionally invalid) Navigation ordinance of 1651. Renewing the East India Company's charter, which Cromwell had also done, he encouraged it to persevere in trading with areas dominated by the Dutch company. Charles established a council for trade and the plantations, and sanctioned companies to organize North Sea fisheries and West African trade, areas dominated by Dutch competitors. At home he would never have used such explicit language, but in negotiating the 1662 treaty he told the Dutch representatives that he would never relinquish anything that they had conceded to usurping regimes.[55]

The king's financial problems left him dependent on loans from members of the commercial and nascent financial interest groups who favoured intimidating the Dutch into making concessions. Few actually believed that a war would result, assuming that Dutch vulnerability to another war at sea would induce them to buy off English hostility. But the strongest pressure on Charles for active anti-Dutch policies came from James and his advisers and associates, men who certainly wanted a war that they assumed they could win easily. As heir presumptive to a newly married king (nobody yet knew that the queen was barren), James had to look for a role. He made the most of the opportunities that followed from his appointment as lord high admiral. He put together an impressive and aggressive group of naval officers, combining officers who had formerly served the Commonwealth with privateering officers who had served the exiled king in Rupert's piratical fleet. By initiating the possibility of positive moves against the Dutch, James attracted the personal support of the most energetic and ambitious politicians – Buckingham, Berkeley and Clifford. Members of the group had connections in every area of official life, at Court, in the council and committee for foreign affairs, in the Commons and the City, among shipowners and contractors. By vigorous, tendentious propaganda they manipulated public opinion.

Charles would have found it difficult to resist pressure from this coalition of interest groups. Although he did make himself out to be reluctant to engage in war against the Dutch, this was in letters written to his sister, the Duchess of Orléans, but intended primarily for Louis' eyes.[56] Charles did nothing personally to prevent war, and, although such senior ministers as Clarendon and Southampton disapproved, they too lacked the resolution to arrest policies that produced a drift into war. Charles seems to have shared the widespread impression that the Dutch would offer concessions rather than fight, and that if it did come to war they would suffer defeats at sea and the paralysis of their seaborne trade. Admittedly in May 1664 Charles responded coolly to a particularly belligerent address from the Commons, calling for action against the Dutch as the obstacle to English commercial expansion, but that was to remind the House that his prerogative powers included exclusive control over foreign policy.[57] In practice Charles agreed to all the moves that, in a classic example of escalation, provoked the Dutch to fight. He lent three royal ships for Holmes's expedition to West Africa to carry out reprisals against the Dutch in 1663–4. In January 1664 Charles accepted the recommendation of the committee of council to take possession of the Dutch colony of New Amsterdam. In March he named James as proprietor of wide territories, including the Hudson valley, and in May despatched the expedition that captured the town that became New York (August). When de Ruyter executed a successful reprisal raid on English posts in West Africa, Charles responded by ordering attacks on Dutch merchant shipping in European waters.[58]

De Ruyter's devastating raid, authorized personally by de Witt, the pensionary of Holland, disproved assumptions about the readiness of the Dutch to capitulate under pressure. It represented such a blow to England's prestige that Charles could not subsequently afford to accept any compromise. The war in European waters got off to a brilliantly successful start. The overwhelming victory off Lowestoft (June 1665) surpassed anything achieved by the Commonwealth navy. The enthusiasm of parliament for the war was reflected in the Commons' acceptance of a Court motion for an unprecedentedly enormous vote of supply – £2,500,000. English confidence in an early and total victory ruled out serious consideration of a belated and inept French attempt at mediation, the preposterously misnamed *célèbre ambassade* (April–December 1665). Buoyed up by naval successes Charles ignored clear warnings from Louis that he would have to enter the war if England continued to reject the terms that he induced his Dutch ally to offer. Charles regarded these terms as inadequate to satisfy the expectations of those who had sponsored the policies that had led to war, and agreed with James in discounting the effects of French naval intervention.[59] In this euphoric period of early and decisive victories Charles demonstrated his personal commitment to the war and the navy by periodically visiting the fleet while it took on supplies during the intervals between offensive operations. He congratulated and rewarded his successful commanders. These short visits provided Charles and James with some of the happiest days of their lives. James was in his element as a fighting admiral. Charles vicariously shared in his glory. At sea in one of the sheltered anchorages he could escape from all the complications of government and politics. It must also have been a relief to get away to the victorious fleet, which remained surprisingly healthy during a long and hot summer, and forget that the plague was devastating London and parts of the provinces.[60]

However the campaign of 1666 proved to be unexpectedly inconclusive. By entering the war the French created a diversion and seriously reduced the flow of overseas trade. The English and the Dutch each won one major naval engagement, but ominous signs appeared that, in what contemporaries called a 'wasting' war – that is, one of attrition – Dutch financial and material resources would outlast those at Charles's disposal. Economic stagnation and commercial disruption, caused especially by the pressing of seamen and embargoes on long-distance voyages, were accentuated by the plague and the fire of London. When parliament met again in September 1666 total victory was no longer possible. Charles made a mildly worded request for additional supply, which the Commons apparently accepted as reasonable and necessary. But a deadlock arose over the means to be used to obtain this money, estimated at £1,600,000. The administration had not worked out in advance how this was to be done – a further sign of a damaging lack of initiative at the treasury.[61] Charles made a serious error by proposing a general excise. This frightened most MPs, who could remember that it had been the mainstay of the Long Parliament's wartime finances, and knew that excises made the Dutch republic the most heavily taxed country in Europe. The Commons responded with a proposal for a once and for all tax to buy out the extremely unpopular hearth or chimney tax, but Charles refused to abandon a taxation device which had been mismanaged but might still prove to be a major source of revenue.[62]

During the 1666–7 session the Court came under constant pressure in parliament. Independent peers and MPs, trouble-makers and factional leaders, discovered new ways of exploiting the increasingly obvious weaknesses of the inadequate and poorly supported Court spokesmen. They used the king's desperate need for supply to get their own way, without considering the possibly dangerous consequences of delay. A strong faction, directed by Buckingham, forced through an Act totally prohibiting the import of Irish cattle into England and Wales. This measure divided the country as well as parliament, making Charles's position uncomfortable. The Act appealed to the cattle-raising regions of the west, north and Wales, but meant higher prices for farmers in the midlands, south and east, who fattened lean cattle for market. It also meant higher prices for consumers. Irish landlords and peasants had already been affected by an Act passed in 1663, which banned imports during part of the year, but permanent and total closure of what was virtually their only market threatened to have catastrophic effects.[63] Made aware of this prospect by Ormonde, Charles at first made it clear that he wanted the Bill to fail. This had no effect. Realizing the strength and determination of those pressing for its passage, Charles then allowed Court dependants a free vote, although the Bill would have passed the Commons in any case. However it was when it appeared likely that the Bill would be blocked in the Lords that Charles came under real pressure. The Commons ostentatiously failed to make progress with supply measures, and some leading country MPs said explicitly that if the Bill did not pass they would not be generous with votes of supply in future.[64] The Commons also insisted on retaining the word 'nuisance' to describe cattle imports from Ireland; this would make it impossible for the king to issue dispensations for imports. The Lords described this device as implying that Charles would give his assent to the Act with an already formed intention of undermining it, by dispensing with its provisions.[65] Charles's own reaction to such blatant distrust of his sincerity was, revealingly, plaintive rather than angry. He complained, 'I do not pretend to be without infirmities, but I have never broken my word with you'. He then directed Court peers to cease opposing either the Bill or the 'nuisance' provision, so that it passed in January 1667. The consequences fulfilled Ormonde's warnings to Charles; the Irish economy suffered severely and the king's revenues were also affected.[66]

During this session Charles remained inactive when the Commons, by initiating an impeachment against Viscount Mordaunt, revived a process that could be used to make ministers as responsive to parliament as to the king. However in the short term the case did not raise major issues: Mordaunt, to whom Charles had great obligations from before 1660, was no longer a person of importance.[67] A much more direct challenge to the king's authority came in the form of persistent attempts by the Commons to establish a statutory commission to inspect and report on the accounts of all taxes voted for the war. Charles resented this as an imposition of unacceptable restrictions on his power to determine and order expenditure. He also knew that any inquiry would expose Southampton's mismanagement of the treasury; this would mean that any change in the administration of royal finances would appear to have been forced by pressure.[68]

As a consequence the Commons delayed granting Charles the money he needed for the war. It was as late as 8 February 1667 before he obtained £1,256,347. This was an adequate sum, but the money would not become available until far too late. Previous high levels of taxation, combined with the trade depression caused by the war, plague and fire, meant that this money would come in slowly. Royal credit was exhausted and all other taxes had been anticipated, so that financiers were in no position to make advances.[69] Aware of these difficulties, and expecting the start of negotiations with the Dutch, Charles and the council had a week earlier made a fatal decision to reduce the scale of naval operations during the summer. Only a 'summer guard' of squadrons to escort merchant shipping would be put to sea, while protection of the east coast was to be effected by newly raised regiments. The opening of peace negotiations at Breda in May persuaded Charles not to reconsider this decision, although it soon became clear that the Dutch would be at sea in strength.

The result of failing to fit out a fleet during the summer of 1667 was disaster. The Dutch had complete control of all the seas around the British Isles. Their victory in the Medway (12 June), which led to the forcing of Chatham dockyard and the capture or destruction of the ships that Charles had laid up, and their blockade of the Thames, brought abject humiliation. Panic gripped London. June 1667 marked the nadir of the restored monarchy.[70] For perhaps two weeks the monarchy, with all its dependent institutions – Court, church, Cavalier Parliament – seemed to be tottering. But as in 1659–60 no practicable and attractive alternative was in sight. Accidentally Charles had insured himself against the consequences of disaster by appointing Monck, Duke of Albemarle, to command the defences. Now in poor health Albemarle's lethargy and indecision contributed to the Medway disaster, but this did not matter afterwards. His very presence, as probably the only man whom everyone could trust, reassured the anxious public.

Conscious of the deplorable contrast between the Medway disaster and the Commonwealth's victories in 1652–3, Charles revealed his internal tensions in unpredictable and temperamental behaviour. To make matters worse his private life was also going wrong at this time of maximum pressure. To his fury his long and (for him) patient pursuit of Frances Stewart had ended in failure when in March she married the Duke of Richmond. Charles quarrelled violently with Lady Castlemaine, his regular mistress. He now moved promiscuously from one woman to another. Similarly his attitude to his ministers and servants changed drastically from day to day. He first countenanced a scheme, concocted by Arlington, to ruin Buckingham who was arrested on charges of having treasonably cast Charles's horoscope with his pet astrologer. When Buckingham was interrogated by the council in June Charles accepted his explanations and dismissed the charges.[71] Within weeks Buckingham was successfully worming his way back into Charles's favour. Arlington had no option but to try to establish a false friendship with a man whose life he had threatened, although in reality this episode made the two men lifelong enemies.

74   CHARLES II: ROYAL POLITICIAN

Charles also showed his teeth to parliament, when it met in a brief emergency session (25–9 July) that actually sealed Clarendon's downfall. Parliament had been prorogued until October, but Charles decided on a session in case the peace negotiations at Breda broke down. Clarendon characteristically argued against recalling parliament, not on the very relevant point that it would be risky to hold a session at a time of continuing crisis and alarm, but advancing the legalistic objection that a prorogation could not be shortened even for an emergency – which revealed his belief that parliament was not an essential part of government.[72] When parliament assembled there was no news from Breda, and Charles therefore ordered a four-day adjournment. To his surprise and fury the Speaker bungled his orders, allowing Tomkins – a former back-bench lieutenant of Bristol – to make an aggressive speech articulating many current suspicions and fears. Tomkins concentrated his attack on the army raised for coastal defence, which had been financed by the constitutionally dubious device of diverting militia money. Other speakers followed Tomkins in denouncing a plan to establish a standing army, which was assailed as a threat to the liberties of the nation. The Commons unanimously passed a resolution for the standing army's immediate disbandment.[73]

This resolution provoked Charles into a menacing response. He wondered that anyone should suspect him of intending to rule by means of a standing army. But, by adding that if others observed the law as well as he did himself 'there will be no need for any such thing', he seemed to reserve the right to do so if their behaviour necessitated it. Learning that peace had been made, he lost no time in proroguing parliament. MPs had travelled to London at a time of crisis, in hot weather and just before the harvest, only to be denounced by Charles and packed off home after four days. They dispersed seething with discontent, and spread their discontent throughout the provinces.[74]

Charles lost no time in disbanding the new forces. This was primarily to save money, but he also realized that he had lost political credit. The blame fell on Clarendon. Charles had really no option but to dismiss him, so as to demonstrate to a discontented nation his intention to break with the men and methods that had produced failure and defeat. Clarendon's personal defects antagonized Charles – his parade of moral superiority, a habitual censoriousness, pedantic hostility to any form of innovation, his open disapproval of the whole younger generation. In public affairs he still tried to monopolize the king's counsels, blocking anything that had not been submitted to him beforehand, but lacked the mental and physical energy to undertake all the business that he reserved to himself. Clarendon's many failings were public knowledge, making him a natural scapegoat on whom Charles could load the responsibility for past mistakes. However

Clarendon's dismissal (30 August) had an unexpected result: it led to Buckingham's emergence as leading minister in his place.[75]

In the autumn of 1667 Charles allowed Buckingham to initiate new policies. In doing so Charles seems to have been led to overestimate Buckingham's likelihood of success by the novelty of his ideas and by his sweeping promises. Buckingham undertook to manage parliament through his lieutenants, notably Richard Temple, Osborne and Littleton, and obtain additional supply.[76] In the longer term they would also get parliamentary approval for a measure of religious toleration, vesting in the king a mitigating power to dispense with the Uniformity and other penal Acts. It was clearly understood that this would enable Charles to use his new powers to benefit Catholics as well as Protestant dissenters.[77] However, Charles made one serious miscalculation in commissioning Buckingham: he did not see in advance how far his new minister would go in pursuit of the old.

Early in October, just before parliament met, Charles agreed that an impeachment should be launched against Clarendon, but the articles prepared on his instructions alleged only criminal misdemeanours which, if proved, would justify no more than banishment.[78] The ministerial faction that was opposed to Buckingham wished to go no further. Arlington and William Coventry saw that to push matters to extremes would create a backlash of sympathy for Clarendon among independent and Country peers and MPs who had wanted his dismissal. It would also provoke a rift between Charles and James, who showed himself determined to defend his father-in-law.[79] Nevertheless Buckingham persuaded Charles to authorize an impeachment on charges of treason, and articles were debated in the Commons on 26 October.[80] By then Arlington had lapsed into silence, seeing the growth of Charles's animosity to Clarendon, but Coventry exposed himself to the king's resentment by criticizing the articles. The Commons received these with some scepticism, because of the blatantly self-interested motives of the prosecutors. By a sizeable majority of 172 to 103, MPs rejected the proposed first article, which charged that Clarendon had advised the king to dissolve parliament and rule by the army, and so was guilty of treason.[81] The Commons did agree to other articles, but these did not amount to treasonable conduct and so would have been insufficient to bring about the judicial murder of Clarendon, which was now the common objective of Charles and Buckingham. Additional charges had to be introduced, alleging that Clarendon had betrayed the king's counsels to the enemy during the recent war, and it was these that swayed the Commons, and were the justification for the general charge of treason which Seymour made on the Commons behalf to the Lords on 12 November.[82]

Charles had to bring a great deal of pressure to bear on MPs to ensure this result, and had to intensify his lobbying when the Lords reacted sceptically to general charges of treason. Seymour demanded Clarendon's imprisonment, pending trial, but the Lords refused unless special (that is, specified) charges were presented.[83] Charles obtained the names of peers who had voted against Clarendon being imprisoned, but his attempts to make them change their attitude do not seem to have been productive. There was now the prospect that the impeachment would collapse and that Clarendon would shortly return to politics as a critic of the Court and his successors. To return to articles that fell short of treason would involve a major loss of prestige. The king had gone too far to retreat. He now broke Clarendon by leaking a project to prorogue parliament and consti- tute the court of twenty-four nominated peers, all of whom would be hand-picked enemies, to try Clarendon on treason charges. This con- vinced Clarendon that his life was now in peril. On 27 November he fled the country, and in December a Bill of perpetual banishment finally eliminated him from English affairs.[84]

In his memoirs James criticized Charles's sacrifice of Clarendon, asserting that all subsequent ministers knew that they could not rely on receiving royal protection against their enemies, and so gave more attention to safeguarding themselves than to serving the king.[85] But in the short term Charles succeeded in significantly reducing political tensions by aban- doning an unpopular minister. In the sixteenth and seventeenth centuries the sudden and brutal destruction of men who had risen to greatness by devoted service to a sovereign provided a recognized way for a ruler to ingratiate himself with his subjects – as the cases of Thomas Cromwell, Philip III's *privado*, the Duke of Lerma, Strafford and Fouquet showed. According to the crude medical concepts of the age, Clarendon's removal represented a purge that ended the constipating blockage from which government had been suffering: on the other hand a blood-letting would have been in the interests of the ambitious Buckingham but not of Charles.

Having freed himself from association with a deeply detested minister, Charles chose to rely on a new set of ministers who were to achieve virtually none of their promised undertakings. More significantly, Clarendon's removal did nothing to free Charles from a state of depen- dence on parliament that was becoming increasingly apparent and restric- tive. It was having the most damaging effects in the area of finance. The financial settlement hastily formulated by the Convention had given the king an inadequate permanent revenue. Expenditure exceeded the esti- mate used by the Convention as their base calculation, while the settled or constant revenue brought in less than they had forecast. Charles's repeated calls for rectification achieved nothing, although these were accompanied by promises and concessions. When asking the Commons to settle an adequate constant revenue, as early as November 1661, Charles joined with a denial of extravagance an offer to let MPs inspect his revenue, disbursements as well as receipts. He also signalled the end of his attempts to modify the Uniformity Bill during its passage through parliament.[86] In March 1662 he asked the Commons to settle a 'real and substantial' revenue, and reaffirmed his love for the church.[87] Charles went to the heart of the matter in June 1663, when he acknowledged that parliaments always preferred to vote extraordinary supply, rather than increase the constant revenue, and the Commons confirmed his expectation by doing nothing about the settled revenue, and voting him only four subsidies – an obsolete form of direct tax.[88] Charles again repeated his offer to allow MPs to inspect his accounts, but this offer had no appeal until the Dutch War began, when charges of massive fraud and embezzlement became current. In December 1666 the Commons adopted a hard line, voting to 'tack' a new poll tax on to the establishment of an investigatory public accounts committee. Charles reacted sharply, threatening a veto. He made it plain that he would forgo the money rather than accept an independent and possibly permanent committee of inquisition.[89] On this occasion the Commons gave up the tack, but used an alternative form of restriction by inserting provisos limiting the use that could be made of the money: in February 1667 Charles, in asking for supply, pleaded for supply Bills 'in the old style, with few provisos'.[90]

The retention of Clarendon as minister had resulted in the shelving of many important decisions. Southampton continued, incapably, at the treasury until his death in May 1667. Only then could Charles, ignoring Clarendon's continuing objections, appoint a vigorous reforming commission.[91] Similarly two junior courtiers, Osborne and Clifford, who represented the Buckingham and Arlington factions, now began to try to organize working majorities for the king in both Houses of Parliament. This new attempt at management followed the failure of the one major project with which Clarendon had associated himself. In the short Oxford session of October 1665 he had attempted to emasculate the parliamentary opposition by imposing a Test on all office holders, peers and MPs.[92] In recommending the Test, Clarendon had claimed that those who wanted political alterations would not now try to stage another rebellion. Instead they were waiting for a 'godly parliament'. The Test would block this possibility: all MPs would have to take an oath not to attempt any change in the government of either church or state. This Test Bill had failed by a narrow margin in a thin Commons. Charles was left with no option but to retain the existing parliament, and to try to influence peers and MPs by intensive management. He does not seem at any time before 1673 to have made a conscious decision to retain the Cavalier Parliament indefinitely, but he and his new ministers were disinclined to gamble on a dissolution. Financial pressures were such that a new parliament would have to be called, and by-elections indicated that a new Commons would be considerably more difficult to manage. As they died, former Cavaliers (and many were elderly) were being replaced by former parliamentarians, or younger men critical of the Court.

By the time of Clarendon's fall the euphoria of 1660 had entirely disappeared. The background to the political difficulties and projects of the intervening years needs to be kept in mind. Most individuals in the kingdoms were affected by a sequence of traumatic events. Charles had absolutely no control over them, but their effects made ordinary people critical of the failings of the king, his ministers and the Court. In the years after 1660 harvests throughout most of Europe suffered from bad weather: the continent was entering a new phase in the 'little ice age' of the seventeenth century. England itself escaped famine, but trade and manufacturers were affected by reduced demand overseas for any commodity other than food. This recession more than counterbalanced the favourable effects when Charles ended Cromwell's war against Spain. In 1665–6 plague devastated London and many of the provinces. The Great Fire of London, from which Charles and James alone emerged with conspicuous credit, for having tried to prevent its spread by pulling down houses to make fire-breaks, destroyed much of the greatest concentration of wealth in the land.[93] London recovered with remarkable speed. But the other principal cause of economic decline, which bred social disquiet and political discontent, was only slowly becoming apparent, and was to last for over half a century. A steady fall in agricultural rents (but not in labourers' wages) made it increasingly difficult for landowners to find or keep tenants, and badly affected the previously active land market. The landowning gentry, politically the most influential of all classes, suffered a reduction in income.

Consequently during the 1660s discontent began to solidify gentry attitudes in forms that already began to resemble those of post–1688 Toryism. They showed a lack of interest in European affairs amounting to isolationism; provincial resentment of both Court and City; violent hostility to bankers and the emergent monied interest; suspicion of ministers, managers and their own self-appointed spokesmen. On the positive side they displayed a fierce loyalty to the church, which found expression especially in enmity to both dissenters and papists.

Having freed himself from Clarendon, Charles had no wish to become dependent on the parliamentary representatives of the gentry. He wanted to develop and follow dynamic policies – a third mercantilist war against the Dutch, a French alliance, religious toleration, fiscal reorganization. None of these policies appealed to the gentry. Still less acceptable was their ultimate, but concealed, objective – an end to royal dependence on parliament and the church.

5   The 'Cabal' and its Projects

The removal of Clarendon produced sweeping changes. He had been the dominant influence over Charles since 1652, although the latter had always consulted others, and taken many important decisions without (or against) his advice. Historians have generally censured Charles for his shabby treatment of an old and loyal servant, but Clarendon had clung to office despite incapacitating bouts of illness, and had ignored accumulating evidence that his policies and governmental methods were no longer working effectively. In the summer of 1667 alarmingly strong and widespread discontent left Charles with little option but to cast Clarendon as the unmistakable scapegoat, loading him with the blame for all that had gone wrong since 1660. This he did by encouraging an impeachment of the man he had already dismissed as minister – brutal and ungrateful behaviour, which was, however, remarkably effective in reducing political tensions and popular discontent in a very short time.[1]

By ruining Clarendon, Charles deliberately broke the mould of politics. A period of political flux and policy gestation ensued, as a new generation of politicians and courtiers engaged in frenzied competition for office, influence and power. At the top, Buckingham and Arlington contested the position of leading minister. A younger generation – Clifford, Edward Seymour, Thomas Littleton, Thomas Osborne, Richard Temple – worked ruthlessly to replace former nominees of Clarendon in offices of middle importance. Downing, William Temple and William Coventry formed another group, of aspirants who sought office in order to bring about fundamental changes both in policies and in the ways in which they were decided and implemented. On the other hand Clarendon's dismissal forced many interests and individuals to go on to the defensive. It caused a temporarily serious rift between Charles and James, who stood by his father-in-law and was seen by many Anglican peers and MPs, as well as by the anxious bishops, as potential champion of the rights of the church and defender of the constitution. In the wake of the dismissal of Clarendon, Charles removed some bishops from the privy council, and forbade others from attendance at Court. In reality the position of the church was even more exposed than Archbishop Sheldon thought: it was at this time that

James's sympathies for Catholicism were developing, and Charles was to engage him in the new policies of an alliance with France and toleration to include Catholics. Ormonde became a belated casualty. His recall as lord-lieutenant in February 1669 was planned as a necessary preliminary to major changes in Ireland. Another project was to be prepared for a union between England and Scotland.

The politicians who had contrived Clarendon's ruin had promised Charles personal freedom of action or, more accurately, freedom from restraints, and an end to a minister's censorious criticisms and pedantic insistence on following only constitutionally prescribed governmental methods. Charles could now follow his own inclinations, and he now assumed a central position in all decision-making, although he continued to delegate most routine business to ministers. The fluid situation at Court and within the council gave him great advantages; there was now no question of a chief minister or a united and homogeneous ministry dictating to him. Ministers and aspirants to high office knew that promotion or survival depended on being able to penetrate Charles's thoughts and intentions, so as to be able to anticipate and implement his wishes – even though they did not believe in the policies and appointments that resulted. Only William Coventry refused to act in this way, and consequently lost influence, and then office.[2]

Charles personally created a state of confusion in public policy in the years after 1667 that operated to his advantage in a tactical sense. Ministers formulated and advised policies and projects, but if these were accepted there was no certainty that the king would give continuing support. Charles frequently took advice secretly from private counsellors, and made promises which he concealed from his ministers. He conducted negotiations and adopted policies (particularly in foreign affairs) that he had to conceal because they were totally at variance with those that were publicly acknowledged. As a result the years 1667–73 constitute a period of changes, ambiguities and deceptions, of almost continuous manœuvring and intrigue, in which Charles successfully misled everyone who mattered, except Louis and William.

However it is possible to detect one central objective underlying all the ambiguities and deceptions, the sudden and drastic changes of policy. Charles shared with his new ministers the aim of significantly increasing royal authority, by freeing the king from dependence on his subjects. This meant primarily freedom from the limits placed on royal actions by the two centrally important institutions – parliament and the Church of England. This can be seen most clearly in Charles's decision not to take up a completely alternative political strategy that unexpectedly became available in 1668–9. The collapse of Buckingham's first attempts to obtain religious toleration, through the management of both Houses of Parliament, gave Charles the option of allying permanently instead with the

Anglican bishops and a majority in Lords and Commons who claimed the title of 'friends to the Constitution', and have often been described as 'Clarendonians', although they had much more coherence and influence after Clarendon's fall than during his term as minister. For eighteen months in 1669–71 Charles gave a deliberately false impression of being ready to work with them, accepting their terms and following their principles – as demonstrated by the 1670 Conventicle Act – but he did so only in order to exploit parliament's willingness to vote him money. Once he became free to do so, Charles turned away from those who thought themselves the natural allies of the Crown, and instituted policies that had already been decided on in secret and were diametrically opposed to those that he had accepted for purely tactical reasons.

Of these new policies, the Declaration of Indulgence loosened the ties that identified the king with the repressive Anglican Church. Charles sincerely wished to institute toleration, but it had to be by means of prerogative powers, not statute, so as to tie the dissenters to the king by gratitude and interest. The declaration also meant that the Catholics could obtain benefits that parliament would never institute. The second substantial departure in policy, the third Dutch War, also involved the total reversal of a policy that parliament had approved – the Triple Alliance of 1668 with Sweden and the Dutch to check French expansion.[3] By attacking the Dutch, to break their power at sea, and allying with the preponderant power of France, Charles infringed the newly formulated principle of maintaining a balance of power in Europe. It could have been argued that if he achieved his objective of winning a naval and then commercial supremacy this would offset French military power. However the main, but concealed, objective of the war was to make the king financially independent. A victorious war would produce prizes and an indemnity. More significantly it was hoped that it would increase the volume of English overseas trade, and consequently the yield from customs. There was also a personal element. Victory would erase memories of the humiliating defeats of 1667, and enable Charles to install his nephew William as sovereign prince in Holland, thus achieving the prize that William II had failed to win by a coup in 1650.

The French alliance accorded with Charles's most deeply felt personal sympathies. Throughout the whole of his life Charles strongly and consistently sought out the friendship of his cousin Louis: it can be said that this was the political principle to which he was most constantly attached. It derived partly from contempt for Spain – the product of his own experience of the feebleness of its ministers and the decline of its army – and for the bourgeois Dutch republic. But it was fostered far more significantly by Charles's admiration for the power possessed and exercised personally by his cousin Louis, and especially for the control that the latter exerted over his ministers and the nobility. The Dutch War of 1672 provided the occasion for the alliance with France, but Charles hoped to establish a permanent connection with Louis.

In the short term the alliance with France also brought about a full reconciliation of Charles with James, who was always even more francophile than his brother. In terms of domestic politics a short and victorious war would immeasurably strengthen the king's position in relation to parliament. Charles would be able to put demands for an increase in his settled or permanent revenue from a position of strength, since MPs would know that it was now at last in his power to dissolve parliament without having to call another, since victory over the Dutch would produce a large war indemnity and, in the longer term, an expansion of trade that would increase receipts from customs. Charles would be able either to exact compliance with his demands from a now submissive Cavalier Parliament, or to choose to rule for the first time without a parliament. In either case he would be able to exact from JPs and corporations an acceptance of religious toleration based on exercise of the royal prerogative. He would also be able to remodel the government of Ireland without risking damaging repercussions, and the army and navy could both be expanded.

These projects or possibilities, all of which feature in the despatches of foreign ambassadors in London, and are obviously based on conversations with Charles, James, and ministers and courtiers who were involved in their preparation, failed when the army and navy failed to achieve decisive victory over the Dutch. But Charles had to abandon his domestic projects even before the end of the war. His ministry, known to contemporaries and posterity as the Cabal, fell apart. By the end of 1673 Charles had to retire behind the screen provided by a newcomer, Danby, who eventually became chief minister, as none of the previous ministry did. Danby initiated new measures and governmental methods that added up to another complete reversal of policies and practices. As he took over management of the king's affairs, so Charles retired into the background, playing a far less active role than in the years 1667–73.

Although the policies of the so-called Cabal ministry all collapsed by the end of 1673, they had lasting effects. Charles's dishonesties and deceptions had been exposed. Virtually everyone with some knowledge of politics could never again trust him or anything he said, either in public or in private. In addition his easy abandonment of unpopular policies and ministers created an almost universal belief that under pressure and coercion Charles could be brought to concede virtually anything.

Charles's two leading ministers reacted characteristically to Clarendon's fate. It reinforced Arlington's caution: although by 1668 he had achieved a major foreign policy success, the Triple Alliance, and Charles relied heavily on his general advice, he went out of his way not to give the appearance of being chief minister.[4] In contrast Buckingham behaved as if he was already chief minister, introducing new policies and launching a campaign of parliamentary management.[5] A major development in the autumn of 1667, which Charles treated explicitly as a direct threat to his power as sovereign, showed how necessary it was for the Court to organize a working majority in both Houses. The prodigiously large sums of money voted in 1665–6 had not brought victory over the Dutch, but had produced serious allegations that very considerable amounts had been embezzled or misappropriated. The Commons attempted to nominate commissioners with the remit of inspecting accounts of extraordinary revenue and expenditure, and with the power to examine witnesses on oath (January 1667). The Commons clashed angrily with the Lords, because the latter preferred to ask Charles to name commissioners. Seeing tactical advantages in doing so, and ignoring Clarendon's objections, Charles responded by nominating an excessively large and heterogeneous body, which he did not expect to do a thorough job. His manœuvre failed. The MPs named refused to act, openly expressing their fear that the composition was being fixed, so that they would be out-voted by royal dependants. Their legal objection that only a statutory commission could require evidence on oath impressed the judges whom Charles consulted. Consequently Charles's nominated commission never began work.[6]

In the autumn session of 1667 parliament established an accounts commission by statute, known as the Brooke House Committee (December), which Charles resented, but had to accept. He rightly appreciated the threat posed by an independent body. Parliament had failed to rectify the original miscalculations of 1660–1, when it had voted him an inadequate permanent revenue. Encumbered by debts from the Dutch war, which the new treasury commission was just beginning to tackle, he knew that further requests would have to be made to parliament for extraordinary supply. Charles already saw himself at a disadvantage compared with all other European monarchs, because he needed parliamentary consent for taxation. If MPs took advantage of his financial weakness to establish an institution to investigate, monitor and report publicly on the expenditure of all money voted in the form of extraordinary supply, the king would be still further restricted. His immediate fears were realized in 1669, when the committee's reports led to furious attacks on the navy treasurer, Carteret, but the Commons failed to turn the committee into a permanent institution and, strangely, the Country opposition failed to revive it in the 1670s.[7]

When parliament met in February 1668 the Court proposed new policies. Charles asked for supply to rebuild the fleet, so as to give strength to Arlington's new alliances with the Dutch and Sweden. More controversially, Charles indicated a significant change in religious policy. On 10 February he asked parliament to consider 'some course to beget a better

union and composure in the minds of my Protestant subjects'.[8] The king
wished to realize the propositions that he had had to abandon in 1662–3,
for limited toleration accompanied by safeguards for public order and the
church, and to return to the principles of the Breda declaration of 1660.
But in the public mind, and certainly in parliament, the new policy
proposals were attributed to Buckingham's influence. As always, the
latter behaved indiscreetly, carelessly allowing leaks of the negotiations
between his representatives and leading dissenters. Archbishop Sheldon,
alarmed that Charles would allow Buckingham to rush bills through a thin
parliament, alerted the Anglican interest to take precautions. The MPs
who collaborated with him very skilfully out-manœuvred the Court.
They poisoned the political atmosphere before Charles's speech by
making great play of a few cases in which dissenters had disturbed Anglican services, and added information on the number of conventicles being
held throughout the country. The Anglican tactic worked, leading the
Commons to ask Charles to restrain dissenters and enforce the laws
against their conventicles. Unwisely Buckingham's managers persisted,
proposing that Charles should be asked to summon leading dissenters, get
propositions from them, and then formulate Bills for toleration and
comprehension. This revealed what had been in the king's mind, but the
suggestion was heavily defeated on 8 April, by 170 to 76.[9]

Buckingham's attempts at parliamentary management provoked a
backlash. Independent MPs in the Commons introduced a new, severe
Bill against conventicles which would have passed had Charles not prorogued the session. Buckingham's lack of skill and general political style
had the effect of uniting the majority of independent peers and MPs in an
effective body. They were the men, mainly former royalists, to whom
Clarendon had failed to give a clear lead; contemporaries called them
'friends to the Constitution in Church and State'. Conservative in all
respects they resisted all attempted innovations – Sir Richard Temple's
mistimed attempt in February 1668 to amend the Triennial Act; a Bill to
allow leaseholders and copyholders to sit on juries; any attempt to relax
the Uniformity Act.[10] They were also profoundly suspicious of royal
requests for supply, fearing a design to introduce a land tax and a general
excise – the first of which they regarded as destructive to the gentry, the
second as involving extensions of an inquisitorial bureaucracy that would
infringe the rights of JPs.

This majority routed Buckingham in 1668, and dominated the sessions
of 1669, 1670 and 1670–1. Three times they passed a stringent Bill against
conventicles through the Commons, but although twice its passage was
blocked by prorogations Charles had to consent to its enactment in 1670.[11]
This represented a public retreat, an even more conclusive check than that
of 1662–3 to his desire for toleration. Clumsy attempts at parliamentary
management deepened MPs' hostility to ministerial corruption and mani-

pulative practices. Buckingham responded by urging Charles to dissolve parliament, in the probably justified expectation that a new Commons would be more favourable to toleration, but Charles (with more far-reaching projects in mind) refused to risk elections that would probably return a Country majority less inclined to vote adequate supply. Instead he prorogued parliament for an unprecedented seventeen-month period from May 1668 to October 1669, giving him time to make some momentous decisions. However, the opposition did not lose its cohesion during this period, and two of Charles's moves provided them with additional leaders.

Buckingham exerted pressure on Charles to remove Ormonde as lord-lieutenant of Ireland, in order to dispose of this most prestigious office for his own advantage. He suggested holding it himself, with the work being done by a deputy, or alternatively giving it to Monmouth, Charles's eldest son, again with a deputy chosen from Buckingham's associates.[12] Perturbed, Ormonde openly approached Charles and received satisfactory assurances in November 1668, Charles telling him, so he reported, '" that no suggestions to my prejudice [had] or [would] have place or credit". And, at my going forth he commanded me to rest confident of his justice and favour to me'.[13] Less than three months later Ormonde learnt that at a 'merry party' Buckingham had persuaded Charles to dismiss him immediately. Again Ormonde tackled the king, who received him kindly and falsely, admitting that he had been considering a change but had not resolved anything – although he had. Charles behaved shabbily in discarding (February 1669) the most outstandingly loyal of all his servants, against whose conduct (unlike Clarendon's) there were few legitimate complaints. But characteristically he used the removal to strengthen his own position. Buckingham dislodged Ormonde but did not get the office, which went to an outsider, Robartes, who went his own ineffective way. Charles shirked telling Ormonde of his dismissal, employing Arlington as his messenger, although the latter had not participated in the decision. This maintained the existing estrangement between Arlington and Ormonde's friends, who might otherwise have coalesced against the other ministers.[14]

Charles had important but unacknowledged reasons for dismissing Sir William Coventry as treasury commissioner in March 1669. Superficially this represented another victory for Buckingham, whom Coventry had foolishly challenged to a duel. Charles disliked Coventry personally, especially for his assertive manner, apparently discounting his proven commitment to greater administrative and financial efficiency. However his main purpose was to eliminate Coventry's influence on James and prevent the coalescence of the 'friends to the Constitution', Ormonde and former associates of Clarendon in a 'duke's party' that would not only dominate both Houses but also exert influence at Court, where overdue but severe retrenchment measures had provoked widespread discontent. Coventry had served James as his man of business since 1660, acting as a counterpoise to a strong group of Irish Catholics in the duke's entourage. Charles knew that Ormonde and Coventry would use all their influence to oppose the two major departures in policy on which he had secretly embarked, and which he now engaged James and Arlington to assist: the remodelling of the Irish administration, which must eventually mean reopening the land settlement; and his central innovation in policy, the negotiation of a secret alliance with France against the Dutch.[15]

The death of Philip IV of Spain in September 1665, that is, while the Dutch War was in progress, raised extremely wide foreign policy issues. Although he was succeeded by a son, Carlos II, uncertainty persisted. The new king was a feeble infant, whose early death was generally assumed. Since there was no other male heir in the Spanish royal family, his death would precipitate a European crisis, with Louis XIV and the Emperor as claimants to the succession. But Louis provoked an acute if more limited crisis, by advancing claims on behalf of his wife to parts of the Spanish Netherlands. This immediate threat to this strategically vital area forced both the Dutch and the English governments into hasty reconsiderations of policy. Louis honoured his treaty obligations to the Dutch by declaring war on England in January 1666, but he made little attempt to engage in hostilities. Instead he prepared his army for what became known as the War of Devolution against Spain (1667–8). The overwhelming success of his invasion of the Spanish Netherlands during the first summer's campaign caused consternation in England and the United Provinces; there seemed to be no reason why France should not conquer the whole territory in a second campaign. Charles's first reaction was to appease Louis, in order to detach him from his Dutch alliance. Although still nominally at war, Charles and Louis exchanged letters in April 1667, using Henrietta Maria as an intermediary. Each undertook not to enter into any engagement contrary to the other's interests.[16] For Louis this meant that England would not ally with Spain against France and the Dutch. In the autumn Charles told Ruvigny, the new French ambassador, that he wished to reach a full understanding with Louis, but added with emphasis that most of the nation feared France. However he turned coy when Ruvigny asked him to state what he wanted from Louis, insisting that the latter should make the first offers.[17]

This exchange led Louis to form conclusions that were to shape all his future dealings with Charles. He realized that although the latter was likely to make difficulties and waste time by protracting negotiations, the weakness of his authority meant that he must always keep open the possibility of an understanding with Louis, because he might need French assistance to preserve his remaining powers, or even his position, as king.

In the extreme case of another rebellion, Louis would give him armed assistance. The more probable eventuality – in 1668 and again in 1678 – was that Charles's ministers and parliament would force him to accept policies which they formulated, and commercial connections with Spain would always incline them to adopt anti-French policies. Louis therefore took the main line of upholding Charles's authority, to prevent him being compelled by his subjects to oppose French interests. In addition Louis appreciated the value of building up an interest in parliament: in 1668 he authorized Ruvigny to spend £5,000 on influencing peers and MPs.[18]

Charles's weakness and impressionability led Louis into direct relations with the leading English ministers. He fought shy of Buckingham's effusive offers to act as his champion, now that Clarendon had been overthrown. He placed no trust in Buckingham's judgement, but satisfied him with some money and a great deal of flattery.[19] Louis deeply distrusted the other leading minister, Arlington, because of his pro-Spanish reputation. As an experienced diplomat he was also less easy to deceive than Charles, James and Buckingham, and by taking initiatives he threatened to create difficulties for Louis, who considered him a negative influence on Charles. Having taken it for granted that Charles and James would agree to an alliance with France, whenever it suited Louis to offer one, the latter was unfavourably impressed when Charles produced a draft treaty composed by Arlington. This was entirely directed against the Dutch (December 1667), but at this time Louis was concerned exclusively with isolating Spain and imposing a peace that would bring him substantial territorial gains in Flanders. He did not want an early breach with the Dutch. Louis therefore responded to Arlington's proposal with an equally insincere and professional gambit, making propositions that would require Charles to seek French approval for any new policy.[20]

Acting very much on his own judgement, and with little support from Charles and James, Arlington engaged in negotiations that were intended to establish a position in which Charles would be tied to neither France nor Spain nor the Dutch, while preserving the integrity of the Spanish Netherlands. He had to persuade Louis to make an early and reasonable peace and, probably more difficult, to induce Spain to make concessions to satisfy Louis rather than prolong a losing war, in the hope that other states would come in as allies. While professionally exchanging mutually unacceptable proposals with Louis, Arlington concluded a defensive alliance with the Dutch (January 1668), known after the addition of Sweden as the Triple Alliance. Sir William Temple, who did the bulk of the negotiating at The Hague, intended the alliance to check French expansion and, more generally, to establish a balance of power in Europe, a concept which he advanced as the guiding principle for English foreign policy.[21] Charles accepted the alliance for much more immediate and tactical purposes. He wanted to ensure an early end to the War of Devolution, before he became involved against his will. He used the alliance to get supply from parliament. However, his main reason was almost certainly to enhance his value in Louis' eyes and calculations. At this stage neither he nor his ministers (with the exception of Clifford who as yet had limited influence) had decided on a new Dutch war, but they placed considerable emphasis on the need to break up the Franco–Dutch alliance of 1662. Paradoxical as it may seem, Charles used his new treaty with the Dutch to achieve this objective. He betrayed to Louis the secret clause in the Triple Alliance by which, if Spain offered concessions but Louis rejected them and continued the war, the English and Dutch would come to Spain's assistance and force France back to the frontiers of 1659. By this revelation Charles signalled to Louis his lack of fidelity to the new alliance, and the latter responded quickly.[22]

In April 1668 a new set of negotiations began between Charles and Louis, but they came to nothing because the latter found it impossible to pin Charles down to specific proposals.[23] The French negotiators blamed Arlington for this failure, and he was certainly wary of the one-sided proposals that they advanced. However Charles's reason for allowing difficulties to arise was devious in the extreme. He wanted to ensure that negotiations for an alliance between the two kings should be conducted by himself. Louis agreed with alacrity, well aware of the advantages to himself of negotiating with a royal amateur. In form he did not participate himself. Instead from July 1668 the previously personal correspondence between Charles and his sister, Henrietta, Duchess of Orléans, became the medium for direct, conclusive and secret negotiations. By using this personal channel Louis virtually eliminated the risk that Charles would reveal anything to the Dutch. It also cut out the English ministers, who might make difficulties. Henrietta wrote in her own hand, but the business portions were not her own work – they were dictated by Louis. Charles's letters were exclusively of his own composition. From the vital political and diplomatic angles this was a correspondence between a lazy-minded amateur (Charles) and the most astute professional in Europe (Louis).[24]

Louis used this negotiation by correspondence to commit Charles to the new line of French policy. By early 1669 this required a joint military and naval war of aggression and aggrandizement against the Dutch republic. The Triple Alliance convinced Louis that the Dutch, but not the English or the Swedes, had the capacity to check and resist him, thanks to their naval strength, their commercial wealth and their diplomatic network. On his side Charles, although he had not originally wanted the second Dutch War, now saw a French alliance as ensuring a quick and decisive victory in a new war of revenge. The greater authority that this would give to the king would enable him to establish religious toleration and declare himself a Catholic – at least this is what Charles told James, Arlington, Clifford and a Catholic peer, Arundell of Wardour, in January 1669.[25]

However, surprisingly little progress was made during the rest of 1669 in agreeing an actual alliance. Charles raised some serious difficulties with Louis, expressing his concern over the spectacular expansion of the French navy, and insisting that a commercial treaty (involving French concessions) must be signed before he would conclude a political alliance. Some historians have concluded that Charles was championing British naval supremacy and commercial interests. The outcome does not substantiate this thesis. The French did not slacken their rate of naval construction. Accepting in principle the need for a commercial treaty, they spun out negotiations so that nothing substantial emerged, and this against a background of vociferous English mercantile protests against Colbert's prohibitive new tariffs.[26] Charles contributed to lack of progress in concluding the political alliance by using too many negotiators, many of whom said different things to the French. The king continued to write to Henrietta. St Albans and Arundell went separately on missions to Paris. Buckingham and Arlington negotiated rather unhappily in London with the French ambassador, the rigid and arrogant Colbert de Croissy, and it did not help the negotiations that the latter did not know Louis' real intentions until October.[27] Charles also ordered both ministers to correspond with Henrietta, but for different reasons – Arlington, so as to commit him and to show Louis that he could now be trusted; Buckingham, for the alarming reason that he had discovered something of Charles's secret correspondence with her. By telling Buckingham and Henrietta to correspond, in very general terms, about the need for Anglo-French friendship and a possible alliance, Charles flattered him and put him off the scent.[28]

In November 1669 Arlington and Colbert de Croissy began serious negotiations, but Louis continued to doubt whether Charles had committed himself irrevocably to a strict alliance. French suspicions were aroused by a treaty (January 1670) with the Dutch and Swedes to provide assistance to Spain if the French attacked Flanders.[29] This treaty can be interpreted as an adroit move by Arlington to ensure that Louis concentrated his enmity against the Dutch and did not resume aggression against Spain. Nevertheless sufficient progress was achieved for the secret Treaty of Dover to be signed in May 1670 during Henrietta's brief visit to England. The shortness of her stay deceived Spanish and Dutch diplomats, who did not know that she came only to conclude, not to negotiate, a treaty.[30]

An entirely aggressive war against the Dutch formed the heart of the Dover treaty, with France and England agreeing to attack simultaneously and not to make a separate peace or truce.[31] Charles agreed to provide auxiliary military forces for the land campaign, and Louis an auxiliary fleet to join the English. French financial subsidies for the war were to amount to 3,000,000 livres per annum, and other indications showed that Charles was tying himself to a partner with far superior power and resources.

Admittedly Louis agreed not to revoke or infringe the peace of Aachen, which guaranteed what was left of the Spanish Netherlands, so that formally Charles would not find himself reneging on the Triple Alliance (which was not a general or comprehensive treaty), but the clause on the vital Spanish succession left Louis with an entirely free hand. Charles undertook to assist Louis in acquiring his rights – which the treaty did not specify – and not to enter any treaty concerning them with any other state. In 1670 this was thought to be a matter of great and imminent importance, since few expected Carlos II to live long. The clause on conquests at the expense of the Dutch in the forthcoming war was also favourable to Louis: the treaty defined, and so limited, English gains – Sluis, Kadsand and Walcheren. French acquisitions were not specified, and so could be decided by Louis. Later, in a rare example of candour, French diplomats admitted that they had not known the geographical location of the English acquisitions (in the Scheldt estuary, commanding the approaches to Antwerp) and so had not appreciated their considerable importance.[32]

The 'Catholicity' clause provides the most mystifying aspect of the treaty. In it Charles stated his intention to declare his conversion to Catholicism: he received a promise from Louis to assist with a subsidy and, if necessary, with an army to suppress disturbances or a rebellion. The timing of the declaration of conversion was left to Charles, that of the declaration of war to Louis. What was Charles's purpose in proposing, and Louis' in accepting, this extraordinary clause? Of course Charles indefinitely postponed his declaration, but pocketed the subsidy which was connected with it, which he spent on the war. Clearly Charles could not declare his conversion formally, as an act of state, until the victorious outcome of the war had strengthened his royal authority in relation to both parliament and the nation. In the interim he showed no sense of urgency in even considering the difficulties that would certainly occur. He displayed no interest in resolving the technical difficulties involved in obtaining formal recognition of his conversion by the Vatican, and when Louis pressed him to open discussions with the Pope, offering clerical assistance, Charles put him off with frivolous objections. For example, Charles insisted that any priest sent to counsel him in the faith must also be able to talk to him about problems in chemistry.[33]

Charles never revealed his mind on this clause, and when he was converted, on his death bed in 1685, this was a private not a public matter. My own hypothesis is that Charles inserted the Catholicity clause in the Dover treaty in order to be able, if it ever became necessary, to exert some leverage on Louis. Charles faced the unpalatable fact that the Dover alliance united him with a far stronger state. By 1670–2 the French navy had increased to a size equal to that of the English and the Dutch combined. Qualitatively it was superior. Louis now led the finest army of modern times and a superbly efficient diplomatic system. Charles and

Arlington knew that all French moves were directed towards exploiting Louis' claims to the Spanish succession when Carlos II died, which would include annexation of the Spanish Netherlands. Charles recognized Louis' rights in vague terms in the Dover treaty, but he had to face the possibility that English and French interests might diverge once the Dutch had been defeated. Any lapse of the alliance would leave Charles in a dangerously exposed position, committed at home to unpopular policies and unable to call on Louis for assistance, either in the form of subsidies to free himself from a refractory parliament or even in the form of the armed support envisaged at Dover. In committing himself to the French alliance and to the policies advocated by James and Clifford, Charles needed to be sure that he would continue to receive support from Louis, although once the Dutch had been defeated Louis would no longer need English naval assistance.

By introducing the Catholicity clause, and postponing the date for the declaration of his conversion, Charles attempted to safeguard himself against any future abandonment of his interests by Louis. This offered the only form of leverage that Charles could exert on his over-powerful ally. Louis, as *le roi très chrétien*, could not easily disavow the obligations of his faith and, by abandoning a Catholic Charles, imperil the survival of Catholicism in England. This stratagem involved the postponement of a public declaration of Charles's conversion. If he made it before the war began it would merely earn him a subsidy. By postponing it Charles had a bargaining counter to use in emergency. Of course this clause exposed Charles to the risk of being blackmailed by the French, but as Temple (who knew nothing about the details of the Dover treaty) saw in December 1673 those who had negotiated it could be damaged by any kind of revelation by the French.[34] In the event Louis and his ambassador in London in 1679, Barrillon, discussed the possibility of making revelations about the Dover treaty, but agreed that although this would provoke public opinion against Charles it would also lead to an outcry against France. Louis did make oblique use of Charles's vulnerability in 1682, when the latter was giving the appearance of preparing to intervene in Europe to check French expansionism. Charles took care to explain to Louis that he was only pretending to intervene, in order to satisfy his subjects, but the French king placed no trust in such assurances. A book appeared in Paris, written by the historiographer-royal, the Abbé Primi, containing references to the Dover treaty and its religious clause. Louis suppressed the book, but only after copies had been sold and left the country. This was an unmistakable warning to Charles, but it was not until the 1770s that the Dover treaty was at last published.[35]

Charles was obliged to negotiate a second secret treaty, the *traité simulé*, to involve the Protestant ministers (Ashley, Lauderdale and Buckingham) in the preparations for the war.[36] Louis welcomed this farce, because it ensured that the Dutch war would take precedence over a declaration of Charles's conversion – of which these ministers knew nothing. However the employment of Buckingham to negotiate the preliminaries in Paris led to a leak. The Dutch chargé sent full reports to The Hague before the treaty was signed in December 1670.[37] It was now too late to start the war in 1671, as originally intended. Military, naval and diplomatic preparations necessitated a delay until 1672, which required from Charles the exercise of considerable dissimulative skill in organizing a series of deceptions. These proved to be effective, but they account for the deep and almost universal distrust of Charles and his speeches that was to handicap the administration in the years after 1672. Charles obtained supply in the 1670–1 session specifically to uphold the Triple Alliance. On the first day, while he said little to parliament, the lord keeper, Bridgeman (who knew nothing about either the Dover or the simulated treaty), asked for money to support the king's allies (who included the Dutch) and to check France, whereas the real reason for naval expenditure was to make possible a war of aggression against the Dutch republic.[38]

Charles had to undertake an equally great deception in terms of domestic affairs. The meeting at Dover coincided exactly with the coming into force of a new and more stringent Conventicle Act. Buckingham's proposals for toleration had provoked the Commons into passing a severe measure in the 1668 session, but it lapsed on the prorogation. But the church and Cavalier interest in both Lords and Commons achieved a unity of purpose and energy that persuaded Charles to allow them to push through a revived Bill, in the hope that this would persuade them to be generous with supply. The result was disappointing – an eight-year continuation of the duty on wine – but he obtained other advantages.[39] The Brooke House Committee lost all momentum. The king and his ministers overcame strenuous opposition in an extraordinary project that could have had far-reaching consequences but eventually proved to be inconclusive. Charles associated himself with the Roos Divorce Bill. Lord Roos had already obtained a church-court divorce from his unfaithful wife: this dissolved the marriage and bastardized children born to her (the whole point of the exercise), but did not allow either husband or wife to remarry. The Act passed with Charles's assistance in April 1670 was the first to authorize remarriage, so initiating the procedure that continued until 1857. Many peers objected on theological grounds, and received a strong lead from the bench of bishops: without Charles's urging the Bill would not have passed the Lords. His intervention made everyone realize that the Bill provided a legal mechanism for him to discard his faithful queen, on the grounds of her infertility, freeing him to remarry and produce legitimate heirs. Buckingham strongly advocated this course. His managers mobilized a majority in the Commons, but there was also a sharp division within the Court. James was naturally hostile. So too were the royal mistresses, who feared that a new and sexually active queen would lead Charles to discard them. However in the end Charles made a private decision not to avail himself of the option that the Roos Divorce Act created.[40]

Observation of the Roos debates gave Charles a taste for attending debates in the Lords: he was to be present at virtually every sitting during the sessions of 1673, 1674 and 1675. But in the adjourned session of October 1670 to April 1671 the main business was financial supply, a matter which concerned the Commons exclusively. The Court spokesmen asked for large grants so as to clear off the royal debts, which were estimated at £1,300,000, in order to facilitate the raising of future loans, and for £800,000 to be spent on the navy, with the explicit objective of upholding the Triple Alliance. In general the Commons responded favourably, but they made slow progress in detail. Consequently Charles summoned them on 10 December to hear a speech of highly inventive deviousness and insincerity.[41] He used the forthcoming visit of Louis to Dunkirk as an argument for expediting supply, so that 'we might owe our safety to our own strength, and not to his courtesy'. He promised that once this money had been voted it would not be necessary for him to ask them for more. He painted a rosy picture of the next session, which would be concerned 'only to provide good laws for the people, and not be spent in providing supplies for him'. When he said this Charles had no intention of calling another session before the war began. Normally parliament would meet in the autumn of 1671, but by then naval and diplomatic preparations would be under way, and it would no longer be possible to conceal their real purpose. Charles did not plan to call parliament again until after the conclusion of a decisive campaign in the summer of 1672. This would immeasurably strengthen his position, enabling him to put demands, not requests, to a parliament that would know that he could now dispense with it.

Charles obtained less supply than he expected, but he prorogued the session (22 April 1671) while a further set of supply proposals were under consideration.[42] These took the form of additional duties on imported commodities, mostly luxury goods from France. Debates on them revealed considerable and increasing hostility to French fiscal and commercial policies, and MPs also expressed concern for the preservation or, if possible, expansion of trade with Spain and its European possessions. Such commercial antagonism to France went against Charles's secret alliance, and the proposed duties amounted to the Commons imposing an alternative and popular commercial policy.[43] Equally unacceptable was an anti-Catholic Bill, which most MPs would certainly have categorized as a 'good law'. Faced with debates in the Commons that generated violent attacks on the Catholics, Charles reacted cautiously. In order to satisfy peers and MPs he publicly conceded that indiscreet behaviour by zealots, particularly the Jesuits and some recent converts, required reproof. But he gave a first hint of his true sentiments by adding that he could not be expected to direct repressive action against old-established familes who had been loyal to his father and himself.[44]

For implementation of the Dover treaty Charles depended on the collaboration of a new Catholic group at Court, although curiously none of its leading members (James, Clifford and Arlington) was as yet formally converted. This group, which also included the very influential Father Patrick McGinn, Richard Bellings, Richard Talbot and two peers, Arundell and St Albans, proved far more effective than its predecessors of the early 1660s. The earlier Catholic advisers associated with the queen mother, and led by the erratic Bristol, had suffered from a well-deserved reputation for intrigue and personal corruption, and had lacked a clear sense of direction. Once Charles revealed his Catholic and francophile intentions in January 1669, James supplied the main drive for what became the policies of the ministry.[45] Arlington, in contrast, was included by Charles so as to commit him to policies that he knew were hazardous. Arlington could not openly disagree with Charles's decisions, for fear of losing the office and perquisites on which he depended financially, and he compromised himself by 'allowing' his wife to accept generous 'presents' from Louis. But he alone of the senior ministers had direct experience of the skill and unscrupulousness with which Louis and French diplomats pursued their dynastic and national objectives. Specifically Arlington feared that a blind attachment to France would produce a break with Spain, which would have serious economic effects.[46]

While Arlington cautiously attempted to preserve some freedom of action for Charles, his caution led to his being eclipsed by his own protégé, Clifford, who quickly established himself as James's lieutenant.[47] James failed to persuade Charles to take the irrevocable step of immediately declaring himself a Catholic, but his own role as the architect of naval victory reconciled him to the war coming first. James prepared the fleet, and Charles gave him supreme command at sea because he would have to undertake the potentially delicate task of ensuring co-operation with (and from) the French fleet. In terms of domestic politics James gave full support to Clifford, whose characteristics of energy and obstinacy, attachment to Catholicism and authoritarianism, so resembled his own.

Most historians have judged Clifford to be the least important of the ministers.[48] Admittedly he rose from relative obscurity as the client first of Arlington and then of James, and his brief career at the top ended in total failure, but he provided the main driving force for the major policies of 1670–3, and successively tackled all the most difficult problems facing the ministry. The evidence of contemporary observers shows that Charles did not share his brother's admiration for Clifford, but he appreciated his energy and determination and gave him completely free scope to implement the decisions agreed at Dover. Clifford made forcible use of his power – it was he who was behind the stop of the exchequer and the sabotage of negotiations for the settlement of minor problems with the Dutch. Clifford was the antithesis of Charles. He would not dissimulate his real opinions and passionate feelings, or compromise and fudge issues. He was a 'plunger', who did nothing by halves. Violently anti-Dutch he did not disguise his determination to wreck the Triple Alliance. He was the roughest and most ruthless of the new treasury commissioners appointed in 1667.[49] Once he became convinced by Catholic claims he moved quickly towards a formal and irrevocable conversion, and after the passing of the Test Act (which he alone openly opposed) he retired into private life for the sake of his new faith. In essentials Clifford resembled his models – Louvois and Colbert, Louis' instruments of absolute authority: he was ambitious, arrogant, hard-working and resourceful. But he suffered from the fact that he served an unpredictable master, who was not yet absolute, and some of Clifford's defects contributed to the failure of the ministry to make Charles independent of parliament and his subjects. In too much haste, Clifford constantly cut corners. Short-term objectives dominated his technically not very proficient administration of royal finances, first as commissioner, then as lord treasurer. His attempts at Court and parliamentary management took the inefficient form of indiscriminate hand-outs. Ignorant of the French language, he underestimated the deviousness of Louis' policies.[50]

Impulsiveness and arrogance also foiled another of James's closest associates, Richard Talbot, who used his influence to obtain Charles's consent privately to initiate another major policy, in Ireland, but Talbot survived to try again in 1684–90. After dismissing Ormonde, Charles had named two lightweights, Robartes and Berkeley, as successive lord-lieutenants of Ireland. He authorized Talbot to return to his native country, where his equally active brother, Peter, an experienced political intriguer, had just become Catholic Archbishop of Dublin. Charles knew that Talbot intended during his visit to rally and activate the Catholic party, and to collect material to justify wholesale amendment of the Irish land settlement. In January 1671 Talbot submitted a memorial to the English council, subscribed by most prominent Catholic landowners, but he made a tactical error by being too explicit at the start in demanding changes to the Act of Settlement. Characteristically Charles countered the alarm that Talbot's activities provoked by issuing an order in council proclaiming the inviolability of the Irish land settlement, but he permitted Talbot's activities to continue.[51]

Talbot's premature disclosure of his aims compelled Charles to use indirect tactics. The king established commissions to examine aspects of the land settlement, but they achieved little. In February 1672 the English council authorized Catholics to reside and work in corporate towns, which would eventually affect the composition of the municipal governments and even of the Irish Commons.[52] But time ran out before Talbot could achieve his major aims. He expected to manipulate the feeble Berkeley, whom Charles had chosen for his Catholic sympathies, but the lord-lieutenant allowed a particularly corrupt group of subordinates to run the government entirely for their own profit, and they obstructed Talbot out of self-interest. Berkeley himself fell into such public contempt that he had to be replaced by Essex, and when the English parliament had to be recalled in 1673, and grants of supply purchased by concessions, Charles abandoned Talbot and his projects. Parliament forced dismissal of the commission of inquiry and expulsion of the Talbots. Charles had explicitly to reimpose the ban on office-holding by Catholics.[53]

These Irish projects originated with members of James's Catholic entourage; Charles allowed them to go forward. By contrast there is no doubt that the major departure in English domestic affairs – the Declaration of Indulgence – represented Charles's own personal and deep-felt wishes. By issuing public declarations and initiating private discussions, Charles had made clear his distaste for religious repression and coercive uniformity. In the Breda and Worcester House declarations of 1660 he had expressed his hopes that religious differences and discontents could be resolved by discussions and compromises, but neither the Convention nor the Cavalier Parliament had accepted his lead. Instead the latter passed the severe Uniformity Act, and refused to concur with Charles's declaration of December 1662, in which he had asked for an Act empowering the sovereign to dispense with penal statutes, in the interests of religious harmony and domestic peace. For Charles this was the essential point in all proposals for toleration: they must confer on the king the determination of both the extent and character of religious toleration. Obviously political tactics underlay this; Charles, like James later, wanted to convert religious dissenters into royal dependants who would repay their benefactor with political and possibly financial support. With responsibility for maintaining order, the king could best judge how far policies of toleration could extend, but this was an aspect on which Charles said little. Rather it was the opponents of toleration who developed the argument that it would necessitate a strengthened standing army.[54]

The experience of the Savoy Conference in 1661 demonstrated the impossibility of obtaining any agreement between Anglican and Presbyterian clergy. Consequently Charles never gave any clergy an active part in his toleration and comprehension projects, although in 1668 Buckingham did informally consult dissenting divines and Anglican moderates while preparing his scheme. This left to the king, assisted by his council, the drafting of legislation for limited toleration and some form of comprehension, which now meant amending the constitution of the church sufficiently to allow those presbyterian clergy who had been rejected in 1660–2 to return. The Commons emphatically rejected this scheme, and the new Conventicle Act represented a reaction to the attempt. This came into effect in June 1670, coinciding with the Dover meeting which took Charles out of London. Most unwisely the dissenters organized mass passive resistance, forcing the City magistrates to call out the militia, and confirming the thesis on which Anglicans based their case for repression, that conventicles were nurseries of sedition and rebellion. Their leading lay spokesmen, Hayes and Jekyll, personally antagonized Charles, first by trying to use legal processes against the magistrates, and then by their defiant attitude when summoned to appear at the council.[55]

The exceptionally severe repression of 1670–1 convinced most dissenters that only the king could protect them. Nothing could be achieved in the existing parliament, in which a maximum of about a hundred MPs could be mobilized to vote for relief measures, but at the cost of provoking double that number to appear in opposition to them. On his side Charles, like James later, greatly overestimated the advantages that the dissenters (and Catholics) would derive from toleration. He interpreted the obstinate insistence of the Anglican bishops and MPs on continued repression as an admission of weakness, a fear that if it became safe and easy to defect from the established church masses of lay people would do so. He also calculated that only under the cover of a general toleration could permanent advantages be conferred on the Catholics. But the immediate context of the third Dutch War provides the main explanation for the Declaration of Indulgence issued on 15 March 1672, two days before Charles declared war.[56]

It would not have been safe for Charles to declare war at a time when the Conventicle Act was having to be enforced with severity. The declaration blocked any Dutch attempt to exploit the dissenters. It nullified Dutch propaganda that Charles was joining Louis in a war of religion, and indeed its publication largely overshadowed the outbreak of war, absorbing most people's attention.[57] The war affected relatively few men directly, whereas the declaration promised to change the existing pattern of life for all men and women. The declaration itself was cleverly worded and skilfully drafted, far superior in construction, reasoning and guarantees to the hastily composed declaration of 1662, and also to James's of 1687 and 1688. It began carefully with a pragmatic justification: 'the sad experience' of the twelve years since 1660 had shown that 'forcible courses' did not work in promoting unity. The Declaration contained the admission that these courses had damaged the economy and particularly trade; this is perhaps the clearest contemporary example of the way in which secular and materialistic values were advancing. Charles, unlike James in 1687, had the wisdom to offer the Church of England elaborate guarantees. It was to remain 'entire in its doctrine, discipline and government, as now it stands established by law'. All its forms of worship, and its revenues, were to be preserved. Only 'exactly conformable' men could be given church appointments. Charles guaranteed the church as an institution, whereas James was to confine himself to confirming the individual rights of existing clergy.

Nevertheless all the guarantees imaginable could not prevent the declaration from provoking suspicions and strong opposition. Suspicions centered on the concession of the right of private worship to Catholics. Although a calculatedly lesser concession than the licensed public worship allowed to dissenters, this legitimated the presence in England of priests to officiate at such worship, thus suspending the penal laws against clergy in papal orders and tacitly accepting an organized Catholic Church. Constitutional opposition to the declaration could not be overcome by the assertions that Charles made about his prerogative right to suspend statutes. He was emphatically explicit about the legal basis of the declaration: it was 'that supreme power in ecclesiastical matters which is not only inherent in us, but hath been declared and recognised to be so by several statutes'. This forthright statement invited (and in 1673 was to get) both angry and reasoned rebuttals.[58] The statutes which Charles claimed to suspend included several passed by the Cavalier Parliament, which was still in being, and it had refused in 1663 to accept the existence of a royal power to suspend statutes. The declaration inevitably appeared to challenge both parliament and statute law.

However, the declaration did achieve its short-term objectives. Dissenters generally welcomed it, although with reservations about concessions to Catholics, and applied for over a thousand licences. Royal agents, many of whom James was to employ again in 1687–8, like Butler and Baber, organized addresses expressing gratitude and promising the king support. London and the provinces remained entirely quiet during the summer campaign against the Dutch.[59] But the success of the declaration was inextricably connected with victory in the war. The latter would make it unnecessary to recall parliament, or alternatively Charles would be able to dictate to parliament from a position of strength. But if Charles became dependent on parliament for money to continue the war into 1673, pressure was certain to mount against the suspending power and for withdrawal of the declaration.

James prepared the fleet during the winter of 1671–2 with great care. Seamen were procured by the imposition of a strictly enforced embargo on sailings by merchantmen – at considerable cost in dislocated trade. By March sufficient warships were ready to implement the strategy of capturing Dutch merchantmen hurrying home before war could be declared. This proved a dismal failure. A weakly escorted Dutch convoy from the

Mediterranean repulsed an attack in the Channel two days before Charles formally declared war. Ominously the failure of this piratical attempt provoked furious recriminations among the disappointed flag officers.[60] However, the junction of the English and French fleets satisfied James's requirements for a joint offensive. Charles paid a special visit to the combined fleet at Portsmouth to encourage the co-operation between the allies on which success depended.[61] Some revisionist historians have exaggerated Charles's personal interest in the navy, which after all he inherited from the Commonwealth. Charles saw the navy as his main instrument of policy in foreign affairs, important because in this area alone he had superiority over France and (he hoped) the Dutch. Although the campaign at sea went badly Charles gave the allied fleet full and consistent encouragement. After de Ruyter's victory at Sole Bay, which inflicted damage that took weeks to repair, Charles publicly praised the French so as to refute the universally credited rumours that they had deliberately failed to engage the enemy closely, leaving the English to incur heavy losses. During the summer Charles twice went out to the fleet to sustain James's authority and prestige and encourage the seamen, but the fleet achieved very little during the remainder of the campaign.[62]

Meanwhile the French military campaign came near to achieving total victory in the single month of June 1672. By 8/18 June the French had routed the Dutch forces, who fell back into the province of Holland. Four days later a Dutch mission met the French ministers accompanying the army to ascertain what terms Louis would accept. Under the shock of defeat, riots erupted in the main cities, with Orangist activists ejecting the city magistrates who represented the republican or Louvestein party. These developments made it a matter of urgency for Charles to establish immediate and direct contact with Louis, who led his victorious armies in person. Charles saw that he must quickly put himself into a position where he could intervene and influence Louis' decisions, now that it seemed likely that all Dutch resistance would suddenly collapse.[63]

The mission sent by Charles to Louis' field headquarters was at the highest possible level, led by the two principal ministers Buckingham and Arlington. To send two such deadly enemies on a combined mission reveals Charles's difficulties: he could not send only one of them, and he knew that Louis despised Buckingham and distrusted Arlington, but both had to go in order to preserve the fragile unity of the ministry. In practice the mission, assisted by Halifax, Godolphin and Monmouth, performed surprisingly well, despite an unpromising start.[64] Before he left England Buckingham started an unauthorized negotiation with the Dutch diplomats interned at Hampton Court. This raised false expectations in Holland that Charles would conclude a separate peace, but the members of the mission managed to convince all those whom they met, including William (now stadtholder), that they were not authorized to break the alliance with France, and they allayed French suspicions on this score. But they found that in his negotiations with the Dutch Louis had not been insisting on the Dutch satisfying English pretensions. This they succeeded in rectifying. The treaty concluded with Louis at Heeswijk (July) provided that neither France nor England would conclude a separate peace, and each would inform the other of offers received. Specific English demands received Louis' approval, including an increased indemnity of £1,000,000; trading rights in east Asia; the annexations agreed at Dover; and sovereignty or a hereditary stadtholdership for William.[65]

Finding that the mission was not empowered to make a separate peace, William concentrated on trying to persuade Charles personally to do so. William had formed an unfavourable impression of his uncle during his first visit to England in 1670. At that time William, aged 20 and barred by de Witt from any governmental role, lacked confidence and experience. His immaturity and introverted personality contrasted sharply with the rough energy and aggressiveness of his father William II, whom Charles had liked and even admired. Charles patronized the youthful William in 1670, giving him gratuitous advice, including (so William later told both Burnet and Sir William Temple) comments on religion that revealed his own Catholic sympathies. Historians have generally discounted these statements, especially on the grounds of Burnet's inaccuracies and sense of self-importance, but Burnet's management and resolution of William's difficulties with Mary gave him an intimacy with William that no Englishman ever achieved, and on such a crucial matter he was not likely to fabricate a totally false story. In any case, there can be no doubt that during this visit William saw through Charles's cynicism and never trusted him at any time in the future.[66]

Consequently there was no likelihood that Charles would deceive William during the worsening crisis of 1671–2. During the winter a belligerent Clifford and a reluctant Arlington, acting on Charles's instructions, scraped together all outstanding grievances so as to justify the planned war. Charles sent Downing to The Hague, to provoke the maximum friction and prevent any solution of problems.[67] Later, when the war was going wrong for him, Charles tried to excuse this behaviour to William by claiming that he had been intent on undermining the latter's republican enemies who kept him from office and power.[68] This claim was transparently false. Charles did not instruct Downing to work systematically to further William's interests, and he rebuffed William's offer to obtain the rectification of all English grievances. Charles expressed his scepticism of William's ability to do so, and broke off the correspondence in April, with a general promise that he would be 'kind'.[69]

With the collapse of the main Dutch land defences in June 1672, William made a desperate attempt to use his family connections so as to detach England from the alliance with France.[70] He made Charles extremely advantageous offers, but his aim of securing a separate peace was too obvious, and the fact that all the decisive victories had been achieved by the French army, while the naval campaign was proving to be inconclusive, gave Charles no opportunity to take independent action. Louis now occupied a position of such strength that he could apparently dictate whatever terms he pleased. Charles needed French diplomatic help to secure even the conditions stipulated in the Dover treaty, and he could not let William use his family relationship to mitigate the harsh allied demands. However, looking ahead, he saw advantages for England in installing William as a client or even puppet prince in Holland and Zeeland. He expected William to betray the Dutch republic without compunction, and to show himself grateful to the allies for conceding to him sovereign powers over what would remain of the United Provinces.

On 4 July William became stadtholder of the province of Holland. Charles rightly claimed that this would not have happened without the war, but William showed no sign of being ready to serve allied interests. Charles deployed more sophisticated arguments. He warned William that if he continued as a mere stadtholder he would find himself in a permanently precarious position, with limited powers, but carrying responsibility for the continuing defeats that a continuation of the war would inevitably produce. Charles unwisely and explicitly envisaged a permanent form of protectorate, with William receiving English support to maintain himself against his domestic republican enemies. Plumbing the depths of cynicism, Charles even tried to justify the drastic commercial concessions which William would have to make as the price of support. These would admittedly damage the Dutch economy, but Charles asserted that they would help William politically by weakening the republicans, whose party depended on the merchants and shipowners of the main trading cities.[71]

Exasperated by William's refusal to collaborate with the allies and sacrifice the independent interests of Holland, Charles began to menace his obstinate nephew. He interpreted the murder of the de Witt brothers by a mob (10/20 August) as a warning to William of his fate if he did not abandon a struggle that could bring only defeats for him, and suffering for the volatile Dutch urban masses.[72] Arlington incautiously went further, explicitly threatening William with the de Witts' fate, provoking an icy rejoinder that William was not easily frightened.[73] But William's arguments met with no positive response. Consequently his letters to Charles and Arlington during the autumn reveal a shift in tactics on his part; he affected to make a distinction between Charles and those ministers who had planned the war and, he implied, were not genuinely concerned to serve the King.[74] By the latter William certainly meant Clifford, and possibly James and Buckingham. In addition to trying to drive a wedge between Charles and the remaining champions of war, William was hoping to invite other ministers (notably Arlington and Ashley) to disassociate themselves. William made a strong disclaimer which indicated that he could turn to rougher methods: he protested that he was not working clandestinely in England against the interests of the king. In truth he was planning a campaign of subversion, but its preparation was taking longer than expected.[75]

During the summer of 1672 the French failed by a narrow margin to overwhelm the defences of Holland. By beginning to construct an anti-French alliance William ensured that the war would not only continue but expand. Consequently Charles was obliged to recall parliament in February in order to get sufficient supply to finance another campaign during the summer of 1673. He had not called a session during the autumn of 1672, in the belief that only the possibility of parliament opposing the war and the king's domestic policies kept William from accepting allied terms. But Charles took decisions in advance of the session that showed his determination to continue the war: on Clifford's advice he took the unusual and brutal course of keeping part of the fleet in commission over the winter, so that the seamen did not have to be paid off. He also ordered the raising of eight new regiments, to be used in an invasion of the Dutch coast. Eventually both moves would cost a great deal, and leave Charles dependent on parliamentary grants; he was behaving like a gambler who doubles his stake after failing to win at the first throw.[76]

The decision to continue the war with fresh determination reflected the increased influence of James's closest political associate, Clifford, whose ascendancy was signalled by his appointment on 30 November as lord treasurer. Charles did not have to appoint a lord treasurer, he could have continued the existing commission, and Clifford had not proved himself to be an outstanding financier. The appointment had exclusively political purposes, and was intended to reassure Louis. However, Charles accompanied Clifford's appointment with the surprising nomination of Ashley, now promoted Earl of Shaftesbury, as lord chancellor, to replace the strongly Anglican and constitutionalist Bridgeman. Of course Shaftesbury was later to become the Whig leader of the opposition, but at this stage in his career he still saw his future in the service of royal projects.[77] He and Clifford advised Charles to adhere to the Declaration of Indulgence. Since Clifford did so because of his crypto-Catholicism, Shaftesbury's sympathies for the dissenters made him useful in maintaining a broader basis for the policy of toleration. Clifford and Shaftesbury continued to advocate vigorous prosecution of the war against the Dutch, whereas Arlington and the mercurial Buckingham were becoming doubtful.

Clifford used his primacy to take charge of all urgent and laborious business, controlling all expenditure, deciding on the allocation of subsidy money received from France, attempting parliamentary management and supervising the raising of the new regiments. Shaftesbury acted as official spokesman, justifying royal policies to parliament on 5 February 1673. Customarily the chancellor followed the king, who on this occasion spoke briefly and defensively. He opened with a totally unconvincing justification of the long prorogations since April 1671, explaining that he had wished to spare parliament demands for supply until these had become absolutely necessary. He asserted that the 'Interest as well as the Honour of the Nation' were involved in the war, and defended the declaration as 'securing peace at home when I had war abroad'. Charles tried to anticipate criticism by emphasizing that the concessions given to Catholics were lesser than those given to Protestant dissenters. He added a disclaimer on another sure subject of contention: the army was not, as seditious rumours said, designed to 'control Law and Property', but to launch a decisive invasion of Holland, and more troops would be needed.[78]

By contrast with Charles's low-key speech, Shaftesbury followed eloquently, aggressively and at length. He put up a superb oratorical performance, long remembered (and held against him), in which he concentrated his attacks on carefully selected and easy targets. Saying nothing about France, he denounced the Dutch in vituperative phrases. They were 'the common enemy to all Monarchies and especially to ours' (that was to please Charles and Clifford), but more generally they aimed at a 'universal empire' (a concept being used increasingly to describe Louis' European ambitions) at sea and in trade. Holland's government must be destroyed, said Shaftesbury, using the words of Cato that had eventually produced the annihilation of Rome's enemy, *Delenda est Carthago*. He also assailed another soft target, the bankers suffering after the stop of the exchequer, when asking for new votes of supply, and tried to depict any hesitation in the granting of supply as the one reason why the Dutch might not sue for peace.[79]

Neither Charles's nor Shaftesbury's speech had much effect. The Commons humiliated the new chancellor by rejecting MPs returned on writs for by-elections which he had issued, and Charles did not wish to pick a fight on this matter.[80] The Commons did resolve to vote £1,260,000 for the war but, after some initial hesitation, decided to delay progress on the supply bill while exerting direct and brutal pressure on Charles to withdraw his claim to a suspending power. This required skilful parliamentary leadership and expert control of procedure, but the unofficial Country leadership totally outclassed the Court, who had derived little benefit from Clifford's experiments in management. On 14 February the Commons confronted Charles with a choice between continuation of the war and retention of his central domestic policy, religious toleration based on exercise of the suspending power.

The Commons used humble language in their address, but their challenge was not concealed:

we find ourselves bound in duty to inform your Majesty that penal
statutes in matters ecclesiastical cannot be suspended but by act of
Parliament.[81]

Charles discussed this challenge at meetings of the committee of council
on 14 and 16 February, and came to the unavoidable decision that financial
supply must be given first priority. Refitting, provisioning and manning
could no longer be postponed if the fleet was to be ready in time, and the
Medway disaster of 1667 showed what might happen if this was not done.
New loans could not be raised unless parliament voted taxes that could be
used as security. But both Charles and his ministers underestimated the
extent of the concessions which would remove parliamentary suspicions
and produce votes of money.[82]

Charles's first manœuvre was to maintain the claim to a prerogative
power in ecclesiastical matters, but explicitly to renounce any power of
suspending statutes concerning the nation's liberties and properties (24
February). He also promised consent to any Bill removing penalties
against dissenters.[83] The Commons reacted unfavourably (26 February),
telling Charles that he had not removed the nation's just fears, and
widened the issue by saying that he had obviously been misinformed
about his powers, an ominous phrase that usually preceded attacks on
ministers.[84] Two days later the Commons opened up a new issue of the
greatest importance by voting *nem. con.* for an address to be prepared
asking Charles to suppress the growth of popery. This vote formed the
basis for a Test Bill.[85] Charles tried to set the Lords against the Commons,
but without success. By 6 March he faced one of the most crucial decisions
of the entire reign. He now knew that the Commons would vote no
money unless he agreed to withdraw the declaration, and that he might be
required explicitly to renounce possession of a suspending power as the
price of money. In addition he would now have to accept a Test Bill that
made major inroads into his undisputed prerogative powers, by preventing him from employing any Catholics in offices. Charles knew that this
would affect James, Clifford and many others.

Charles's own instinct was to dissolve parliament, sacrificing the
Supply Bill, and to apply to Louis for increased subsidies. All the leading
ministers except Arlington advised him to maintain the declaration and his
claim to a suspending power. James went further in urging severe repressive action against a parliamentary opposition that he asserted was now in
treasonable contact with the Dutch.[86] Before dissolving parliament
Charles thought it wise to consult the French ambassador, Colbert de
Croissy, who effectively imposed a veto, making it clear that Louis could
not now afford additional subsidies on the scale that Charles would need to
replace the Supply Bill that would fall with a dissolution. He also stressed
Louis' expectation that England would collaborate fully in further cam-

paigns – a hint that Charles must realize that the existing subsidies had to be earned. This veto on a dissolution of the Cavalier Parliament represents the first occasion during the reign on which Louis intervened in English affairs with decisive and long-term effects, but it was not to prove the last: in 1678 and again in 1681 Louis was to act as the secret arbiter in English politics, first supporting the country opposition to wreck royal projects, and then intervening to make it possible at last for Charles to rule without parliament.[87]

Charles's decision not to dissolve a parliament temporarily dominated by the opposition forced him to beat a retreat on his central policies, but the naval and military campaigns which this retreat made possible turned out to be disappointingly inconclusive. Charles agreed to withdraw the Declaration of Indulgence, although he did not renounce his claim to a royal suspending power.[88] He allowed the Test Bill to progress, giving it his royal assent on 29 March, but this concession did not reassure either parliamentary or a now alarmed public opinion. Clifford's vehement attack on the Bill in the Lords confirmed suspicions that a design had been conceived by the ministry to benefit the Catholics and increase the king's authority. By refusing to take the Test and resigning as lord high admiral (17 June) James confirmed the fears that he, the heir presumptive, had embraced Catholicism.[89] His resignation also contributed to the meagre results of the war at sea. His replacement, Rupert, fought three bloody but drawn engagements; his failure to destroy or bottle up the Dutch fleet forced the abandonment of the war plan to invade the coast of Holland or Zeeland, using the newly expanded army. Rupert created great embarrassment for Charles by publicly and repeatedly blaming the French naval squadron for his failure, going out of his way to raise storms of anti-French hatred, which only Charles and James dared try to refute.[90]

By the end of the summer of 1673 the ministry had disintegrated. Clifford refused to take the Test, resigned (19 June) and died soon afterwards in retirement. Arlington and Buckingham openly and ferociously attacked each other. Charles discovered that the latter, like Shaftesbury who resented his abandonment by the king on the issue of the writs for by-elections, had established links with the Country opposition leaders. Only James remained constant, urging Charles to persist in the French alliance and to fight another campaign in 1674. This represented the king's own preferred policy, and Louis certainly wanted him to continue the war, but there was now a startling change in the advice that Charles received from Louis. In March the latter had advised strongly against a dissolution, but in the autumn he urged Charles to dissolve parliament and offered him a subsidy of £700,000. The imminent entry of Spain into the war against France caused this change. Louis needed English naval assistance in the Mediterranean. By ensuring English participation in the 1674 campaign against the Dutch, Louis aimed at involving Charles in war against Spain. In the longer term this would have the added advantage for France of making Charles an accomplice in the conquest and annexation of, at least, further valuable parts of the Spanish Netherlands.[91]

It is clear that the dissolution of the Cavalier Parliament, and consequent reliance on French subsidies to finance a Dutch and Spanish war, would have converted Charles into a French dependant. Charles showed remarkable persistence in wishing to continue the war, but Arlington warned him of the widespread discontent that would be caused by the loss of trade that would inevitably follow from war against Spain. The consequent loss of customs revenues would partly offset the proposed French subsidy.[92] Charles could have scraped together enough money to finance another naval campaign, but his new lord treasurer, the future Earl of Danby, fell seriously ill after his appointment in June and could not begin the urgent task of financial reconstruction for several months.[93] Charles had to make the crucial decisions himself. He rejected James's advice, playing for time by proroguing parliament until January 1674. However there was no disguising the fact that the collapse of the ministry and its projects represented a heavy defeat for Charles personally. What are usually referred to as the policies of the Cabal were really his, in terms of formulation and initiation. The Dover treaty and the Declaration of Indulgence originated with the king himself.

All the members of an extraordinarily heterogeneous ministry had agreed to the major policies of 1670–3, but for significantly diverse and indeed contradictory reasons, and only some knew what Charles really intended them to achieve. Shaftesbury supported a primarily commercial war, and for him the Declaration of Indulgence brought the Protestant dissenters toleration, but gave Catholics only limited connivance.[94] For Clifford, a mercantilist in his crude, rough way, commercial expansion following the defeat of the Dutch represented only a means of achieving the political end of increasing royal power and authority, and the declaration formed the first stage in the establishment of Catholicism.[95] Arlington cautiously, Buckingham wildly, sought personal prestige and advantages by serving a victorious king.[96] James thought that at last he had pointed Charles in the direction of asserting and realizing the rights inherent in the Crown.[97]

As always when he took the trouble to exert the full range of his political skills, Charles had no difficulty in deceiving and manipulating all his ministers and advisers. Their diverse principles and ambitions made his task easier, as did the similarly differing characteristics of the various and often conflicting interest groups that Charles managed to mobilize in support of his policies. By applying the age-old maxim of 'divide and rule' Charles ensured his own mastery over all his subjects. He was less successful in his relations with foreigners. Charles's comparative lack of resources kept him in a secondary position in relation to Louis. But it has to be added that, as in 1678, Charles was personally no match for Louis' superior skills in machiavellian statecraft, and towards the end of 1673 disquieting evidence showed Charles that his freedom to act according to his own preferences had been undermined by his nephew William.

Divisions among ministers and in parliament would not have mattered if the war and its accompanying policies had succeeded. Their failure produced demoralization, suspicion and confusion. The Venetian diplomat Alberti, who got his information mostly from James's entourage, only slightly exaggerated the dismal situation:

the king calls a cabinet council for the purpose of not listening to it; and the ministers hold forth in it so as not to be understood. Thus there is an end of that mutual understanding which is so necessary. [98]

6 Charles and Danby: Crown and Church

During the first months of 1673 Charles found himself being subjected to intense and various forms of pressure. The French ambassador virtually dictated the crucial decisions not to dissolve parliament but instead to withdraw the Declaration of Indulgence and accept the Test Bill, in return for money that made possible another summer's campaign. In the following months there was no relaxation of pressure, although it changed in character. The Test Act produced the resignations of James and Clifford: this evidence of their conversion to Catholicism provoked great alarm. It apparently authenticated the assertions of a conspiracy to introduce Catholicism and absolutism which were being made in current Dutch propaganda. The war at sea did not go well in 1673, with Rupert blaming the French for the allied fleet's failure.[1] This prevented the enlarged army being used to invade Holland or Zeeland: its idleness bred undisciplined behaviour, but attempts to impose military law fuelled allegations that the ministers really intended to employ this army at home, to establish arbitrary government.[2]

With most things going wrong, the ministry became bitterly divided into hostile factions. Each minister, assuming (rightly) that Charles either could not or would not defend him, prepared to save himself by attacking others, regardless of the effects on governmental business, or the king's reputation, of such self-justificatory efforts. The financial position deteriorated sharply, with war expenditure and depressed overseas trade being compounded by Clifford's incompetence and his indiscriminate payments to shore up the Court interest in parliament.[3] These financial difficulties faced Charles with the unavoidable necessity of allowing another parliamentary session that would certainly prove difficult to manage or control.

The difficult situation in which Charles found himself inevitably led to speculation and intense political intriguing. Most politicians expected major changes in policies and of ministers. Knowing that all his ministers and advisers were thinking primarily of defending their own interests and safety, Charles acted very much on his own judgement. Unexpectedly he chose not to undertake wholesale and drastic alterations. Charles did not wish to abandon the current projects, and tried to ignore pressures on him to do so. He failed to maintain this stand. What can at first be described as defensive, cautious behaviour, designed to preserve his freedom to make decisions, tended to deteriorate into a series of short-term improvisations. Charles was slow to realize the strength of anti-French feeling, but persisted in a policy of continuing the war, for fear that by abandoning the French alliance he would make it unlikely that Louis would offer him subsidies again. Charles tried to persuade parliament to vote money for another year's campaign, arguing that the Dutch peace offers were neither honourable nor satisfactory in detail. Parliament simply ignored him.[4] Similarly Charles showed himself unperceptive in failing to make James break off negotiations for his remarriage to Mary of Modena. He should have anticipated the serious effects in parliament, and on opinion generally, of a marriage to an Italian Catholic, arranged by French diplomats. It provoked a storm of anti-papist hostility, which helped to frustrate Charles's attempt to continue religious toleration, despite his formal withdrawal of the Declaration of Indulgence, by ensuring non-enforcement of the penal laws by the magistrates.[5]

Charles did not reconstruct his administration, although several combinations were forming themselves in readiness for major changes. He limited himself to two moves involving a single individual. The first seemed at the time to be merely a temporary arrangement: on 19 June 1673 Charles named Thomas Osborne to succeed Clifford as lord treasurer.[6] This promotion of a very secondary politician surprised contemporaries, but the other move, the dismissal of Lord Chancellor Shaftesbury (9 November), was not unexpected.[7] Shaftesbury's behaviour in the Lords clearly invited royal action, but at this time neither Charles nor the informed public had any reason to suppose that Shaftesbury would now devote the rest of his life to organizing and leading political opposition to the Crown. In the event these two isolated decisions determined the shape of politics for the next six years. But in 1673 observers interpreted Osborne's appointment as a stop-gap. Although ambitious and able – Charles had tried to recruit him as a servant in 1667 – Osborne was not yet a major, or even an independent, political figure. His enemies decried him as Buckingham's creature. He did serve Buckingham as his (much-needed) man of political business, doing the detailed routine work which that erratic grandee found tedious. At first courtiers believed that Osborne was merely exchanging masters.[8] He had to undertake, or at least initiate, an essential but laborious and difficult reconstruction of royal finances. Many expected that he would then have to make way for a minister who possessed a major interest of his own: none foresaw Danby's durability as a minister, or that he would have more authority delegated to him than any other royal servant in England during the reign.

Danby at first lacked a personal interest at Court, in parliament and in the country. He did not have (and in fact never developed) any warm or intimate personal relationship with Charles. Danby was a tough and insensitive Yorkshireman, ready to take on the most difficult tasks under unfavourable circumstances, in order to advance himself and his rapacious family.[9] For a time this remained his main aim, but he was eventually to succeed to such an extent that he changed the whole character of English politics, with Charles acting as a generally supportive but not very active partner. In establishing an interest of his own, Danby from 1675 developed most of the techniques of patronage and management that became essential tools for all chief ministers over the next 150 years.[10] But this development only partially explains Danby's success in making himself Charles's chief minister. After he had become established, Danby explained to his master the principles that he had set out to apply ever since his appointment. He told Charles candidly that the king could never become 'great or rich' until he fell into the 'humour of the people'.[11] By the latter Danby meant not popular whims, but the general outlook of the nation – a compound of prejudices (above all anti-popery), fears (especially of France and rule based on an army), and interests (particularly the Anglican). In Danby's view these set limits, which Charles must accept, to what could safely be attempted. Danby was not a courtier, like Arlington. He regarded himself as the indispensable intermediary between the king and his subjects, explaining royal policies to the latter, and reciprocally making the king take notice of the interests, grievances and views of at least the Anglican section of the 'political nation'.

Now Shaftesbury similarly based his political career after 1673 on his 'knowledge of England', but he set out to exploit this knowledge, together with his connections and influence, to form and lead a systematic opposition which developed into the first Whig party. He aimed to impose tight and permanent restrictions on the powers of the king and his ministers. In contrast Danby made himself the indispensable servant of the king by tackling the most difficult and time-consuming governmental and political tasks – restoring the royal finances, managing parliament and eventually handling relations with foreign states. From 1674 his success increasingly relieved Charles of the pressures that had been imposed on him by the Cabal's failures, and in practical matters the king delegated to Danby control over day to day business. Charles had the wisdom to see that other ministers, more acceptable to him in personal terms, did not possess the courage or stamina to take on such an onerous role. But he never gave Danby his entire confidence and trust, and consciously prevented him from achieving anything approaching a monopoly of power and patronage. Danby retained predominant influence as chief minister because, and provided that, his policies continued to be effective. But throughout his ministry Charles retained alternative ministers – Arlington especially – who stood outside Danby's system of patronage. Even more disturbingly, Charles from time to time explored the possibilities of instituting alternative policies that diverged significantly from those that Danby was following. In consequence Danby's ministerial position was never as strong as it outwardly appeared, especially to an increasingly frustrated Country opposition which remained impotent so long as Charles maintained the 'standing' Cavalier Parliament.

Throughout his life Charles consistently wished to enjoy friendly relations with Louis XIV, an attitude that increasingly separated him from almost all his subjects, who came to fear France as an expansionist and over-powerful neighbour, the model for designs to introduce absolutist methods of government, and the new champion of militant Catholicism. During 1673 Charles experienced the serious disadvantages inherent in the auxiliary role that the Dover treaty had assigned to him. The fleet, which absorbed most of the available finance and was manned at the cost of virtually embargoing long-distance commercial trade, failed to win command of the narrow seas. This made impossible any major landing on the vulnerable Dutch coast, and this meant that a quick and decisive defeat of the enemy now became unattainable. Consequently the newly expanded army spent the summer in a ludicrous expedition that got no farther than Great Yarmouth.[12] Charles added to his problems by appointing a French officer, Schomberg, as general. This intensified suspicions that the army would be used at home, to increase royal authority. It also antagonized Buckingham, who had pressed Charles to give him the command, converting him from being the most vociferous champion of the French alliance into a raging francophobe. The appointment also infuriated Rupert, who actually used a dispute over protocol as an excuse to open fire on a ship carrying Schomberg. Rupert's personal enmity made co-operation with the army more difficult, and his frequent denunciations of French naval officers for cowardice and treachery made it clear that Charles could not retain him as fleet commander if the war continued into 1674.[13]

William ensured that England did not continue in the war, by organizing a campaign of propaganda and political subversion.[14] Charles never forgot this, and never really forgave his nephew for this unprincipled but decisively successful intervention in English politics. Self-preservation justified William's tactics, and he in turn, like a true Stuart, never forgot or forgave Charles for plotting the destruction of the Dutch republic, and for arrogantly rejecting all William's initially desperate appeals in 1672. Dutch propaganda, notably du Moulin's pamphlet *England's Appeal*, aimed at stimulating parliamentary and popular suspicions. The French alliance and the Dutch War were depicted as part of a conspiracy to establish absolutism and Catholicism by means of the army. French subsidies would make Charles independent of parliament. Toleration was intended to facilitate the growth of popery. Dutch propaganda proved effective because it articulated fears and suspicions that many already felt.[15] By concentrating on the king's domestic policies, rather than on the war itself, which was represented as a cover for the conspiracy, it ensured that obstruction of the war and co-operation with the king's enemies, so far from being unpatriotic or treasonable, could be justified as being for the defence of the nation's liberties and the Protestant religion. After an initial failure, Dutch agents established a network of correspondents and collaborators whose influence Charles failed to overcome.[16] He tried privately to reassure both ministers and Country opposition spokesmen that he wanted only one more year's campaign, for the sole purpose of compelling the Dutch to offer better terms, but no one believed him. When he showed an edited version of the 1671 simulated treaty to parliament, a concession that he had earlier refused, the archtypical Cavalier, Strangways, commented: 'France has entangled us; the public articles are ill enough: what are then the private articles?'[17] The better-informed William Temple believed that Charles ran the danger of becoming trapped: continuing the war meant a break with Spain and the ruin of what overseas trade continued; breaking with France might provoke Louis into publishing details of the agreements between himself and Charles.[18] Had the full truth about the Dover treaty become known, the repercussions would certainly have been devastating.

Only James characteristically advised Charles to seek an additional French subsidy to continue the war, and to dissolve parliament: in financial terms nothing would be lost, since the Commons had voted not to consider any additional votes of supply until August 1674, 'unless the obstinacy of the Dutch shall render it necessary', and of this MPs would be judges. But although many contemporary observers considered that James's influence was growing during the last months of 1673, Charles wisely declined to opt for what his brother described as 'resolute courses'.[19] As yet Danby's personal influence and advice carried little weight, but the inescapable facts of the situation forced Charles to conclude a hurried peace in February 1674. The previous December Danby argued that neither the present nor any new parliament would vote any money so long as Charles maintained the French alliance. He added that in the currently inflamed state of public opinion it would also insist on enforcement of the laws against Catholics. Revealingly he demonstrated the impracticability of making any attempt to rule by means of an army: if it was a foreign force, or one partially foreign and Catholic in composition, the nation would unite against it – and the king. Charles could hardly use the existing army, for lack of money, and the events of 1659 had shown the unreliability of unpaid soldiers, and the depth of popular hostility against troops living at free quarter.[20]

Charles ignored James's general advice, but he protected him on two issues. He dismissed renewed suggestions by Shaftesbury for a royal divorce and instant remarriage.[21] He rejected addresses from the Commons against James's marriage to Mary of Modena as constituting an illegal invasion of royal prerogative.[22] Charles could not stop the marriage once it had been concluded in Italy, by proxy, without dishonouring his brother in the eyes of the ruling families of Europe. But the Modenese marriage had the gravest consequences, both immediate and long-term. It provoked a spectacular outbreak of anti-papist feeling, seen in the revival of widespread pope-burnings on the anniversary of Elizabeth's accession in 1558 – 17 November. James's marriage to a young wife, selected partly for her breeding qualities, created the spectre of a Catholic dynasty. The question of the succession became the central issue in politics, and was to remain crucial right into the eighteenth century. Politicians began to discuss a range of measures to guard against the now visible dangers of a Catholic successor: a provision that the children of the new marriage should be educated as protestants (but fortunately until 1688 they all died in infancy); the placing of restrictions on the powers of a Catholic sovereign; a prohibition on all future marriages to Catholics by members of the royal family; and, most ominous of all, the exclusion from the succession of all Catholics, or of James by name.[23] It is clear that Charles and James did not foresee any of these possibilities, but for them the whole matter was exclusively personal and dynastic. Addresses by parliament, or even the expressions of opinion by their subjects, were impertinent. They disregarded all but their own wishes, exactly as James I and Charles I had done during the protracted negotiations for the latter's marriage to the Spanish infanta.

Despite the difficulties that James created for his brother by his conversion to Catholicism, his marriage and his bad advice, he remained an important influence at Court, although no longer a formal member of the administration. Danby knew that he had to obtain James's backing in order to secure his hold on office against challenges from within the Court. Arlington constantly sniped at the lord treasurer, but he shied away from the responsibility that would accompany ministerial primacy.[24] A more serious threat to Danby came in the autumn of 1673 from a combination headed by Ormonde, the personification of old Cavalier loyalty and Anglican steadfastness. He had his own man of business, Sir William Coventry, formerly James's secretary and then treasury commissioner, who would manage royal finances in Danby's place. This combination appealed to many independent peers and MPs.[25] It promised honest and efficient administration, and a return to Anglican principles that attracted the bishops, whereas Danby was untried in treasury business and was only beginning to adopt the role of Anglican champion. For Charles the Ormonde-Coventry combination would be unacceptably restrictive. He detested Coventry personally, and associated him politically with the attempts made in 1668–71 to limit the financial freedom of action of the

Crown by appropriation and accountancy controls. Charles was not yet ready to give up his attempts to continue religious toleration by unofficial methods, that is, by letting magistrates know that he did not wish the laws to be enforced against Catholics and dissenters. Ormonde stood for reimposition of the Anglican supremacy, Coventry for an equally unacceptable and immediate break with France. To appoint them would signal a complete and public reversal of all the policies and principles associated with the previous ministry, and the dismissal of all those who had been committed to them. Danby, in contrast, had been merely inserted as an individual into an existing, composite administration. So far from dictating to the king, as Coventry would do, he needed royal support while he busied himself with the technical problems of restoring royal solvency and systematically managing parliament so as to bring it under effective control.[26]

The parliamentary session of January–February 1674 showed how much management work needed to be done. Charles began with a lamentably ineffective speech to both Houses in which, as everyone noticed, he fluffed his lines (7 January). This was not surprising since most of what he said consisted of lies or, at best, half-truths.[27] A week later Buckingham proved equally unconvincing when he created a sensation by appearing before the Commons (without Charles's leave) to explain his ministerial conduct, mainly by shovelling the blame on Arlington.[28] The latter made a more effective case in reply, although he failed to prevent the Commons voting for a debate on his impeachment. He had asked Charles's permission to go to the Commons, but this eagerness of ministers (who were also peers) to satisfy the Commons revealed a total lack of trust in the king's ability or willingness to protect them.[29] For months ministers had improperly leaked information about council and cabinet council proceedings so as to clear themselves and denigrate colleagues, but Buckingham outraged ministerial obligations to the king by breaking his oath of secrecy in revealing official transactions to the Commons. Charles also infringed a convention that at other times he strenuously defended. Questions of war and peace belonged exclusively to the royal prerogative, but Charles for tactical reasons asked the Commons for 'speedy advice and assistance' on a peace offer from the Dutch (24 January 1674).[30] The Commons reacted negatively, making no attempt to give either constructive counsel or money, which left Charles with no option but to conclude peace (9 February).[31] Without consulting Danby he then prorogued parliament until November, and later extended this to April 1675.[32]

  This sterile session, in which not a single Bill passed, revealed the dominant influence exerted by a loosely organized but extremely articulate Country opposition. Danby convinced Charles that nothing would be gained by a dissolution, since a newly elected Commons would certainly be even more critical, but they realized that a prorogation in itself would not diminish the influence of Country politicians.[33] Charles commissioned Danby to act during the recess to limit and restrain criticism of the king and his ministers. A proclamation was issued against all attempts to stir disaffection and disseminate calumnies. It ordered private persons not to 'intermeddle' in state affairs. Instructions were given to tighten controls over the press.[34] However, it is clear that Charles seriously underestimated the significance of the increased activity and influence of the Country opposition. In particular he had no understanding of the reasons why most of his subjects, the educated élite as well as the masses, feared Catholicism; for him anti-popery was always a cover for political ambition and activities that would otherwise be quasi-rebellious and politically inadmissible. He condemned leading Country spokesmen as mercenaries actuated by ignoble greed for money and by the hope that the Court would buy them off with offices. Charles blamed Spanish money for the Commons' refusal to vote him supply to continue the war, and attributed the basest motives to those who had worked with William to bring the war to an end.[35]

William's triumph in forcing Charles to quit the war rankled for a long time. Williamson, an English representative at the Nijmegen peace conference, succeeded in obtaining information about William's secret network of agents and propagandists. Charles vehemently pressed him to discover more, and above all to get the names of those peers and MPs who had worked for William.[36] Later, at the end of 1674, Charles returned to the issue, instructing Arlington to press William personally to disclose the names of his contacts, as a pre-condition of the restoration of good relations between them.[37] On both occasions Charles disclaimed any intention of punishing the guilty, and he may have meant this. But his main purpose was to get information with which he could discredit the entire opposition by publicizing the treasonable behaviour of some of its members. Moreover if William revealed any names this would ensure that in future no politician would think it safe to establish a secret connection with him. William revealed nothing, but maintained contacts with opposition leaders as an insurance policy. Charles remained cold and distrustful. He vetoed a visit to Holland by Ossory, who later served William as a general, and refused to allow William to visit England. He also prohibited the levying of troops in Britain for the Dutch service, although men were being recruited for Louis.[38]

Having been forced to make peace himself, Charles now concentrated on trying to make William agree to a general peace. He hoped that this would rehabilitate him in Louis' eyes, and he did obtain French authorization to take on the role of mediator between the warring states.[39] In November 1674 Charles sent Arlington and Ossory on a mission to William to get him to agree to Charles being mediator. They were instructed to use as an inducement the suggestion, which was to be hinted as a possibility rather than stated as a promise, that once peace had been concluded William would be permitted to make an approach to marry Mary, James's elder daughter. The mission proved a dismal failure.[40] First, in pseudo-machiavellian fashion Charles concealed this last point from Louis, to whom the purpose of the mission was explained as exclusively concerned with mediation. But James wanted to sabotage the possibility of William marrying his daughter, in the absurd hope that Louis would accept her for the dauphin; he informed the French ambassador. Louis can never have considered a child of Anne Hyde's as suitable for his heir, but he realized that William would gain in influence through such a marriage. Then, Ossory exceeded his instructions, making what was virtually the offer of an early marriage. Arlington also departed from his brief, agreeing to take back with him the project of an Anglo-Dutch defensive alliance.[41] Charles rightly saw this as a first move by William to draw him into the war as part of the anti-French confederation. He also knew that William's friends in parliament would work to this end: he therefore extended the prorogation until April 1675, too late in the year for the organizing and financing of active English intervention.[42]

Danby also needed a longer interval to formulate his own distinctive set of policies, and to strengthen his influence with Charles. It can have come as no surprise to the king – none of whose ministries were homogeneous – that the line being energetically pursued by Danby during the recess diverged at all points from that being followed by James. During late 1674 James negotiated with the moderate leaders of the so-called Presbyterian party, for religious toleration and the dissolution of parliament. He also approached the French ambassador for a subsidy in return for the dissolution, representing this as a major blow for William, showing him that no help would be forthcoming from England. James did not see the dissenters as allies, but as royal dependants. They would receive toleration by prerogative means, not by statute, and so would have no option but to 'love and fear' the king.[43] In sharp contrast Danby put together a new political alliance, by appealing directly to the Anglican bishops and clergy, together with the old Cavaliers who had formerly accepted Clarendon's lead. He convened meetings of bishops and prominent laymen in the king's name, asking their advice on how to proceed so as to protect the Protestant religion. The bishops responded eagerly – Charles had left them in the political wilderness since 1670, and Sheldon's uncompromising stand against the policies of toleration later created a deep rift with the king and his brother.[44] The first Anglican objective was to obtain a complete, public and formal repudiation of the 1672 Declaration of Indulgence, with explicit instructions to all JPs to resume enforcement of the laws against dissenters and Catholics. The Anglicans wanted the latter excluded from Court, and their pressure via Danby achieved a first move by Charles: in February 1675 he issued a proclamation ordering all Catholic clergy to leave England, and rejected the protest which the Catholics sent him through Elliot, one of his confidential servants. Although James reacted uneasily to this, and maintained his contacts with the opposition right up to the eve of the session, he could not prevent Charles from committing himself to Danby's policies.[45]

In his opening speech to parliament (13 April 1675) Charles promised to show his zeal for the Church of England, 'from which I will never depart', in unveiling what was to form the royal and ministerial strategy for the next few years – an alliance with the Anglican loyalists, based on the indefinite continuation of the existing Cavalier Parliament.[46] Danby introduced a well-prepared project to institutionalize and perpetuate this alliance. This took the form of a new Test, to be imposed on all peers and MPs, and later extended to cover all holders of offices. A Bill 'for preventing the dangers which may arise from persons disaffected to the government' required the taking of an oath not to resist royal authority or to endeavour the alteration of the government in either church or state, that is, not to attempt fundamental changes of any kind. Charles spelt this out explicitly: 'the pernicious designs of ill men have taken so much place' (that is, in parliamentary proceedings) 'under specious pretences, that it is high time to be watchful in preventing their contrivances'. He and Danby meant the Test to make systematic and popular opposition illegal. Introduced in the Lords, the Bill was energetically pushed forward by the Court, with Charles appearing daily at the exhaustingly long debates to display his commitment. Opposition peers resisted tenaciously, but were overborne, although the Court majority shrank at one point to a single vote.[47] In the Commons the opposition MPs failed miserably in an attempted counter-attack – a badly prepared impeachment of Danby – and their attacks on Lauderdale were mere sound and fury.[48] Charles disregarded addresses for Lauderdale's removal, riding with him in the royal coach in the Hyde Park parade to demonstrate his support.[49]

The one major Court concession during six weeks of hard-fought debates actually improved the Bill's chances: the Test was not to encroach on the parliamentary privilege of 'debating any matter or business which shall be propounded . . . or repeal or alteration of any old, or preparing any new laws'. However, consultation about proposing any fundamental change in a forthcoming session, or discussions outside Westminster would still be illegal.[50] Only a violent dispute between the Lords and Commons thwarted enactment of the Test. Undoubtedly the opposition exacerbated this dispute, over a legal case (*Shirley* v. *Fagg*), but it concerned a genuine and important issue on which each House believed that it was defending its own right against encroachment by the other. The dispute aroused virulent recriminations and provocative actions. It made Charles attempt to save the Test, in a strongly worded speech (5 June), written carefully in advance so as to spell out his denunciation of those whom he stigmatized as contrivers, the ill men who set the Houses against each other and wanted to force a dissolution. This diatribe clearly had Shaftesbury as its target, but the speech failed. On 9 June Charles had to prorogue parliament, and this meant abandoning the Test.[51]

Some observers expected Charles to abandon Danby also, but despite the lord treasurer's failure his position improved. The casualty turned out to be Arlington, Danby's rival. Charles bitterly resented his noticeably half-hearted support for the Test, and his failure to prevent some of his connections in the Commons helping the attempted impeachment of Danby. Charles had no compunction in retaining Arlington to balance Danby, and to show the treasurer that an alternative chief minister existed, but he would not tolerate an attack at such a critical moment on a servant who was trying to increase effective royal authority. Arlington resigned as secretary of state and went into semi-retirement.[52] This gave Danby one great advantage, which Charles probably failed to foresee. He used the opportunity to strengthen his private connection with William. Realistically he did not plan to reintroduce the Test, but ever-resourceful he turned his attention to developing new managerial techniques so as to ensure his own political control within parliament.

The joint campaign to pass the Test had seen Charles commit himself in public to Danby, and its failure did not cause him to move away from Danby's general political strategy. Previously Charles had shared James's often-stated belief that anti-popery was a form of political fraud, a cover for unacknowledged if not subversive aims, as objectionable in the case of ministers and bishops as in that of opposition politicians. The devising and introduction of the non-resistance Test covered Danby from such criticisms when he began to enforce the laws against the Catholics, as he had to do in order to satisfy Anglican opinion. Moreover his anti-papist measures made nonsense of the opposition argument, which formed the main theme of Marvell's satirical pamphlets, that Charles and Danby were merely continuing, by the use of new devices and disguises, the conspiracy initiated by the so-called Cabal for the establishment of popery and absolutism.[53]

There remained one major weakness in Danby's position as chief minister: he could not dissuade Charles from renewing and continuing serious negotiations with France. The king had rejected a French approach in February 1675 because Louis offered him insufficient money, and demanded a dissolution in return – which would have meant abandoning the then hopeful project of the Test.[54] In August, with the Test lost and parliament prorogued, a new subsidy agreement was reached with Louis. This was largely due to James, who acted as both the intermediary and the strenuous advocate of a renewed French connection. Louis promised money in return for either a further prorogation or, if an autumn session was held and proved unsatisfactory, a dissolution.[55] Louis had very clear objectives: he wanted to ensure that parliament did not force Charles into anti-French courses of action. Bribing the king would be a surer way of blocking the Dutch, Spaniards and Imperialists than the alternative of countering the lobbying of their diplomats by the distribution of money to peers and MPs. Charles had rather longer-term objectives; it would be wrong to see him as nothing more than an endless opportunist and improviser. First, Charles accepted Louis' assurances that he had only limited objectives in the Spanish Netherlands; these were entirely dishonest. Secondly, Charles felt dishonoured by his enforced abandonment of France in 1674, and now as always he preferred a French orientation to the alternatives of understandings with the Dutch and Spaniards. He knew that many of his servants, notably William Temple, were working more assiduously to serve William's interests than his own. Danby himself was trying hard to ingratiate himself with William. Charles faced a real danger that William would exploit his English connections to drag the kingdom into war against France, whereas an agreement with Louis left him free to remain neutral and act as mediator.

Charles excluded Danby from the negotiations with France. By assuming personal charge of the treaty Charles ensured a bad bargain. Ruvigny, the French ambassador, took advantage of his carelessness and impatience, and obtained Charles's agreement to a subsidy which was considerably smaller than the one Louis had authorized him to promise.[56] Charles's slovenly behaviour was inexcusable, since apart from negotiations with Ruvigny he had little official business to do. He spent the summer at leisure, mostly at Windsor, but Danby devoted himself to intensive preparations on an unprecedented scale for a session in the autumn. He despatched standard letters instructing Court MPs to attend from the start, and began to make systematic use of all forms of Court patronage.[57] The aim was to construct a working majority in both Houses, and specifically to persuade the Commons to vote supply, so as to clear sizeable anticipations of revenue that he had not been able to avoid. This first major attempt at parliamentary management on Danby's part proved to be inadequate. In the Commons the opposition used the size of the anticipations (put at £1,000,000) as a reason to refuse supply. In the Lords the Court party defeated an address for a dissolution only by using proxy votes collected by Danby beforehand. With his hopes frustrated, Charles reacted sharply, proroguing parliament on 22 November for the unusually long term of fifteen months, and did so without making the customary closing speech – in order to register his disapproval of parliament's behaviour.[58]

Apart from punishing parliament, this long prorogation was intended to persuade France to pay the agreed subsidy as if for a dissolution: the absence of a session in 1676 meant that no English intervention in Europe could be mounted until the summer of 1677 at the earliest. Louis at first tried to wriggle out of his undertaking. It needed further serious negotiations, and an initiative from Danby who proposed approaching the Dutch for an alliance, to persuade Louis to pay up.[59] The French were at first inclined to interpret Danby's suggestion as a feint or manœuvre to put pressure on them. But in fact it marked the first sign of spreading ambiguity and uncertainty in English foreign policy, or rather policies. Charles continued to follow his preference for an understanding with France. But he allowed Danby, his chief minister, to move in the direction of co-operation with William. Charles maintained three diplomats as mediators at the interminable Nijmegen peace conference. Berkeley and Jenkins acted on their instructions to favour French interests, but the king took no action to check Sir William Temple, who worked assiduously in William's interests. Charles wanted to bring the war to an early conclusion, but he allowed Temple to use his influence to prevent the Dutch republicans responding to French offers of a separate peace.[60]

In terms of domestic affairs the fifteen-month prorogation largely achieved its main objective of sharply reducing unofficial or independent political activity. Without a parliament to act as a focus, the opposition could no longer exploit grievances, and its members had to disperse to their homes, although Shaftesbury resisted personal pressure from Charles to leave London for Dorset.[61] Danby's administration behaved in an increasingly authoritarian fashion. He went too far in attempting to close down all the popular new coffee houses, because they operated as centres for political discussion and the dissemination of pamphlets. They were required to obtain licences.[62] Prosecutions were brought against unauthorized and seditious publications. The council ensured intensified enforcement of the laws against the dissenters. The Court intervened in East India Company business to prevent candidates linked with the opposition being elected to office. Responsibility for this activity, and for intensive, new and more elaborate preparations to mobilize peers and MPs for the next session, which began over six months beforehand, fell to Danby. In contrast Charles enjoyed 1676 as a year almost free from pressures. Conscious of the relief that he owed to Danby, he gave no encouragement to Court intrigues, in which James became involved, for a dissolution and a change of both policies and ministers.[63] But he followed one of his chief political maxims, the necessity of keeping London under close control at all times, by intervening to stamp out an attempt to create disaffection there. Jenks, a City radical, made a speech at the June election of sheriffs calling on the lord mayor to convene a common council to debate both City and national grievances. He based his demand on inflammatory allegations about a papist conspiracy to burn London and to assassinate Charles in the interests of his Catholic brother: the speech was a dress rehearsal for the Popish Plot of 1678. Charles took the matter seriously enough to lead the interrogation of Jenks at the council board, but the latter boldly defied the king's rough and brutal attempt at intimidation. Charles failed to obtain evidence that Shaftesbury or Buckingham had inspired, or even directed, Jenks. He had to be content with keeping Jenks in custody without trial, evading writs of habeas corpus by legally dubious means.[64]

After being at ease during 1676 Charles found himself beset by critical pressures from the early months of 1677. He now faced the first of two major crises, but whereas the second – the Exclusion crisis of 1678–81 – concerned domestic issues, the first crisis of 1677–8 arose from developments in Europe. The main influences brought to bear on Charles, Danby and parliament were those of William and Louis who intervened systematically and with great effect in English politics. In the short term victory went to Louis, whose intervention in England contributed significantly to his success in making a separate peace with the Dutch at Nijmegen, and so destroying William's confederation. However in the longer term William built up the connections and acquired the reputation that were eventually to bring him a quick and decisive success in the Revolution of 1688.

A major and sudden alteration in the balance of European power precipitated this first crisis. Believing that William represented the main obstruction to an early European peace, Charles had welcomed his run of military setbacks: he said in 1676 (admittedly to the French ambassador) 'this little man needed correction to give him some wisdom', a most revealing hint of Charles's contempt for his physically insignificant and immature nephew.[65] But as parliament met in February 1677 the French launched a surprise offensive that swung the war decisively in their favour. Louis captured Valenciennes, Cambrai and St Omer, defeated William at Cassel in April, and seemed to be on the point of overrunning the entire Spanish Netherlands.[66] These sweeping French victories created great alarm in England, but Louis had already made preparations to neutralize it. He had offered Charles subsidies to prorogue parliament for yet another year, until 1678. A recess of over two years would have been unprecedented, and would almost certainly have turned into a dissolution.[67] Charles had refused. Louis blamed this refusal on Danby, and became concerned with the strength of William's interest in parliament. He instructed his ambassador to distribute money to peers and MPs, to counter the payments being made by Dutch and Spanish diplomats.[68] As a result parliament, and especially the Commons, became one of the decisive battlefields in the European campaigns of 1677–8. Louis and William also struggled to gain influence over Charles, enlisting the services of courtiers, servants, mistresses and intimate friends, acting on the assumption that Charles was highly impressionable and unfixed in his principles.

James acted as the principal French partisan, arguing against allowing a parliamentary session. Characteristically he warned the king against trusting Danby and the other ministers, because they thought primarily of their own interests, not his, and would defer to public opinion and criticisms rather than unflinchingly obey him. James agreed with Louis that Danby would align himself with anti-French sentiment, and consequently push Charles into adventurous foreign and war policies that ran counter to royal interests.[69] It was necessary for Danby to meet these criticisms: it was not enough to contend that the protection of national interests demanded action to contain the growth of French power. He also had to show that the prestige and prerogatives of the Crown would suffer unless Charles took action. The need for money supplied Danby with his main argument. The additional excise expired in 1677, royal debts had mounted and the navy needed new ships. He convinced Charles of the financial impracticability of James's advice to live without a parliament, and he got the Commons to vote £600,000 for naval construction. But he failed to commit the king to specific policies: the opening speech from the throne, and Charles's reply (17 March) to a first address, were phrased in deliberately vague generalities.[70] Nor would Charles give an immediate and satisfying answer to the 30 March address from the Commons, which specifically referred to the danger of French power, and asked him to secure the kingdom and preserve the Spanish Netherlands by concluding alliances, and particularly one with the States General.[71] By doing so the Commons encroached on the prerogative, but most MPs by now suspected Charles of asking parliament for money to finance a war he had no intention of fighting, 'a cheat, a pick-pocket war', like that of Henry VII in 1492.[72] Only after damage had been done did Danby persuade Charles to try to retrieve the position. Speaking on 23 May the king openly referred to current suspicions that money would be used for purposes other than those announced; he ended with a plea, 'I do assure you, upon the word of a king, that you shall not repent any trust you repose in me for the safety of my kingdoms'. He made clear his own fear of being manœuvred into a position of dependence on parliament, saying that unless the Commons voted money first it would be dangerous to take any open steps against France.[73]

The Commons went near to expressing openly their total lack of trust in Charles. They demanded that he enter into a defensive and offensive alliance with the States General, and passed a resolution (by 182 to 142, with some 50 abstentions) refusing supply until alliances had been concluded.[74] Predictably Charles responded by adjourning parliament until July (1677), rebuking the Commons for a dangerous invasion of his prerogative which might lead foreign princes to think that in future they must treat with parliament, not with the king.[75] These stances were to be maintained throughout the crisis, Charles saying that he would not enter a war unless he first received adequate supply, the Commons declaring that they would not vote supply until he had committed himself irrevocably by declaring war.

Charles was in fact playing a double game. He received reports from Montagu, his ambassador in Paris, that opened up the prospect of receiving substantially larger amounts in French subsidies than parliament was likely to vote. Charles personally conducted the negotiations, through the French ambassador in London, giving the latter an inflated statement of the services that he could provide. In June Charles suggested that parliament should be prorogued until March (or May) 1678, so as to dishearten William and Spain by showing them that English aid would not be forthcoming. Charles as mediator would persuade them to accept French conditions. Difficulties arose only over the amount that France was to pay, because Danby and Montagu belatedly discovered what had been happening. They found that with lack of attention to detail Charles had once again got himself a bad bargain. They dared not expose themselves to his anger by disrupting the agreement itself, but tried to haggle for a larger subsidy, with little success. In virtually pleading for French assistance Charles had carelessly revealed the precariousness of his financial position. He had made the mistake of assuming that Louis shared his own eagerness for an early peace, and failed to understand that French diplomatic strategy was concerned with forcing the States General into a separate peace, abandoning their allies, and so breaking up William's confederation.[76]

Yet after reaching a subsidy agreement with Louis, by which parliament was not to meet until early in 1678, Charles unexpectedly consented to an autumn visit by William, during which he overrode James's objections, and seriously disconcerted Louis, by suddenly concluding William's marriage to Mary, James's elder daughter and next in line of succession.[77] At first sight this politically sensational marriage appears to represent an abrupt reversal of the summer's secret pro-French policy, or it can be interpreted as such an inconsistent move as to indicate that Charles's policies lacked direction or even coherence.[78] For Danby the marriage was a first step in breaking free from the secret connection with France, but Charles had a very different intention. He greatly overestimated the influence that it would give him over William, believing that he could now induce the latter to agree to an early peace. Charles and William discussed a set of proposals during the visit, which a special envoy, Feversham, took to France.[79] For Charles these first proposals, even if they failed, were intended to draw William into negotiations. The latter had no intention of accepting peace on terms that he regarded as disastrously inadequate for Dutch (and British) security. Instead he now thought himself better placed to draw Charles into the war, which would restore the flagging morale of the Dutch, prop up the defences of the

Spanish Netherlands, force Louis to evacuate Sicily and postpone the conclusion of peace until France could no longer dictate its terms.[80]

Not everyone welcomed the marriage and a defensive treaty with the States General. Some opposition MPs who had connections with William's republican opponents claimed that he and Charles would now aid each other to establish arbitrary government in both Britain and the Netherlands. Danby's close working relationship with William increased their suspicions.[81] But most contemporaries interpreted the marriage as a major defeat for France. Charles tried to reassure Louis, explaining his approval in terms of the need to lighten his domestic difficulties. He argued that his friendship with France made his subjects suspect, as they had done in 1672–3, that he planned to change the established religion and the constitutional system of government. The marriage showed them that he had no such intention, but he promised Louis that it would not diminish his desire to remain on the best possible terms. Charles even claimed explicitly that he would now control and direct William.[82] But the more Charles explained his difficulties, the less trust Louis placed in his assurances. He regarded Charles as inherently weak: politically because of his need to take account of the interests, opinions and prejudices of his subjects; personally as a result of his impressionability. His attitude in consenting to closer links with the Dutch demonstrated all his failings. Charles had repeatedly promised James that Mary would not be disposed of in marriage without his consent, and James had passed on the assurance to Louis. Overnight Charles changed, requiring James's consent for political reasons.[83] Yet he assured Louis that the marriage would not change his policy of friendship with France. Having said this, Charles then concluded an alliance with the States General on 31 December 1677, and brought forward the meeting of parliament to 28 January.[84] Although exasperated, Louis did not turn irrevocably against Charles, whom he rightly thought he could always influence and manipulate, but these developments did identify Danby as the major obstruction to French policies. Characteristically Louis first made Danby the offer of a massive bribe, but after this had been reluctantly declined, the French ambassador began to concert with opposition MPs' attacks on the lord treasurer that were in December 1678 to culminate in revelations that finally destroyed his position.[85]

The crisis in the low countries absorbed almost all Charles's attention during the first seven months of 1678, and dominated the proceedings of parliament which met for longer (although fragmented) periods than in any year since 1663. The king tried desperately to bring about a general European peace, but lacked the influence and diplomatic skill and patience to succeed. As pressure mounted on him to enter the war – from Danby, parliament and William – and his attempts to persuade Louis to hold back further military offensives failed, Charles had to take action to prevent the French from occupying the whole of Flanders. But even then he tried to maintain his good relationship with Louis, and by all means to avoid a breach.

Charles was in almost continuous contact, by correspondence and ambassadorial conversations in London, with Louis and William during the months from January to August 1678, but he failed to make any significant impact on either's policy decisions. Quite the reverse: Charles had to react to moves which were intended to manœuvre him into positions in which he could be manipulated. William believed that a settlement providing security for France's neighbours could be obtained only if England became involved in the war as a combatant. Charles knew that William's English associates agreed and were working to this end. Their influence and the state of public opinion after the royal marriage would make it very difficult for Charles to change his policies if William manœuvred him into an actual war against France – a war whose difficulties and dangers were greatly underestimated. Louis, occupying a much stronger position than William, operated a more subtle policy. He deliberately prolonged negotiations for peace so as to take maximum advantage of all differences between enemy states, and intervened systematically in their internal affairs to create difficulties for their rulers.[86]

Warnings from Charles that public and parliamentary pressure might force him into the war failed to impress Louis in a military sense, although he did evacuate his forces from Sicily, for fear of English naval intervention. But he knew that English entry into the war might enable William to overcome increasing Dutch war-weariness, and postpone indefinitely the possibility of the States General making a separate peace. Louis skilfully deployed a variety of tactics in his political campaign to neutralize England. He kept Charles on the defensive, eliciting from him responses that were not always the result of consultation with Danby and the cabinet council. Rifts between king and ministers helped Louis. English confusions bewildered the allies. Opposition MPs, remembering the cynical royal deceptions of 1670–2, suspected that another attempt was being made, using the French threat to Flanders as a pretext, to obtain money from parliament to raise an army which would then be used to change the system of government into an absolute monarchy. In fact, during the early part of the crisis, events and pressure from Louis drove Charles from one expedient to another: only as late as June 1678 is there (not entirely conclusive) evidence that serious consideration was given to the option of using the army to increase royal authority.

At the end of 1677 Louis showed Charles who was master, by suspending payments of the agreed subsidy and rejecting Charles's proposal of a lengthy truce which would enable him to set to work as mediator.[87] Charles subsequently failed to formulate terms which came near to being acceptable to either William or Louis. In detail the differences concerned which Flemish towns the latter should retain: at stake was the wider issue of the defensibility and integrity of the Spanish Netherlands, and the security of its neighbours.[88] Louis took precautions against the possibility that parliament might force Charles into the war, although he realized that the latter was exaggerating the danger. In January 1678 Louis sent Ruvigny to London, ostensibly on family business, but really to work with the opposition in the forthcoming session. Montagu warned Charles in advance of Ruvigny's purpose and named his principal contacts, Holles and Russell. Charles took no action, probably because the exposure of French tactics would have been exploited by Danby to engineer an open breach with Louis.[89] But knowledge of the alliance between Louis and part of the opposition led Charles to make a cautious and defensive speech to parliament (28 January). He claimed that the alliances with Holland would preserve Flanders, but added provisos – unless prevented by Spanish negligence, or by 'want of due assistances' from parliament. He asserted that the crisis required a fleet of ninety ships, and an army of thirty to forty thousand men, a far larger force than had been expected.[90]

Charles immediately encountered deep-seated and offensively expressed distrust. Ruvigny's opposition contacts had worked out an effective strategy with him. They did not oppose war preparations directly, but encumbered all offers with unacceptable conditions, and deliberately provoked Charles by infringing his right over foreign policy. The Commons address of 31 January demanded inclusion in any new treaties with the allies of two calculatedly impossible war aims: a pledge to continue fighting until France had been reduced to the frontiers of 1659; and agreement by the Dutch to a total embargo on trade with France. An offer of supply was linked to a demand that Charles inform the House about the terms of his alliances.[91] The king replied by rebuking the Commons (4 February) and repeating his demand for immediate supply.[92] But his real reply took the form of a new, but hopeless, approach to Louis. Knowing that Louis had instigated this blackmailing and obstructive Commons strategy, Charles sent him an astonishingly naïve proposal, that he should conclude an early peace and then tie Charles to the French interest by a permanent treaty that would include an annual subsidy of £600,000.[93] It is not clear why Charles expected Louis even to discuss such a one-sided and long-term arrangement in the middle of a crisis for the allies, in which Louis possessed all the advantages over his enemies.

Louis was now within reach of inflicting a major diplomatic defeat on William, by persuading the States General to make peace separately, abandoning the interests of their allies, which would inevitably break up the confederation. A surprise offensive in March 1678, which produced the capture of Ypres and Ghent, showed the Dutch that the war was unwinnable and even a successful defence of the Spanish Netherlands doubtful.[94] It also created alarm in England. Charles could not afford to remain inactive. He sent a token force of 3,000 men to secure Ostend.[95] On his instructions Danby proceeded to raise an army of nearly 30,000 men with impressive speed – but on the negative side many MPs publicly complained that this provided an ominous demonstration of the ease with which military government could be established. Naturally Danby used the opportunity of the army's formation to expand his patronage system, but contemporaries were impressed by the apparently high quality of the units raised.[96] The prospect of the French overrunning the entire Spanish Netherlands also forced the Commons to adopt a more constructive attitude. They voted a poll tax to finance the army and fleet, which got the royal assent on 20 March, and passed a Bill prohibiting the import of most French commodities, which Charles had to accept, although it would lessen the customs revenues significantly.[97]

Swept on by events over which he had no control Charles found himself teetering on the edge of a war that he did not want. Surprisingly James now switched to enthusiastic support of Danby's advocacy of war, in the hope of being given command of the army that would have to be sent to Flanders.[98] Charles persisted in his attempt to conclude a secret agreement with Louis, but the latter responded coldly. Ruvigny demanded the immediate withdrawal of the troops sent to Ostend: if this had been done Charles would have been signalling to the world his intention of deserting the allies, and virtually proclaiming himself the paid pensioner of France.[99] At this late stage Charles also discovered how far Louis had got in persuading the war-weary Regent party in the States General to make a separate peace: Dutch procrastination was holding up progress in negotiations that Danby was pressing for a new alliance. Opportunistically, Charles tried to exploit Dutch war-weariness to justify his own inaction, and to gain more freedom of action, by telling parliament (29 April) that the Dutch were making haste to leave the war.[100] This proved to be a tactical mistake. Although Charles tried to win the confidence of MPs by explicitly asking their advice on what should now be done, and by showing them the text of the existing alliance with the Dutch, his transparent eagerness not to become involved in the war confirmed suspicions that he had never intended to enter the conflict, but had raised an army in order to establish arbitrary government. Consequently the Commons reacted sharply, blaming Charles and Danby for the way in which the war was going in Louis' favour, and resolving that the alliance with the Dutch was not 'pursuant to addresses of this House, nor consistent with the good and safety of this kingdom'.[101] Charles wisely refrained from answering, but on 7 May the Commons went further, addressing for the removal of those ministers who had advised the content of the king's replies to their foreign policy addresses of 26 May 1677 and 31 January 1678. Danby rallied the Court party to resist these resolutions, but they passed in a series of close divisions on 10 May, which revealed the weakening of his own influence, and the depth of suspicion of royal policies, although as yet neither Charles nor Danby realized that the Country leaders were concerting their opposition with the French ambassador.[102]

The Commons addresses showed Charles that a majority of MPs would concentrate on taking advantage of his necessity if he embarked on an expensive war against France. Instinctively he returned to negotiations with Louis, who was just sufficiently impressed by the new English army, and William's use of its existence to persuade the States General to remain in the war, to make him a new offer. In a secret agreement (17/27 May) Charles put himself in Louis' hands.[103] He undertook to disband the new forces, and to recall all those abroad, except for the garrison at Ostend. He added an apparently gratuitous promise, which it is hard to see how he could fulfil, to procure the States General's consent to peace within two months. This clause displays French policy at its most devious. Louis had already won over enough Dutch deputies to obtain a majority in the States General; but by getting Charles to intervene in Dutch internal politics, Louis would poison Anglo-Dutch relations. Finally Charles had to earn his subsidies by proroguing parliament, a move that would reflect on Danby, for his failure to maintain a Commons majority.

Charles expressed his reluctance to prorogue parliament at Louis' dictation, but he preferred to depend on Louis rather than enter the war and find himself helplessly dependent on a Commons dominated by the aggressive and unscrupulous Country opposition. However, although Charles instructed Danby to warn William that no help would be forthcoming from England, even to save Flanders from French occupation, he did not formally ratify the 17/27 May agreement with Louis or fulfil all its terms. His reasons were financial. He needed money to pay off the army and the fleet, and he and Danby calculated that parliament was so eager to disband the new forces that it would immediately vote supply: then the French subsidies could be used to discharge royal debts.[104] In other words Charles was hoping to be paid twice over for disbanding the new forces, by Louis and by parliament. In the event Charles lacked time; he ignored clear warnings that Louis expected disbandment by 17/27 July. Danby showed even less eagerness for disbandment. Although the evidence is incomplete, there are indications that he formulated a project (in which James concurred) to retain permanently a part of the new army, citing the unreasonable behaviour of the Commons as justification for the need to increase royal authority. Louis gave him a pretext, and inconsiderately plunged Charles into a new set of difficulties, when France unilaterally refused to implement the peace terms agreed with the Dutch until France's ally Sweden had been given restitution of its lost territories. This threatened a resumption of general hostilities. Danby independently worked with William to bring this about, concluding a new treaty with the States General on 15/25 July, but the Dutch republicans were not deflected from their aim of an early peace; the Treaty of Nijmegen was signed on 31 July/10 August.[105]

Only at this late stage did Charles realize that Louis did not now intend to pay him the subsidies stipulated in the unratified May agreement. But neither he nor Danby would cut their losses, and they proceeded to increase their difficulties by continuing to gamble. Parliament voted £380,000 in June for disbanding the new forces, but this money was used to keep the forces in being, and no units were disbanded during the rest of 1678.[106] It is now impossible to penetrate Charles's and Danby's intentions, to know whether they were seriously considering a project to dissolve parliament and use the army to strengthen royal authority. By failing to disband the army they certainly confirmed parliamentary suspicions of a design to establish absolutism. They also devastated royal finances. Parliament had voted £600,000 to raise the army, and £380,000 to disband it, while the assessment of 1677 and credit on the excise had financed the fleet. But all these sums had been spent by the end of July 1678, and the maintenance of the army into 1679 cost over £750,000. This could not be covered by existing revenue. Danby's final legacy to his master in March 1679 consisted of a floating debt of just under £2,500,000. The weakness of the Crown in relation to parliament during the early stages of the ensuing Exclusion crisis stemmed directly from the financial consequences of the unsuccessful gambles of 1678.[107]

A curiously naïve and hopelessly ill-timed move by Charles shows that he was aware of his financial predicament. Without giving Court spokesmen in the Commons any advance warning, he proposed on 18 June 1678, when suspicions were at their height, that his permanent revenue should be increased by £300,000 per annum, and that he should receive compensation for the reduction in customs receipts caused by the ban on French commodities. The Commons rejected the proposal summarily.[108]

With the end of the European crisis in sight Charles meant to return to his normal and easy routine, spending August 1678 at Windsor and the autumn at Newmarket, leaving Danby to cope with business. He made no change in these plans when he was informed of a plot against his life, on 13 August, by Christopher Kirkby, an amateur scientist who was acting as front man for the prime movers, Israel Tonge and Titus Oates. Since it did not appear to be a matter of great urgency Charles delegated its detailed investigation to Danby, who proceeded slowly.[109] Tonge and Oates interpreted his leisurely proceedings as indicating that they were not being taken seriously. Consequently Oates tried to make a bigger impact by forging letters, ascribed to an alleged plotter named Bedingfield. These were brought to Charles at Windsor (30 August). Seeing that they were crude fakes, the king would have dropped the investigation altogether, but James seized on the forgeries as providing an opportunity to discredit what he believed was a move by the Country opposition to mount an anti-Catholic campaign. He pressed for the council to continue the examination of the informers in order to expose their falsehoods. Danby agreed, so as to protect himself against future criticism for lack of investigative zeal. Between them they persuaded a sceptical Charles.[110]

On 28 September Charles presided over a council examination of the informers. In the morning Tonge's allegations made an unfavourable impression, but in the afternoon Oates convinced everyone except Charles that there was sufficient truth in what he alleged for emergency action to be ordered. With brazen confidence he named the Jesuits allegedly implicated, and said where they were to be found, in disguise and under assumed names. Their arrest impressed all present the next day, effacing any impression made when Charles cleverly trapped Oates in lies about details that he used to embroider his allegations: Oates fancifully described Don Juan as a fat, swarthy Spaniard (he was tall and fair), and misplaced the location of the main Jesuit church in Paris. In the event Charles made no attempt to convince the council that a serious plot did not exist. By leaving for Newmarket he forfeited any chance of influencing its proceedings; in his absence the alleged plot became a great matter of state.[111]

This began when Oates named Coleman, secretary to the Duchess of York, as a leading plotter. A versatile and imprudent activist, Coleman was actually James's confidential man of business, a renowned lobbyist for the Catholics at Westminster and an agent for the French embassy. He assured the ambassador that all incriminating papers had been destroyed, but a search produced a mass of correspondence with France, mostly in cipher. His letters were a few years old, but when deciphered they raised such delicate issues in relation to James that the cabinet council excluded the clerks before examining them on 5 October.[112] Rumours about the plot now began to sweep London, and were intensified by the mysterious disappearance of the capital's best known JP, Sir Edmund Berry Godfrey, before whom Oates had twice sworn informations. Yet Charles remained at Newmarket and, when he returned on 16 October, showed himself out of touch by openly expressing a scepticism about the plot that few now shared. On the next day Godfrey's body was found, apparently murdered by the plotters, and hysteria exploded among the people in and around London. On 18 October the council could not think what should be done. Charles was continuing to treat the plot as a criminal matter, to be dealt with by the courts. The councillors found that their inaction was being popularly interpreted as an attempt to stifle the evidence and hush up the plot. Danby realized how vulnerable he would be if stern action was not taken before parliament met, and that it was politically impossible to defer its meeting. Only on the day before that happened, 20 October, did he persuade Charles to authorize a proclamation, encouraging informers to come forward with new evidence.[113]

By his scepticism about the plot Charles put his chief minister in a false position. In his speech to parliament on 21 October the king made only a passing reference to 'a design against his person, by the Jesuit's, whom he would leave to the law, and a veiled reference to Coleman 'tampering to a high degree with foreigners, and contriving how to introduce Popery amongst us'.[114] Charles's sceptical attitude prevented Danby from taking the initiative; inevitably opposition peers and MPs made every effort to widen the issues, especially by suggesting that the plotters had aimed at undermining liberties and the constitution as well as the protestant religion.[115] Coleman's letters bore this out, and necessarily raised the question of James's position, despite Oates's ill-considered and premature statement that James was not implicated in the plot. Danby asked himself the question that over the next two years all politicians had to consider: would Charles preserve James and his right to the succession? Danby's uncertainties were further increased by the knowledge that James was engaged in a negotiation with the Holles group of the opposition for his dismissal, to be followed by the dissolution of parliament, and the grant by a new parliament of supply in return for religious toleration, and he suspected that such a change of policy might well appeal to Charles.[116]

Initially Danby failed to give parliament a clear lead. Court spokesmen remained conspicuously silent on the first day of the session, because they had not received instructions, leaving Country MPs to monopolize debates. Consideration of the plot and of action needed to safeguard the king's still-threatened life, dominated proceedings to an unprecedented extent: from 21 October until 8 November the Commons discussed no other major business. Consequently parliament virtually took over investigation of the plot, its committees repeatedly interrogating Coleman and other suspects. Oates, Bedlow and other informers received encouragement, and spoke to the Commons from the bar of the House.[117] The momentum being assumed by these investigations made it essential for Charles to lay down the limits within which MPs and peers might act, but such was the excitement generated by the plot, to be intensified by further sensational developments in December, that the very firm, clear and reasoned line of policy laid down at this time by Charles had little effect. Nevertheless it must be emphasized that Charles explicitly declared his position on the central issues raised by the plot as early as November 1678, and that he was to adhere to this position throughout the subsequent Exclusion crisis.

In a short, pertinent speech to parliament on 9 November Charles put forward a proposal for imposing limitations on a Catholic successor.[118] This was to remain on the political agenda for the next two years as the royal alternative to Exclusion. He promised to give his consent 'to such reasonable bills as should be presented, to make them safe in the reign of any Successor, so as they tend not to impeach the right of Succession . . . in the right line'. Indicating that he was prepared to agree to the new Test Bill, excluding Catholics from parliament, Charles insisted emphatically that James must be exempted by name. This emphasis at last decided Danby on his own line. Discarding earlier reservations, he directed his followers to pass this exemption, but there was a majority of only two (158 to 156; 21 November).[119] Charles continued in an assertive mood to defend his prerogative rights. The Commons sent secretary Williamson to the Tower for issuing army commissions to papists: Charles peremptorily released him because he had been following royal orders.[120] Parliament actually passed a Militia Bill, ignoring clear indications from the king that he considered it unacceptable because it would infringe his exclusive control over the armed forces, although only for a limited time. Charles vetoed it.[121]

This burst of royal self-assertion and personal activity stemmed from a belated but acute realization on the king's part of the dangers that he now faced. Danby's detached attitude made Charles act in his own interests and make his own decisions, without taking the advice of any other ministers. Despite his intense repugnance for a man whom he categorized as a perjurer, Charles met Oates privately. He picked up disquieting information. In what must have been an extraordinary private interview Oates boldly informed Charles that the queen had solemnly sworn to take revenge on Charles for his sexual infidelities by commissioning his murder by poisoning. Maintaining tight self-control, Charles chose not to react to this impudent allegation.[122] But he acted quickly to ensure that the queen's innocence was vindicated, first at council, then in the Lords. His honour was involved. However, he had important additional reasons for protecting her. The queen employed as her secretary Richard Bellings, an experienced and prudent Catholic agent, but one whose exposure would be even more devastating than that of Coleman because Charles had employed him on secret missions and, above all, because he had signed and helped to negotiate the secret Treaty of Dover. Using his uncanny political instinct, Oates was already sniffing at Bellings's trail, and he was also concentrating on one of the five Catholic peers accused of participation in the Plot, Arundell of Wardour, another Dover signatory.[123]

Charles also reactivated secret and personal negotiations with Louis, a line that was never to be far from his mind during the years of crisis, and was ultimately to bring him independence from parliament in 1681. Early in December he renewed private discussions with the French ambassador: eight meetings took place before the first week of February 1679.[124] Two major obstacles impeded agreement with Louis: the army had still not been disbanded, and Danby remained as chief minister, with no intention of giving up office. Charles needed him to manage parliament and repair royal finances, and no alternative at first appeared. Additionally Charles could not abandon a minister who knew so much about his recent secret dealings with France. Danby would have had little hesitation in using this knowledge, if necessary, to blackmail the king, or even to save himself by ruining James. He would not have been likely to acquiesce in his own destruction, like Strafford in 1641, to save his master – whom he always seems to have despised.

In fact the decision to destroy Danby politically had been made already – by Louis. The new French ambassador in London, Barrillon, concerted a scheme with country MPs by which Ralph Montagu (who had been dismissed as English ambassador in Paris as a result of Danby's influence) would publicly reveal evidence showing that Charles and Danby had been secretly negotiating with Louis earlier in the year, when they were simultaneously asking parliament for money to finance a war against France. Charles and Danby knew that many MPs had been collaborating with successive French ambassadors, and with Coleman, to obstruct business. However they had no hard evidence, and Coleman refused to reveal anything. A case was prepared against Montagu, charging him with contact with the papal nuncio in Paris, which it was hoped would discredit him at a time when anti-papist hysteria was at its height. Even more important and urgent as an objective, the allegation would justify the seizure of Montagu's papers, so that any evidence incriminating Danby (and Charles) of having deceived parliament and the nation could be suppressed. The attempt failed. The production of selected correspondence in the Commons by Montagu's friends discredited Danby, against whom articles of impeachment were voted on 21 December, despite strenuous Court resistance.[125]

Danby's support in the Lords was sufficiently strong for him to defeat an impeachment – provided of course that Charles continued to retain him in office. But his loss of control in the Commons made him useless to the king, and it would take time and money to try to rebuild a working majority. Instead Charles decided to prorogue parliament (from 30 December to 4 February) to give himself time to decide what to do, and also to check the momentum that a new crop of informers was giving to parliamentary investigation of the Popish Plot.[126] His reasons for wanting to prevent an impeachment of Danby were entirely selfish. He could not permit a public trial in which Montagu, speaking for a prosecution managed by the Commons, not the king's legal officers, and Danby acting in his own defence, would certainly make damaging revelations about royal policies. Furthermore even an unsuccessful impeachment would occupy all parliament's time, poison relations between Lords and Commons and postpone indefinitely any vote of supply.

Danby's loss of control over the Commons forced Charles to think how to carry on the government without him. During the prorogation Charles thought he found the way: he took over the clandestine negotiation initiated earlier by James with the Holles group in the Country opposition, even though its leading members could not be regarded as dominant political figures. But they offered Charles an escape route from appalling difficulties. They said they would be satisfied with Danby's resignation as treasurer, provided that Charles dissolved the Cavalier parliament and summoned a new one without delay. They also promised supply for an early disbanding of the new forces. Events were to prove that Holles and his associates promised more than they could deliver, and Charles was rightly uncertain about the proposed deal. Only after considerable hesitation did he take the irrevocable step of dissolving the eighteen-year-old parliament, and so shattering the mould of politics.[127]

7 *The Contest with the Whigs*

The prorogation on 30 December 1678 (a year that had already seen more prorogations than any other) was interpreted as yet another Court tactic, intended primarily to give Danby time in which to regroup. Some observers perceived a wider purpose, suspecting that Charles was concerned to safeguard James and the queen from reportedly imminent attacks. But the dissolution of the Cavalier Parliament (24 January 1679) was a much more fundamental development. By this decisive and irrevocable move, on which he alone decided, Charles totally transformed the character of politics.[1] By discarding the 'standing' parliament, in which Danby had patiently constructed working majorities, Charles effectively terminated Danby's ministry. For politicians electoral skills now appeared to replace parliamentary management as the key to success: after a period of eighteen years without one, there were now to be three general elections within two years. Inevitably Charles and a new set of ministers quickly felt the impact of excited public opinion. In place of a largely static political situation, with ministers entrenched at Whitehall and Westminster against a Country minority that was powerless to eject them, but could at times block legislative proposals and deny the king money, there ensued several months of extreme fluidity, with major changes occurring weekly, or even daily. Sweeping changes transformed Court and Commons. Danby and many of his assistants lost office, to be replaced by a new generation of younger and largely untested ministers – Essex, Hyde, Sunderland and Godolphin. The first elections of 1679 swept away most of Danby's parliamentary dependants. Half the new MPs had never sat before, and it was on them that Shaftesbury made such an impact that it sustained his campaign for Exclusion for over two years.[2] Whig propaganda was beginning to instil in the nation generally, and not just in the electorate, a high level of political consciousness.

At first Shaftesbury seemed to be the chief beneficiary of the torrent of changes that marked the first quarter of 1679. Danby lay in the Tower. Charles sent James into exile overseas.[3] Shaftesbury became president of a privy council, organized on entirely new principles, that included several of his close associates. It seemed (not least to Shaftesbury himself) that he was to fill the political vacuum created by Danby's fall and the ruin of his system. Indeed Shaftesbury was now acquiring the primacy, power and influence that were to make him the undisputed leader of the first Whigs. Eventually, of course, his policy of Exclusion was to fail, and in the wider context it can be seen that it was not Shaftesbury but Charles himself who filled the vacuum left by Danby. The king, using his prerogative powers, played the decisive role in defeating the Whigs. After years in which the direction of policy had been largely delegated to Danby, Charles now asserted himself, making all the major decisions himself during the fight to resist Exclusion, often without consulting his new ministers, or in the face of their contrary advice. Never again during his reign did he entrust power to a single minister, as he had done with Clarendon and Danby. Instead Charles created and carefully perpetuated a heterogeneous ministry, so as to maximize his own freedom of action.

At first Essex had the key role, as minister, of restoring royal finances which Danby had left in a state of confusion and indebtedness.[4] He never trusted Charles, certainly not to the point of making him financially independent of parliament, and seems to have had limited ambitions – unlike his brother Henry who increasingly dominated him. Lawrence Hyde, the most junior new minister, needed, as Clarendon's ablest son, to justify himself by success. Eventually he emerged as the king's closest adviser, and kept contact with James on his behalf.[5] Halifax can best be described as the consistently negative influence within the new administration, who excelled at countering and blocking others, initially Shaftesbury within the council and later in the Lords, later James and Hyde.[6] Sunderland received charge of foreign policy, tutored by William Temple, in which the main feature was to be the formation of an alliance to contain France. He also assisted Charles in negotiating with Louis for subsidies. Since he also corresponded with William this meant that he was voluntarily (and characteristically) taking on an inherently contradictory role – unlike Danby who had gone along with Charles reluctantly.[7] Shaftesbury's appointment horrified James, but the new president quickly realized that Charles had given him only the illusion of power and influence in order to compromise him with his political associates.[8]

Relegated to the background, and afraid that Charles would abandon them, Danby and James separately bombarded the king with provocative and mistaken advice, which he rightly ignored: both treated the crisis as one of incipient rebellion and urged him to take drastic repressive action, arresting opposition leaders, dissolving the new parliament, overawing the City by reinforcing the Tower.[9] Neither appreciated the essentially political nature of the novel challenge that emerged as Shaftesbury organized and led the first Whig party, and committed its members from an early stage to the parliamentary and electoral struggle to enact a Bill excluding James from the succession. Charles saw this and made the right response by rallying opinion against the Whigs. It is superficially tempting, but it would be simplistic, to depict Charles as the original Tory, confronting Shaftesbury, the first Whig. But Charles acted as a partisan only in self-defence: he had to have Tory support to contain and resist Whig pressure, to check the momentum which Shaftesbury developed. Tory support made this possible, but then it was Charles's skilful employment of the prerogative powers – prorogation, dissolution, proclamations, influence over the judiciary, actions of *quo warranto*, patronage – that brought him total victory over the Whigs.

Charles can be described as a father figure in relation to the Tories. He made no attempt to act as party organizer, and he did not try – as James did so disastrously in 1687–8 – to mount a campaign to influence parliamentary elections. In the first elections of 1679 he did not respond to appeals from courtiers for assistance in constituencies. They mostly bore the taint of having been Danby's dependants and had little chance of success. Neither the king nor his new ministers tried to reconstruct a working majority in Lords and Commons by the kind of managerial techniques that Danby had used – such methods would now be counterproductive, and financial resources were lacking. The Whigs drew support from describing themselves as honest spokesmen for the country against a corrupt Court, and Charles rightly saw that the royal Court (in the sense of all the servants of the Crown – ministerial, household, professional, army and naval) provided far too narrow a base on which to rely. Charles realized that he had to rally and lead unofficial and independent supporters, to persuade a significant proportion of the nobility, gentry, farmers and townsmen (the clergy needed no persuasion) to commit themselves voluntarily and publicly to him.[10]

Charles worked consistently to inspire the Tories, but he could not allow himself to be seen as a party king. This would make it far more difficult for him to emerge credibly, as he did in April 1681, as the sovereign who demanded from his subjects the abandonment of all party politics, so that all could unite in submission to royal authority and the rule of law.[11] The Court actually became the weakest component in the combination that opposed Exclusion. Denied supply by the Whig parliament in 1679 Charles had to authorize drastic retrenchment, which Essex executed. Hungry courtiers affected by these economies privately favoured making a deal with the Whigs by which, in return for Exclusion or a royal divorce, parliament would vote supply, of which a proportion would go to courtiers. This sentiment was also shared, in 1680, by the faction centered on the Duchess of Portsmouth. In contrast another distinct Court group embarrassed Charles by showing greater loyalty to James than to the king, but could not be discouraged too far because several of them had constant access to Barrillon, the French ambassador.

Unlike courtiers most Tories were independent peers and gentry, few of whom had held salaried or central office. They prided themselves (often self-righteously) on their rectitude and tradition of loyalty, enshrined in their devotion to the memory of Charles I. However, many of them never felt entirely confident that they could trust Charles II absolutely or rely on his consistency and determination to stand by his principles and friends. This faced Charles with perhaps his most urgent task, to establish his credibility and trustworthiness, and counter the Whig arguments that under intense pressure he would always give way.[12] It was significant that most of those closest to him, who thought they knew him well – James himself (and never more than in the spring of 1679), Shaftesbury, Sunderland, Barrillon, the Duchess of Portsmouth, Gilbert Burnet, William – predicted that his impressionability and inconstancy would lead him to concede Exclusion.[13] It is not surprising that Charles's past record made many of his loyal subjects hesitate before putting themselves in his hands as leader and protector. He had abandoned ministers (Clarendon and Clifford) as well as policies (the Declarations of Indulgence, the Dutch War in 1674), when they ran into severe difficulties. Consequently the king's first emphatic statement, as early as November 1678, that he would never accept a distortion of the rightful succession, received comparatively little attention and virtually no acceptance.[14] The unexpected admission of Shaftesbury and his associates to the new privy council increased misgivings among loyalists.

The bishops and Anglican clergy were without doubt the staunchest of all loyalists. They feared that any weakening of royal authority would infallibly lead to the destruction of the established church, but their experience made them distrust Charles's intentions and integrity. The two Declarations of Indulgence, and the king's frequent attempts to mitigate the severity of the Uniformity and Conventicle Acts, had led Archbishop Sheldon to organize the friends of the church in its defence, and to keep a vigilant watch on all moves at Court. But he had been succeeded by the far less aggressive Sancroft and the defence of clerical interests had been entrusted to Danby. The clergy feared that the fall of their champion would lead to the church suffering damage, and this seemed to be confirmed by the disturbing development that few JPs were now enforcing the laws against dissenters. James's curt refusal to consider reconversion increased their depression, but Sheldon had left them a saving principle to which they clung; he had always emphasized the necessity for the clergy to establish the closest possible links with the principal landowning laity. In these links, which Charles had nothing to do with, is to be found the origin of the Tory party.

Charles had also to counter the persuasive Whig propaganda that he was still intent on ruling arbitrarily. He had to convince independent lay and clerical opinion that he would rule within, and by, the laws. It was for this reason that he did not pardon those condemned for taking part in the

Popish Plot: although he knew that the evidence against them was largely perjured, they had been convicted according to the forms of justice. This stand as a constitutional ruler was essential to give credibility to his offer to consider limitations on a Catholic king as the alternative to Exclusion, which he repeatedly emphasized was legally as well as personally unacceptable. Although in private Charles expressed his aversion to any form of limitations, he publicly paraded his willingness to accept them as proof of his own good intentions, and to underline Whig intransigence as unreasonable and dangerous. Similarly he made public moves in 1680 to form an anti-French alliance, a policy that he did not believe in but adopted in the attempt to dissipate suspicions that he really wanted a new alliance with Louis.[15]

Charles achieved only partial success in convincing his subjects (and even his ministers) that he would never consent to Exclusion. Whig propaganda proved to be extraordinarily effective. It maintained belief in Shaftesbury's totally erroneous argument that, whatever Charles said to the contrary, he really wanted to be coerced into accepting Exclusion. Until as late as the Oxford parliament in 1681 it continued to be a Whig theme that Charles was only looking for the excuse of intolerable pressure to justify him in abandoning James's right. Shaftesbury's entire political strategy was based on the assumption that Charles did not mean what he said in his repeated declarations against Exclusion. Not only would he accept it himself, but he would ensure that the Lords passed the Bill. The Whig arguments failed to take into consideration the contexts of Charles's earlier abandonments of policies. All of them – the Declarations of Indulgence, the Dutch Wars, the new army in 1678, the Test Bills of 1665 and 1675 – had been intended to increase royal and ministerial power and authority. In contrast, during the Exclusion crisis, Charles believed that he was having to fight defensively to protect the essential prerogative powers inherent in the Crown, his own right as well as that of James to the succession. Similarly Tories and clergy interpreted the Whig campaign for Exclusion as a design to subvert the constitution and the church.

Having the advantages of historical hindsight, knowing that after Charles's final rejection of Exclusion at Oxford the whole Whig position collapsed in a matter of months, it is easy for us to underestimate the severity of the crisis, and the pressures that Charles had to withstand. But an examination of the skill, determination and ruthlessness that Charles employed during the crisis makes apparent the extent to which the intensity of the struggle against the Whigs brought out in him latent qualities and political ability that he had not chosen to exert in the past. The Charles who emerged triumphant and vindictive in 1681 is hardly recognizable as the easy-going saunterer of the Clarendon years, or the king who remained in the background as Danby apparently ran the administration. Forced by the crisis to descend into the political arena, he routed the Whigs, manipulated his ministers and held off James and William in a virtuoso performance as a machiavellian ruler.

Intense speculation and continuous private negotiations filled the time between the prorogation of the Cavalier Parliament (30 December 1678) and Charles's announcement of its dissolution (24 January 1679). With a vote for an impeachment against him, Danby took the lead for the last time in the reign, while Charles wisely stayed in the background giving his treasurer a minimum of support, but easing himself into a position in which he could discard him. At first Danby fought bitterly in the hope of retaining his office, but even he came to realize that the most he could achieve was to step down as treasurer and take a household office (reportedly as lord steward) which would confer considerable but informal influence. Charles tacitly accepted this possibility. He did not object to Danby bargaining with the Holles group. Danby should have realized that Holles had neither the strength nor the skill to fulfil his undertakings, and that no agreement with opposition groups would have any value without Shaftesbury's approval.[16] Charles also knew about James's clandestine approach to Shaftesbury, which stood no chance of success because the latter needed to be able to exploit anti-papist excitement, and he established his own clandestine contacts which were to lead to Shaftesbury's unexpected nomination as president of the reconstituted privy council in April.[17]

During the weeks before parliament assembled on 6 March, all Danby's actions displayed the weaknesses of a failing minister. Charles did not interfere, but carefully distanced himself from such actions as the dismissal of all government servants who had voted for an impeachment. Fighting for survival, Danby neglected even urgent business, such as the need to restore royal finances to some kind of order. Increasingly he was boxing himself into positions in which he was becoming a liability to the king. However, he did persuade Charles to make one major move that created a sensation throughout Europe. On 3 March Charles ordered James to leave the country, and privately vetoed his characteristically stupid choice of France as his country of exile. Although the order was accompanied by a solemn statement that the king had never been married to anyone but the queen, rebutting growing rumours of Monmouth's legitimacy, most people interpreted James's exile as the prelude to his abandonment.[18] Danby increased James's feelings of insecurity by claiming credit for his exile in terms suggesting that severe restrictions should be placed on him, or any Catholic successor. James responded by angrily directing his associates not to help Danby against his enemies.

Charles could not afford such major rifts within the Court at such a critical time. He suffered further and gratuitous damage when Danby involved him in a personal dispute on the first day of the new parliament.

Edward Seymour, Speaker since 1673 and renominated on 6 March, had quarrelled bitterly with the treasurer and was putting himself forward as a member of the replacement ministry. Unfortunately Charles allowed Danby to persuade him to use his prerogative power and veto Seymour's nomination (7 March). The ferocity of the Commons' reaction came as a surprise. In five days of debates MPs insisted on their nominee. Charles talked affably with them, and disclaimed any sinister intentions in vetoing Seymour, but he adamantly refused to give way on the constitutional issue of the right to veto.[19] This dispute made him aware of the intensity of feeling against Danby. When parliament reconvened on 15 March a compromise Speaker was agreed on, but the next day Charles arranged that Danby should resign on 25 March, giving him time to make up the treasury accounts, and should be succeeded by a treasury commission. By then even Danby saw that he must abandon the idea of a household office that would enable him to act as 'minister behind the curtain'. But as a careerist driven by his highly developed acquisitive instincts, and by his rapacious wife, he wanted compensation (a key concept in his patronage system). Charles made a serious misjudgement in accepting his claim and in calculating what he should receive. The king's announcement that as well as a pardon he was giving Danby a pension of £5,000 per annum for life and promoting him to a marquessate provoked almost everyone.[20] The Lords resolved that the impeachment voted in December was still effective, despite the dissolution of the Cavalier Parliament – which raised an important constitutional issue. In the Commons eighteen full-scale debates on Danby and the impeachment took place over the next eight weeks. The virulence of MPs' attacks matched anything said against Strafford in 1640–1, and by the end of these weeks Danby was in the Tower, anxiously preparing a defence to save his life.[21]

Aware of his mistake, Charles stubbornly defended the main issue at stake. He withdrew the pension and the new peerage, but on 22 March told the Commons that the pardon must stand. He added that if it was found to be technically defective, and he knew that the frightened lord chancellor had not affixed the great seal to it, although naturally he did not say so, the pardon would be promptly reissued.[22] Charles could not allow his prerogative right of pardon to be questioned and set aside. Having taken such a firm line on the issue of principle, it was perhaps a mistake for Charles to continue with the statement that all the ministerial actions that formed the basis of the articles of impeachment had been taken by his express order. In any case MPs paid no attention; if anything Charles's speech worsened their tempers.[23] The next day Charles instructed Danby to go into hiding to avoid arrest; this the Lords ordered the next day. Later Charles again anticipated parliamentary action when he advised Danby that for safety's sake he should leave England, but this the latter would not do, rightly fearing that (like Clarendon) he would never be allowed to return.[24] When the Lords introduced a Bill of Banishment the Commons went further, bringing in a Bill of Attainder. Although often very confused, the debates disappointed any hopes that Charles and Danby may have entertained of differences developing between the two houses: they agreed on a Bill stipulating that Danby must surrender by a named day, or be attainted. By a very clever tactical move, the Bill did not specify the date, but left it to Charles to decide. This committed the king to completing a Bill he had not initiated, and frustrated his very devious tactic of trying to edge Danby out of the country so as to prevent a trial in which all kinds of damaging revelations might be made, while pretending that his concern was to save his minister's head. By dropping the threat of attainder the Bill achieved its objective: Danby surrendered, and on 16 April was committed to the Tower.[25]

Of course it was Danby, not Charles, who paid dearly for the royal miscalculations: he spent the next fifty-eight months in custody. But no impeachment ever took place, although Charles's action eventually resulted in a clause in the Bill of Rights (1689), providing that no pardon could be issued to bar, or stop, an impeachment. In a more limited sense the case taught Charles an important lesson. Never again did he make a major move without calculating in advance its likely effects on parliament or general opinion; never again did he allow any minister to use him, as Danby had done.

The successive outbreaks provoked by Danby's case and by the veto on Seymour reflected the volatility of the new Commons that confronted the king. Virtually all Danby's relations and most of his dependants had been eliminated, but there remained between a quarter and a third of the members of the House who waited for a lead from whomever were to succeed Danby as ministers. On the other side Shaftesbury, who had taken great pains to ascertain its composition, and the likely attitudes of MPs, initially lacked the ability to organize or direct those who were hostile to, or suspicious of, the Court. In its first confused weeks the new Commons was uncontrollable and ineffective, wasting time and energy in furious but incoherent debates. Country opposition MPs showed significantly less method and discipline than in the Cavalier Parliament. Some of the more far-sighted and responsible had hoped for a process of 'reformation', a programme of legislation to rectify grievances, and Charles had indicated in general terms his readiness to accept such measures, provided they did not affect the succession, but he did not undertake any initiatives. Country disorganization meant that very little was put forward, and only one Act (the Habeas Corpus Amendment) actually passed. Debates exposed the inadequacy of the Court spokesmen, Ernle and Coventry, making Charles realize the need for reinforcement. Shaftesbury showed what was in his mind early (25 March) in a widely publicized speech in which he emphasized the necessary connection between Catholicism and absolutism. This indicated his intention of reviving the succession issue, on which he was actually preparing to stake everything, but it was not until 27 April that he began to control and exploit the undisciplined zeal of Country MPs, and concentrate their attention on James and the succession issue. However, he had been busy preparing the case for Exclusion, using the secret committee of the Commons to collect and examine material linking James with the Popish Plot.[26]

Charles faced a delicate problem in planning and timing a pre-emptive move. He had expected the exiling of James to have had a much greater effect, and he knew that the rejection of Seymour as Speaker and Danby's case had alienated moderates. Demoralized and virtually leaderless peers and MPs looked in vain for official guidance. Charles had no alternative but to execute a clean break with Danby's discredited methods. To establish his credibility with moderates, waverers and the uncommitted he had to substantiate his promises of new and good administration. In a bold and sweeping innovation, announced on 21 April, Charles dissolved the privy council, replacing it with a smaller council organized on new principles.[27] He had unavowed and indeed devious political reasons for this drastic change. It broke up all existing patterns of politics at the highest level. It was also designed to compel many leading Country peers and MPs to reconsider their positions and intentions, and gave them an opportunity to change their attitudes.

Following fashionable contemporary ideas of balance and interest, and elaborating an idea suggested by William Temple, Charles limited the council to thirty members in the hope of more effective consultation and decision-taking. Half sat by virtue of holding office: the rest comprised independants; ten peers and five commoners, 'whose known abilities, interest and esteem in the nation [should] render them without all suspicion of either mistaking or betraying the true interests of the kingdom, and consequently of advising [the king] ill'. Charles promised that this combination of official and independent members would prevent him from resorting in future to a single minister (and that was to be so), or from taking private advice or employing an inner group of ministers – two undertakings that he neither meant nor observed.[28]

The announcement of the names of the new council caused a sensation. Shaftesbury became lord president, ostensibly being given the highest position because he had previously served as lord chancellor, the first office in terms of precedence. In reality it was because he was emerging as the foremost party politician, with Charles laying a two-way bet. It was possible that Shaftesbury could be bought off with this office. Alternatively, if he intended to continue working with the Country opposition, the offer, and still more its acceptance, would compromise him with the zealots. For the same reason Charles offered membership to four MPs with records of consistent opposition to the Court (Cavendish, Capel,

Russell and Powle). Halifax similarly possessed the reputation of a harsh critic of the Court; initially Charles reportedly resisted suggestions for his inclusion. Monmouth served by virtue of his office. The inclusion of two bishops – Archbishop Sancroft and the aggressive Bishop Compton of London – gave them the responsibility of protecting or furthering church interests now that its former champion Danby had disappeared. Only one close associate of Danby (Bath) gained membership, and some prominent politicians felt aggrieved at being omitted. Charles excluded Ralph Montagu and Buckingham, and many Country MPs thought they had superior claims to membership than the four selected, which caused some discord in the Commons. Two deliberately underplayed points should have shown the observant that Charles did not intend to capitulate to pressure and become a nominal king, a Doge of Venice. He did not include the exiled James, but by saying that princes of the blood would be entitled to sit reserved his right to include him later. In addition the king nominated Lauderdale as a supplementary member, although he had been the target for repeated Commons addresses demanding his removal from the royal counsels.[29]

The unforeseen establishment of an entirely new kind of privy council did not enable Charles to regain the initiative. He had made a clever move, but the growing intensity of the crisis limited the effects of even such an adroit and novel tactic. It has often been depicted as primarily a move to gain time, but within a week the Commons passed a decisive vote (27 April) that Shaftesbury designed as the prelude to an Exclusion bill. The short-term gain came in the form of reinforcements for the Court in the Commons in the persons of Capel, Cavendish and Powle. Charles also placed high if perhaps temporary value on the services of Essex, the former lord-lieutenant of Ireland (1672–7) who also became first commissioner of a reconstituted treasury, with the herculean task of restoring order and solvency to royal finances, partly by the invidious method of selective retrenchment. Essex suppressed pensions to former dependants of Danby, whose system of patronage he regarded as constitutionally dangerous. But he had developed distrust of Charles's own attitudes: in November he resigned as commissioner largely because the king took decisions without consulting his council. This left the main work of financial reorganization to two apprentice ministers with long careers ahead of them, Lawrence Hyde and Sidney Godolphin.[30]

The king's most unexpected gain from the new council proved to come from Halifax's inclusion. Formerly an inconsistent but at times highly irresponsible associate of the Country opposition, he now became the most outspoken and effective parliamentary opponent of Exclusion. James greatly feared his likely influence on Charles, regarding him as a republican because of his apparently serious advocacy of limitations, the reduction in the power of a Catholic sovereign. Aware of Halifax's reputation as a most subtle and machiavellian politician, Charles was at first averse to naming him to the council, but he had no difficulty in containing and outwitting him. Two of Halifax's main attributes helped Charles: he lacked stamina, and periodically left the political scene, and he contemptuously disregarded even the most virulent criticism. Consequently he could always be relied on to fight when things were at their worst, as in the 1680 session, but he did not apparently want to share in the fruits of victory.[31]

As well as the council and the treasury, Charles reorganized the admiralty. He appointed a new commission, composed entirely of politicians, that proved to be lamentably incompetent, undoing most of the constructive work of the past decade. This political character was no accident. James had continued to influence, if not control, naval policies and appointments since his resignation as lord high admiral in 1673. Charles nominated opposition politicians to direct a largely laid-up fleet, and accepted their maladministration as the price he had to pay in order to refute opposition charges that the navy, as a 'Yorkist' institution, posed a threat to the nation's liberties.[32]

Exclusion as an explicit issue moved into the central arena of politics with the Commons preparatory vote on 27 April

> that the Duke of York being a Papist, and the hopes of his coming as such to the Crown, have given the greatest countenance and encouragement to the present conspiracies and designs of the Papists against the King and the Protestant Religion,

before adjourning the debate for three days, for a report to be made on Coleman's letters.[33] Charles now had to organize a defence of the rightful succession. On 30 April he and the lord chancellor addressed both Houses with an offer that spelt out in detail their alternative of limitations on a Catholic successor, which would have significantly enhanced the relative position of parliament. If Charles died before James, and at this time their medical history suggested that this was unlikely, an existing parliament was to continue, or his last one was to reassemble, even if it had been dissolved. Parliamentary approval would be needed for the appointment or dismissal of privy councillors, judges, lords-lieutenant and deputies, and naval (but not army) officers. But such approval would not be necessary for secretaries of state, and admiralty, ordnance and household officials. This apparent inconsistency betrays Charles's machiavellian design. The omissions do not seem necessary or logical. They were intended to lead the Commons into time-consuming and untidy debates on points of detail, which would reduce the likelihood of any actual legislation passing – and parliament would have itself to blame if that happened. In a further attempt to involve the Commons in contentious discussion of detail Charles added that he would be ready to agree to any additional restrictions that parliament suggested, but with the proviso that these must not alter the succession itself.[34]

The Commons responded with little enthusiasm. They did not even vote thanks, but adjourned an inconclusive debate to a day when a furious debate on Danby swept it aside.[35] The king's offers were not seriously discussed until the fateful debate on 11 May, when royal spokesmen (including three of the four MPs brought into the new council) were briefed to offer objections to Exclusion and to explain the alternative of limitations. They spoke skilfully but were unable to prevent a crushing defeat for the Court: they started to divide the House but quickly realized that they would suffer an ignominious defeat. They therefore yielded the question, so that a resolution for a Bill to be brought in 'to disable the Duke of York to inherit the Imperial Crown of this Realm' passed *nem. con.* This vote of 11 May marked the beginning of the Exclusionist, or Whig, dominance of the Commons that soon became impregnable and was to continue until the Oxford session of 1681.[36]

Charles realized the necessity of taking early action to check increasing Whig momentum in what now emerged as a systematic campaign by Shaftesbury to compel him to accept Exclusion. The king had nothing to lose by terminating parliament's life. When he asked for money (14 May), Whig speakers responded with a long list of impossible demands, including revocation of Danby's pardon, a total alteration of naval and military officers, expropriation of Catholic estates, Lauderdale's dismissal, and a dangerously vague securing of the Protestant religion. The debate ended without money being voted.[37] The debate on the second reading of the Exclusion Bill (21 May) showed that Charles could expect nothing from this parliament: it passed by the convincing (but not overwhelming) majority of 207 to 128. This made a third reading a formality.[38] Of course the Court majority in the Lords remained, and most observers expected it to reject Exclusion. However, Shaftesbury planned to change the political atmosphere before the Lords came to debate Exclusion. He intended to postpone introducing the Bill until after the Lords had dealt with the formidably complicated judicial questions of Danby's pardon and impeachment (voted by the last parliament). He also wanted it to undertake the more straightforward trial of the five Catholic peers accused of involvement in the Popish Plot. He and Charles knew how explosive much of the evidence in these cases might be, and clearly James's reputation might suffer from witnesses whom Charles suspected of operating under Shaftesbury's direction.[39]

The relation between the king and his ministers during the summer of 1679 was, even by the standards of Charles's reign, extraordinary and unstable. Shaftesbury, as president, was sponsoring the policy of Exclu-

sion which not only Charles but most of his colleagues feared was a design
to subvert the monarchy, or at least to make it elective. Monmouth
commanded with success the army sent to suppress the Covenanting
rebellion in Scotland, while the radical Whigs in London who were
spreading rumours of his legitimacy and consequently of his right to
succeed Charles (as a puppet king) were openly sympathizing with the
rebels.[40] Sunderland, Hyde and Halifax kept a distrustful eye on each
other, suspecting plans to achieve ministerial primacy. Essex developed a
profound distrust of Charles, and does not seem to have noticed how
cleverly he was being manipulated by Shaftesbury. The council possessed
no unity or coherence. Charles consequently had to make all major decisions
himself, and to rely entirely on his own judgement.

The principal reason why Charles prorogued parliament on 27 May was
to avoid becoming involved in a set of complicated politico-legal cases that
would have further divided his ministers, isolated his allies the bishops,
and probably given Shaftesbury new and dangerous arguments to use in
favour of Exclusion. On that day the five Catholic peers came to
Westminster Hall, ready to stand trial by the Lords.[41] If this set of trials
was begun, it would become virtually impossible for Charles to bring the
session to an end, for fear of being accused of stifling the prosecution of
those implicated in the Popish Plot. Five trials could occupy several
weeks. Any convictions would undesirably enhance the credit of Oates,
Bedlow and other witnesses. Any renewed attempt to bring Danby to trial
would also create formidable difficulties for Charles. The royal prerogative power of pardon would come into question. The new ministers all
hated the fallen minister – it was one of the few points they had in common
– and they rightly feared that Charles was continuing to maintain clandestine contact with him, and was receiving advice that was not confined to
Danby's own case.[42] They wanted a trial so that, if pardoned after conviction, Danby would be permanently barred from administration and politics, preferably by life-long banishment such as had been imposed on
Clarendon. On the other hand the bishops had committed themselves to
Danby's defence. Their effectiveness as royal auxiliaries would be greatly
reduced if they became hopelessly isolated, fighting an unpopular cause.
Unlike them, Charles had no intention of allowing himself to be drawn
into defending a detested and discredited former servant.

Charles, therefore, had many good reasons to avoid any major political
trials taking place in the Lords at this delicate time. He took immediate and
decisive advantage of a disagreement between the two Houses. The Lords
declared that they wanted to begin on 27 May with the first of the five
popish peers: Danby's case would have to wait. The Commons insisted
that Danby's case must be decided first, with the five peers coming later so
as to ensure a long session. This disagreement gave Charles a pretext for
the prorogation on 27 May, so avoiding at least the appearance of doing so

to defeat Exclusion. With tongue in cheek he announced his regret that the differences between the Houses had disappointed the great fruits he had hoped for from the session.[43]

The prerogative powers of prorogation and dissolution provided Charles with the decisive weapons to check Shaftesbury, but they had to be employed skilfully (above all in their timing) if they were to have decisive effects. The decision to prorogue was made by Charles personally. He did not consult the new council, which would certainly have advised against the action. Wisely Charles prorogued parliament without indicating his further intention of dissolving it well before the date fixed for it to reassemble. The Whigs were vocally indignant, but not really surprised by the prorogation. But with their eyes concentrated on Exclusion, they failed to detect in full the reasons for Charles's action.[44]

Charles prorogued parliament because he urgently needed to regain exclusive control over the investigation of the Popish Plot. A new crop of witnesses had recently come forward, some of whom were obviously operating under Shaftesbury's protection. The prorogation abruptly terminated the proceedings of the parliamentary committee that the Whigs were using to find material that could be used against James. It was replaced by a committee of council, named by the king. But the most important reason for ending the session related to the pending, in fact long-delayed, trial of Sir George Wakeman, the former Catholic physician to the queen.[45] Although Wakeman had been accused by Oates as far back as the previous November, the officers of the Crown had not taken action to bring him to trial. The preparation of his defence did not necessitate such a long delay. It was the personal involvement of Charles and some of his most intimate servants in organizing Wakeman's defence that made it impossible for the trial to take place while parliament was sitting. He was accused of undertaking to poison the king, the charges being based on the very unsatisfactory general evidence given to the council in November 1678 by Oates and Bedlow. Oates had been feeling his way in what he knew was a sensitive area, and at that time he had made only insinuations about the queen – although these were designedly in a form that permitted him to elaborate them later (his characteristic technique). When he did denounce the queen it had been in private, to Charles himself, a mistake since it alerted the king to the danger. Bedlow had publicly gone much further than Oates, and was reported to Charles to be boasting that he had the power to destroy the queen, and was only concerned that as a result his own life, and those of the other witnesses, would be forfeit. In order ostentatiously to put himself under royal protection, he asked to see the king. Charles agreed that the three principal witnesses – Oates, Bedlow and Prance – should appear at council. He used the opportunity to discover how far their allegations affected the queen, and was relieved to find that they would not endanger her.

Charles's fundamental loyalty to his wife was usually ignored by wishful thinkers among both courtiers and Country politicians.[46] They put excessive emphasis on the king's sexual unfaithfulness, not realizing how superficial were most of his relations with women. Politicians had flirted with the project of a royal divorce since 1668, but Shaftesbury had never committed himself to it. As a solution to the problem of the succession it had only limited attractions for Opposition politicians. It recalled the precedents of Henry VIII's time, which had contributed to the Reformation; it was strenuously opposed by the bishops, who would thereby isolate themselves further; it held out the probability of a regency in the not very distant future, since children born to a new queen would be unlikely to have attained their majority by the time of Charles's death (he was now 49), and would need effective protection from their wicked uncle, James – this could provide an appropriate role for Monmouth or William. But from a Whig point of view a divorce could not be compared with Exclusion in the political possibilities it opened up. It could only be a project, the subject of manœuvres by individual politicians, not an issue that could be used to involve and mobilize the nation. Unlike James, the queen was not a major and unpopular political figure. Her divorce would mean only the displacement of an individual (the idea was to banish her to a convent overseas). It would not necessitate, nor could it be used to justify and legitimate, significant constitutional changes that would have the effect of reducing the powers of the monarchy.

The trial and conviction of the queen on criminal charges would be a very different matter. With their standing and confidence greatly increased, the witnesses would be in a position to make charges against James, and so confront Charles with a set of very difficult decisions. The king decided to take a personal part in organizing the queen's defences before Wakeman came to trial. To an inner group of ministers, formed specifically for the purpose, he confided his anxieties about the potential threat to the queen, and with them organized intervention in Wakeman's trial that saved him, and so stifled the intended attack on the queen. The intervention organized by Charles and his advisers was largely cloaked by the behaviour of Lord Chief Justice Scroggs at the trial, which attracted universal surprise and frantic Whig denunciations.[47] In previous Popish Plot trials Scroggs had assisted Oates and other witnesses for the prosecution; in Wakeman's trial he disparaged and obstructed them, and summed up very clearly for an acquittal. The royally inspired moves were less obvious but unusual: the council sent messengers to ensure the attendance of a key defence witness who, unlike prosecution witnesses, could not be compelled to attend by a subpoena. Wakeman had been told what Oates had alleged to the council and the Lords the previous autumn. He was not allowed to produce the council registers or the Lords Journals in evidence, but a clerk of the council testified to what had been said.[48]

Wakeman's acquittal was an even more severe blow to the Whigs than the prorogation, or the dissolution announced on 10 July. It ended the series of easy convictions that the witnesses had secured since November 1678 and so created a possibility that the excitement provoked by their revelations about the Popish Plot might now begin to subside. Shaftesbury found himself in an increasingly false position. He protested at council that Charles had not attempted any consultation before proroguing parliament, and that the dissolution followed a debate (3 July) in which a majority of councillors had advised against it. He was right in concluding that this action made nonsense of the declaration that the king had made on establishing the council, but Charles replied very firmly 'that in matters of this nature, which were so plain, and wherein he was so fully convinced as to the necessity of dissolving this parliament, he could not divest himself of that power of resolving without the plurality of votes in the council'.[49] In other words he would take his own decisions on major matters.

In announcing the dissolution Charles had proclaimed that a new parliament would assemble on 7 October, but Wakeman's acquittal made it inevitable that its start would be delayed. Once again the king did not actively intervene in the general elections, which disappointed his hopes that the new Commons would be less committed to Exclusion than the last. Given the limited electoral influence at the Crown's disposal, Charles was wise in not attempting to influence either voters or candidates, but the inactivity of his ministers (with the conspicuous exception of Shaftesbury) exposed a flaw in the arguments underlying the reorganization of the council earlier in the year. The new ministers proved not to have an interest in electoral terms that could strengthen the king's position. Nor did any of them have the inclination to engage in electoral competition with Shaftesbury and the Whigs. Halifax, who held no office, and Essex, because of his reservations about royal intentions, lapsed into virtual inactivity once the session ended and Wakeman had been cleared. This established a pattern that lasted for the rest of the reign. As pressure on the king lessened (on this occasion paradoxically at the time when the elections were going disastrously wrong from a Court angle), so the usefulness and influence of ministers declined. With a meeting of parliament postponed Charles had little current need of either Essex or Halifax, and he became irritated by the former's scruples, which centred on an abortive scheme to form an élite bodyguard to protect Charles, but which Essex suspected might be used to provide cadres for a future strengthening of the standing army.[50]

Charles now made a serious attempt to negotiate a secret agreement with Louis, in the hope of gaining subsidies that would give him at least temporary independence from his subjects. He did this by personal negotiations with Barrillon from which he excluded all his ministers, even Sunderland, whom he had earlier represented to Louis as being appointed secretary of state on account of his francophile tendencies. These private negotiations proved to be an abject, indeed humiliating, failure. Charles made the initial mistake of implausibly exaggerating the gravity of the crisis, warning Louis that the monarchy might be overthrown in the immediate future and replaced by an aggressive republic; Louis at this time calculated that a prolonged crisis in England would serve his interests, since internal weakness would prevent Charles from intervening in European affairs. Charles responded unskilfully to the practised moves of Barrillon. When the latter said that Louis considered that the weakness of the English monarchy stemmed directly from the policies of 1678, Charles rashly hastened to agree in order to demonstrate that he would never repeat the mistake of adopting, even for show, anti-French policies. This convinced the French that he could be bought cheaply. Charles disassociated himself from the policies of 1678, blaming them on Danby and, surprisingly, on James.[51] Attributing to Charles the combination of subtlety and chicanery that marked their own conduct of business, Louis and Barrillon wondered if this slighting reference to James represented a signal by Charles that he might abandon his brother, but in reality it was nothing more than a careless comment. In the second of these four meetings, which took place in July and early August, Barrillon lectured Charles that he must do something to regain Louis' confidence.[52] In the third Charles belatedly put forward specific proposals. He asked for 4,000,000 livres so that he could manage without having to call parliament to vote supply. He argued that such a display of independence would impress his subjects, and mark a first step in reasserting his royal authority. In return he promised a general undertaking that never again would he allow himself to be persuaded or coerced into adopting anti-French policies. Otherwise he could make no concrete promises. He ended by asking Louis simply to trust him.[53] In their fourth interview Barrillon's arrogant behaviour, which accurately reflected Louis' own current attitude, reflected his consciousness of French power and Charles's weakness. He passed on a warning from Louis that a meeting of parliament would not be helpful; no money would be forthcoming unless Charles agreed not to allow it to assemble. Then he admonished the king, telling him that no French assistance would be forthcoming unless he kept all the engagements into which he entered. In reply Charles complained that he was cutting himself off from getting money from parliament before he knew whether Louis would give him adequate assistance. Then the king swung to an opposite extreme, making promises that went beyond what the French were demanding – that he would not call another parliament for several years, and then only if Louis explicitly agreed. He ended with another appeal for subsidies. Barrillon replied by lecturing him on the cause of his current poverty – the abandonment of the Dutch War in 1674 – before offering the expectant king the pitifully inadequate sum of 500,000 livres, in return for the prorogation of parliament until March 1680.[54]

This offer shook Charles. He rightly complained that a seven-month prorogation would achieve nothing for either party, but would certainly embitter parliament. He vainly argued for a longer period without a parliament, suggesting three years, in order to justify a larger subsidy. This inconclusive negotiation with the French shows Charles at his very worst, bargaining incompetently, although of course it can be added that he was negotiating from a position of almost humiliating weakness. He needed French help, but there was nothing that he could offer in return that Louis wanted at this time. Perhaps conscious of his humiliatingly weak position as a virtual petitioner, Charles showed none of the skill and resolution that he had displayed in confronting and out-manœuvring the Whigs during the past four months. However his facile assumption that Louis would come to his rescue is consistent with his frequent and over-optimistic assumptions on previous occasions that an alliance with France must accord with his own best interests, even if it was concluded on what were basically French terms.

One possible explanation for Charles's lamentable performance in the personal negotiations with Barrillon is that they took place in the period just before serious illness struck the king on 22 August 1679. Charles had not been critically ill since before 1660, but this briefly dangerous sickness, in which he seemed to be on the point of death for two days, made everyone realize that the succession issue was a real and not hypothetical one. Overnight the nation could find itself with a papist ruler. Although Charles recovered quickly, this sickness demolished the easy belief that he would certainly outlive his brother, and it undoubtedly reinforced the Whig arguments for the necessity of Exclusion. Public composure was also shaken by a growing realization that during the king's sickness the country had stood briefly on the edge of civil war.

Charles's new ministers seem to have been at a complete loss to know what to do during his sickness. Acting on some kind of feverish hint from Charles, one of James's closest friends (Feversham) sent to him to return from exile in Brussels. James did not arrive at Windsor until 2 September, by which time Charles was convalescing, but even then his return took the ministers by surprise and abruptly changed the balance of influence at Court. Most courtiers ostentatiously rallied to him. The new ministers feared that the Whigs would gain popularity by exploiting widespread fears of the effects of a resurgence of James's influence. Indeed this resurgence was immediately reflected in an unexpected development: Monmouth had to go into exile in Holland, because James insisted that he would not go out of England again unless Monmouth was sent away.[55]

Charles's acceptance of this demand by James was partly to establish a balance, but it was also intended to check Monmouth's increasingly public pretensions. For two years James had been made uneasy by the roles which

Charles gave to his son. Admittedly the king consistently rebutted suggestions of Monmouth's legitimacy, but he had allowed him to build up considerable influence in the army.[56] James had advocated war against France, with himself in command, in 1678 in order to reduce Monmouth's influence and build up his own, but since then the successful suppression of the Scottish rebellion had further increased Monmouth's military standing. During Charles's illness some of Monmouth's rasher associates had approached fellow officers, and sounded opinion in the ranks, to ascertain their likely attitude if the king died. At the same time London radical Whigs had debated what should be done to prevent James's instant proclamation as sovereign: one suggestion had been to announce that the king had been poisoned, a plausible claim in the light of the Popish Plot revelations, and one that was to be made in 1685. James would come under suspicion, and would be ordered to remain overseas until a partisan investigation had been completed.[57]

Although Monmouth had not made any explicit statements or moves during the king's illness, he had clearly been the intended beneficiary of those that had been made by his friends. Although Charles could not ignore this, he was still ready to show his son favour, but on conditions and within certain limits. He only suspended Monmouth's tenure of most of his offices, and promised their restoration after a shortish period of exile. But reasons of state led Charles to deprive Monmouth of the key post of general, which was left unfilled, and he explained that the period of exile must extend over the next parliamentary session. He also decided that when Monmouth did return, so would James, and he modified the latter's exile. Instead of Brussels, James was now to go to Edinburgh, and he was given control of the government of Scotland, where of course the Test Act did not apply.[58]

The resurgence of James's influence, and Monmouth's decline, had the effect of further polarizing the nation. James's return led to a postponement of parliament, initially by a prorogation from 30 October to 26 January 1680, although the change in political atmosphere was such that few expected it to sit then. Inevitably Shaftesbury lost his office, Charles dismissing him on 14 October.[59] The king had decided on this action in August, before he fell sick, but he had thought it wise to wait until Shaftesbury provided him with reasons. He was right in predicting that Shaftesbury would court dismissal; while the king convalesced at Windsor, his president had convened extraordinary meetings of council to discuss James's return, a blatant attempt at making mischief. But after dismissing Shaftesbury, Charles surprisingly made an approach offering him a high office (it is not clear which), on condition that Shaftesbury abandoned his insistence on Danby being tried, and on the bishops being barred from acting as judges in the trials. It is now impossible to say what was in the king's mind in making this offer, but Shaftesbury had no hesitation in rejecting it.[60] He made political capital out of it, claiming that Charles had wanted to make him treasurer, but that he had refused unless the king abandoned James and the queen. This misrepresentation showed Charles that Shaftesbury valued his image as 'tribune of the people' more than any office. Confident that he could ultimately compel the king to surrender on the issue of Exclusion, Shaftesbury henceforward put all his energies into leading the Whigs to victory.

Shortly afterwards, but in a characteristically confused manner, Monmouth followed his example. He made an unauthorized return from exile and obstinately refused to obey Charles's peremptory and repeated orders to leave. Monmouth greatly over-valued both the popular welcome that greeted his return, and his father's love for him. He failed to realize how far Charles had shed his easy-going readiness to allow private feelings to come before public duty, and was astonished when he refused to allow him a private interview.[61] Monmouth now lost all his offices, and was to find popularity a poor compensation for them. He justified his return on the ground that he had to defend himself from possible charges of disloyalty arising from a new plot, the Meal Tub Plot. This sham plot showed dramatically how the political tide was turning. Catholics had wisely adopted the lowest possible public profile ever since Oates first came forward, but in the last week of October the council was made aware of a plot by zealous Catholics to plant forged papers in the houses of leading Whigs, implicating them in treasonable plans to seize power. What made the affair extremely dangerous was that James knew about it, and could be said to have given encouragement to the Catholics concerned and to the principal agent they employed, Dangerfield, whom he had actually introduced to the king. This affair made it imperative to delay a meeting of parliament for as long as possible, since Dangerfield changed sides and stood ready to reveal all that he knew (and more) on behalf of the Whigs.[62]

On 11 December Charles announced in a proclamation that he intended to order a series of prorogations that would postpone the first meeting of parliament until the following November. Again he failed to consult the council before making the decision, and overrode the protests that his announcement provoked.[63] His primary purpose was to gain time, in which political excitement would largely subside, so weakening Shaftesbury, and demonstrating to his subjects his ability to live without financial aid from parliament (which he knew would not be forthcoming). The prorogations also gave him the freedom to experiment with two concurrent, but entirely contradictory, policies – the formation of a (largely Protestant) league of states to check the advance of French power, and a new and more sustained secret approach to France for a subsidy treaty.[64] This double policy decision represented an unfortunate return to the labyrinthine policies of 1678, which had proved disastrous. This time the policy simply failed to have appreciable effects. Although a great deal of ministerial time and energy were absorbed neither policy made any impact on the intended targets – domestic opinion, and Louis.

Shaftesbury and the Whigs frustrated Charles's hopes that the long prorogations would significantly reduce, or even eliminate, the prevailing levels of political consciousness and abnormal excitement. The Whigs anticipated the announcement of the prorogations: they organized a petition from sixteen Whig peers asking that parliament should be allowed to meet on 26 January 1680. Charles snubbed the delegation that presented it on 7 December, but he knew that Shaftesbury had tried to get a companion petition presented from the City. This had failed, but many petitions were being canvassed in the counties. The king tried to halt the Whig campaign by issuing a proclamation on 12 December underlining the illegality of 'tumultuous and seditious' petitions.[65] He also hoped that by announcing prorogations until November 1680 he would show that an irrevocable decision had been made, and that petitioners would be wasting their efforts. The results showed that it was Charles who was wasting his breath. He failed to stem a wave of massively subscribed Whig petitions, and he achieved little by rebuking those who presented them. In contrast, he gave encouragement to those who organized and presented loyal counter-addresses, known as 'abhorrences', that deplored petitioning, and thanked the king for his protection of the laws and the church, often using language that could be interpreted as reflecting on the behaviour, and even the institution, of parliament. Charles had no option. It was essential to encourage the abhorrers, or Tories, so as to refute the Whigs' claim to speak for the nation, but by doing so the king inevitably accentuated the polarization of the nation into two hostile camps, and maintained popular excitement at undesirably high levels throughout 1680.[66] By insulting the Whigs and trying (with comparatively little success) to institute renewed prosecutions of dissenters, he helped Shaftesbury to keep his party confident and active. Charles had thought that without a parliament the Whigs would lack a focus. Whig peers and the newly elected MPs remained dispersed throughout the provinces, but by using them to organize petitions and canvass support in their own counties, and so binding them more closely to their constituents and neighbours, Shaftesbury deprived the king of the advantages that the latter had expected from the prorogations. He succeeded in keeping the nation's attention on Exclusion: in form petitions called simply for parliament to meet, but this was stated to be for the purpose of securing religion and liberties and, as Whig organizers and canvassers explained, only Exclusion could achieve this.[67]

By maintaining constant pressure on the Court, the Whigs effectively sabotaged the anti-French diplomatic activity that Charles inaugurated and Sunderland tried to negotiate. They did so for propaganda purposes, but at home the policy attracted little attention away from Whig petitioning. By keeping up pressure on the king, Shaftesbury deterred potential foreign allies from taking seriously approaches by the former for an alliance, and he convinced Louis that the king was in no position to obstruct or oppose French policies. Consequently there was no current need to buy Charles off at the valuation that he placed on himself. A negotiation conducted by Sunderland, assisted in the later stages by Hyde who was added at James's insistence, came to nothing because of the inadequacy of the subsidy that Louis was prepared to pay (1,000,000 livres).[68]

Charles also ordered Sunderland to institute negotiations with the Dutch, assuming that this would make Louis more eager to offer larger subsidies. In doing so Charles naïvely underestimated French subtlety and ignored the lessons of the negotiations that had led to the peace of Nijmegen in 1678. By inducing the States General to ignore William's vehement protests against concluding a separate peace which would ignore the interests of the allies, Louis had smashed the confederation and won himself a virtually free field for manœuvre in Europe. His first priority was to keep William isolated and powerless. This could be best achieved by maintaining a close connection with his domestic enemies among the republicans. Consequently in November 1679 he offered the States General a formal treaty of alliance, which in effect would be directed against William. Charles and Sunderland were slow to appreciate the danger of this bold move. Not only would it virtually annihilate William's prestige and influence – in Europe generally as well as in the United Provinces – but it would isolate England. With the Dutch allied to France no other states would combine with England against them, and Louis would therefore have no reason to buy English neutrality or support.[69]

Self-interest compelled Charles to help William to defeat the French approach, but in doing so he learnt how unscrupulous French diplomats could be. The French envoy at The Hague (d'Avaux) circulated a letter from Barrillon saying that Charles was opposing a Franco-Dutch treaty only because he wanted to conclude a treaty with Louis himself. This showed that Charles had actually made an approach to France, obviously for money. D'Avaux also tried to convince his Dutch republican contacts that Charles and William were forming a combination against constitutional liberties in England, Scotland and the United Provinces, allegations that were passed on by republicans to their Whig contacts.[70]

In February 1680 Sunderland, who now aspired to manage Charles, and had already succeeded in the easier task of gaining an ascendancy over both James and the Duchess of Portsmouth, pompously claimed that as a result of his direction the king had become steady, and was actually applying himself to business. He asserted that the king's affairs were daily improving.[71] This improvement was what Charles and Sunderland had hoped to achieve by a mixture of firmness and conciliation. Charles made no effort to hide his contemptuous pleasure when the four remaining Whig councillors asked to resign (February).[72] He put his public duty above his personal inclinations when, in a private negotiation, he demanded that Monmouth should reveal all his dealings with the Whigs as the price of recovering his offices and sources of income.[73] James's recall from Scotland was cynically balanced by the renewal of prosecutions of Catholic recusants.[74] Charles ordered an extensive purge of the commission of the peace, dismissing most JPs who were connected with petitioning.[75] He also ordered prosecutions of Whig journalists, pamphleteers and publishers: these had only a temporary success. When parliament met in October 1680 the flood of Whig propaganda resumed.[76] The king took care to cover Whig moves. Whereas in 1678 he had left to go racing while Oates was making his initial allegations to the council, he now returned from Newmarket to be present when Shaftesbury presented it with preliminary information about an Irish plot.[77] In May James attended the council, on his brother's instructions, while it examined the crude but persuasive stories being circulated about the Black Box, which was alleged to contain evidence of Charles's secret marriage to Monmouth's mother.[78] In June a treaty of alliance with Spain was concluded, and became the subject of much royal propaganda. Spain was now such a weak power that such an alliance was of little practical value, but ministers proclaimed that it proved that Charles was not tied by any secret connections with France.[79]

Contrary to Charles's expectations the prorogations did not significantly reduce the level of Whig political activity. The petitioning campaign extended to the provinces the high levels of political excitement and consciousness previously prevalent in and around London. Shaftesbury now achieved a major victory by gaining control over the governmental institutions of the City. Whig candidates won the key elections of sheriffs twice over: the Court treated the matter as a trial of strength and disqualified the successful candidates on the first occasion because they had not taken the necessary oaths, but they did so and routed the Tories a second time.[80] Shaftesbury stunned everyone by an extremely bold move: on 26 and 30 June he tried to get the Middlesex grand jury to present James as a papist, and the Duchess of Portsmouth as a prostitute. Technically the attempt failed, because of intervention by Lord Chief Justice Scroggs, but by this attack Shaftesbury ruined all the king's hopes of a manageable parliamentary session in October.[81] It was now clear that the Whigs would immediately reintroduce a Bill of Exclusion, and it was also rumoured that they would impeach James. The Whig insult to the heir presumptive showed any potential European allies that Charles was likely to continue under such heavy pressure at home that he would be unable to fulfil his commitments abroad. Shaftesbury's inventive malice and intransigence boosted Whig confidence, puncturing the complacency of the ministers, who had hoped that widening divisions among the Whigs would produce a readiness in the new Commons to consider new offers of limitations.

When parliament met, on 21 October, the Whig tide began to run so strongly in the Commons that all Charles's careful preparatory steps were quickly rendered ineffective.[82] Indeed not only most MPs but some of his ministers now became convinced that the king would give way on the issue of Exclusion. The main reason for this belief was the way in which he had come to the decision to send James back to Scotland (15 October). When Charles had first asked advice from the council, two days earlier, a majority had been opposed. But he had manufactured a majority in favour on the 15th by putting a loaded question: should James be sent away, or should he stay and parliament be dissolved? Those who began to think that Charles would concede Exclusion, under pressure, saw this as the forerunner of another loaded question: should James's right be sacrificed, or should the king accept the likelihood of another civil war?[83]

Consequently the administration was falling into serious disarray as the session began. Sunderland and Godolphin, assuming that Charles wanted to give way on Exclusion, were already working to ensure that William would be the beneficiary (through Mary's right) and wanted William to come over and take a seat in the Lords. On the side they had persuaded the Duchess of Portsmouth, whose influence on Charles in political as distinct from personal matters they overestimated, that passage of Exclusion could result in her son by Charles, the Duke of Richmond, being recognized as heir.[84] Personal rivalries and differences separated the other leading members of the ministry. Essex was moving into the Whig ranks. Sunderland wrongly thought that Halifax was also wavering, because he had remained inactive in the country during the summer. But when Halifax returned to London it became apparent that he and Hyde so loathed each other that it was doubtful whether they would work together.[85] The other prominent anti-Exclusionist, Seymour, alienated everyone by his arrogance and the crude determination with which he pushed his pretensions to high office. Charles certainly did not take him at his own valuation.[86]

Ministerial divisions forced Charles to rely on his own judgement in making all the crucial decisions during the session. By giving James a pardon before he left for Edinburgh, the king effectively blocked the Whig option of an impeachment to strengthen the case for Exclusion: as in Danby's case the question of whether a pardon could be issued before the trial of an impeachment would have impeded progress.[87] This made the Whigs revive an Exclusion Bill, the progress of which dominated Commons proceedings. They totally ignored a lame and unconvincing royal speech which opened the session on 21 October. Charles defended the series of prorogations, claiming that they had given him time to prosecute his 'Protestant' foreign policy, and warned MPs that all Europe was watching their debates; only if they behaved constructively would foreign states ally with England. He added an urgent plea for money to raise soldiers to reinforce the Tangier garrison which had recently suffered heavy casualties in an ambush by the hostile Moors.[88] The Whigs took no notice. They clashed angrily with a now well-organized but numerically weak Tory minority whose leaders – Hyde, Seymour and Jenkins – tried bravely but ineffectively to get the House to consider the royal alternative of 'remedies that may consist with the preserving the succession of the Crown in its due and legal course of descent'. However, Tory critics scored one important success, forcing an amendment to the Bill, so that, instead of the question of who should succeed being left open, only James's right was now abolished: the Crown would go to the next legitimate heir, that is, Mary.[89] But although the Tories showed themselves far more active in the Commons than in 1679, and Charles reiterated his determination to accept only measures that maintained the rightful succession (9 November), the Exclusion Bill got its third reading two days later without a division being forced at any stage.[90]

This time the Bill was taken up immediately by the Lords, whose debate on 15 November represented the visible turning point in the struggle against the Whigs, and contained many surprises. The size of the majority that refused the Bill a first reading, 63 to 30, was a direct result of Charles's open, personal stand. Sunderland, Godolphin and the Duchess of Portsmouth (all frightened by Whig intransigence) had predicted that Charles would find an excuse to give way, and that he would advise the Lords to allow the Bill to progress while discussions took place that would determine its eventual form. Sunderland claimed that he had told the king that the interests of the monarchy necessitated passage of the Bill, whatever his own personal sentiments, and Charles seems to have let Sunderland conclude that he would accept this advice. In fact Charles totally refuted the line advocated by Sunderland by attending throughout the Lords debate, and putting on a theatrical performance that left the peers in no doubt as to his royal wishes – scowling at speeches in favour of the Bill, expressing his approval of those against.[91] Halifax scored an oratorical triumph, eclipsing Shaftesbury and demolishing his arguments. This earned him virulent Whig hostility. Claiming that he had a malign influence on the king, the Commons demanded his removal from Court and council (Halifax held no office of state) in an address (22 November) to which Charles gave an understandably cold answer – that he could see no crime alleged, and so would take no action.[92]

Halifax served a useful purpose by acting as a lightning-conductor. Charles could disregard the Whig-dominated Commons, because the violence of excited MPs' speeches in debates was not being reflected in popular disorders outside Westminster. On 17 November, two days after the Lords debate, the Whigs celebrated Elizabeth's accession in 1558 with another huge propaganda demonstration, a kind of politicized lord mayor's show, with floats depicting popish tableaux and culminating in a pope-burning. It passed off without disturbances, and may indeed have had a cartharthic effect: Charles was said to have watched it incognito.[93] Whig attacks on other prominent Tories also had little effect because they were too obviously malicious and personal. They generated a great deal of partisan fury in the Commons, but they could not disguise the increasingly lame-duck character of a parliamentary session that Charles showed no sign of wanting to end. Whig frustration and intransigence suited the king's political strategy. He encouraged Tory peers and MPs to advance various proposals for limitations on the powers of a Catholic successor, causing equal alarm to James and William. Both had to be reassured privately with explanations that these were only tactical moves, and that Charles would never agree to drastic reductions in royal powers.[94] Charles dramatized Whig intransigence. On 15 December he addressed parliament on the need to have money with which to support alliances and preserve Tangier, knowing that the Commons would not vote supply unless Exclusion was conceded. He again promised to accept any remedies put forward to secure liberties and the Protestant religion, so long as they preserved the succession in its 'due and legal course'.[95] Despite this the Commons presented him with another address on the dangers from popery, which implied that only Exclusion could provide security. This gave him an opportunity for displaying his displeasure: he refused to say a word when a delegation presented the address, leaving it to retire in total silence.[96]

Charles again made his position absolutely plain in a final message to this parliament, on 4 January 1681, when he deplored the Commons' fixation with Exclusion. He added that the Lords rejection of the Bill confirmed his own opinion, and yet again recommended consideration of 'all other means for the preservation of the Protestant religion', knowing that he would be ignored.[97] The Whig rank and file, buoyed up by Shaftesbury's continuing confidence in ultimate victory, waited impatiently for a prorogation that would allow the reintroduction of an Exclusion Bill and, rightly confident of re-election, did not fear a dissolution. However, some of their leaders, former office holders who were becoming impatient with Shaftesbury's autocratic style of leadership, tried to make a bargain with the king. In a secret negotiation they promised him ample money in return for their own admission to key (and lucrative) offices, but they also expected him to declare that he would not oppose Exclusion. Charles's main aim in entertaining this approach was probably to split the Whig leadership, and this objective was partly achieved when the existence of these negotiations leaked out, forcing the Whigs involved to clear their reputations as 'patriots' by moving resolutions in the Commons against any MPs taking office.[98]

By the beginning of 1681 Charles occupied an immeasurably stronger position than he had at the beginning of the session. He had repaired the rift within the administration caused by Sunderland's advocacy of Exclusion, emerging with a more homogeneous and reliable set of ministers who were united by the fact that all had come under censure or the threat of impeachment by the Whig Commons. Hyde now became the king's manager of day to day business. Seymour and Littleton replaced Sunderland and Godolphin. Halifax continued in a detached position which gave him opportunities to controvert the case for Exclusion, while evading ministerial office and responsibilities. Sunderland remained in office for the time being, although Charles had decided to dismiss him, because his immediate removal would have alarmed William prematurely. The king had managed so far to prevent direct intervention in the crisis by William. Although Sidney (envoy at The Hague and associate of Sunderland) had procured a letter from the States General urging Charles to unite the English nation, if necessary by conceding Exclusion, this had been disavowed after its abject failure to influence events – it had arrived too late for the Lords debate – and formally William had no responsibility for it.[99]

Shaftesbury continued to launch bitter attacks on James and the Court, but even the trial, conviction and execution of Stafford, one of the five peers allegedly involved in the Popish Plot, aroused surprisingly little parliamentary or popular excitement.[100] It largely confirmed old allegations, whereas Shaftesbury now needed new revelations to arouse and activate his followers, loyal as they remained to the cause of Exclusion, and to excite the masses. Commons attacks on ministers and leading Tories failed to intimidate them. The inflammatory Whig resolutions passed by the Commons on 10 January were intended to rally the party, but they also confirmed the line that Charles had carefully laid down – that he was faced with intransigence that prevented all reasonable discussion of how best to secure the nation.[101] On 10 January he announced a prorogation (to the 20th), but two days before that date he dissolved parliament. With confidence Charles calculated that the Whigs would continue to adhere to Exclusion during the forthcoming elections, and to insist on it as the only way in which security could be obtained, at the session at Oxford, where the next parliament was ordered to meet on 21 March.[102]

8   *The Years of Personal Rule*

The decisive victory that Charles won at Oxford by dissolving the third and last Exclusion Parliament was overwhelmingly a personal triumph. Charles made all the crucial decisions. He personally and finally refuted the Whig argument, on which all the chances of Exclusion depended, that under pressure he would concede the passage of the Bill. Instead he followed the dissolution by speaking authoritatively and convincingly to his people, in a skilfully composed declaration emphasizing (and exaggerating) his own respect for the constitution and the laws but making it clear that he would expect all his subjects to respect them also.[1]

During the last four years of the reign Charles at last emerged as an unfettered sovereign. He now ruled personally, without a chief minister. He kept the Court and administration in a fluid state, playing off one minister against another so that nobody (not even James) became predominant, or could feel secure in relation to the king. Charles also systematically reduced his need for active Tory support, first in the counties and then, after the Tories had helped him dislodge the Whigs from the governing positions, in London also (September 1682, when Tory sheriffs assumed office). Charles regarded the defeat of the Whigs as freeing him from having to allow the Tories to act independently in a political role. Although he had had to act as a politician himself in order to defeat the Whigs, Charles did not want to have to continue in this novel fashion, using the Tories as auxiliaries. Obviously he had first had to destroy the Whigs as a party, but that was only the first if decisive step towards reducing and eventually eliminating all forms of spontaneous and independent political activity, including that of those who claimed to be acting as his partisans and in his interests. That is why it would be incorrect to describe Charles as a Tory. He had many reasons for wanting Tory activism to subside. It kept alive tensions in the localities. Tories often delayed or prevented repentant Whigs from submitting, because they were personal rivals. The Tories became divided into factions, particularly in London and several provincial towns where populist leaders emerged. They and their local rivals tried to involve the king in their local disputes, and there was a danger that these provincial divisions would extend to the Court. In letters and directives Charles stated his attitude: all discussion of public affairs by unofficial persons who did not hold positions of responsibility was likely to disturb the public peace. He instructed magistrates to confine themselves to resolutions, addresses and petitions to matters directly related to their localities, and not to interfere with affairs of national concern.[2] Similarly once the Whig press had been silenced, Charles discouraged Tory journalists, reducing the number of newsheets and pamphlets that were published.

Charles, in this last phase, can be described as having as his principal objective a kingdom at last free from the abnormal and potentially dangerous excitements caused by popular and, still more, party activity. His achievement of this objective by the beginning of 1684 seems to us, knowing what was to happen under James, a very temporary and precarious achievement, a futile exercise in turning the clock back. But after the tensions of 1679–81, and the growing fears of another civil war developing out of Shaftesbury's campaign for Exclusion, Charles's advocacy of passive loyalty had considerable attractions. Like his father, Charles angled his appeal particularly to the wealthy, to those who had most to lose from disturbances. But he also cleverly argued that political excitement and party activity did damage to a much wider section of the nation, acting as a distraction from the daily and profitable following of trades and manufactures by all industrious people. Private persons should concentrate on their own callings and business, leaving magistrates with the exclusive duty of making any representations – which the king would consider, coming to a judgement free from all external pressures.[3] The structure of the Court, with its lobbyists and intermediaries, made this an unrealizable ideal, but Charles derived great advantages from the economic prosperity of these last years. Buoyant overseas trade gave him sufficient revenue not to have to follow his father's fatal policy of developing and levying extra-parliamentary taxes, nor was he tempted to interfere with the course of trade and business, for example by reverting to the hated policy of monopolies. After March 1684 Charles was also, if temporarily and precariously, free from his earlier dependence on Louis XIV. The expiration of the French subsidies surprised him, but he could subsist without them, and for the immediate future there seemed to be no danger of a major European crisis. Consequently for the last year of his life Charles enjoyed an ease that he had never previously experienced.

When Charles dissolved the second Exclusion Parliament (18 January 1681), and ordered a new one to meet at Oxford on 21 March, he did not expect the general election to produce any significant weakening of Whig strength in the Commons, or any modification of the party's insistence on Exclusion. As in the two elections of 1679, the king and his ministers did not intervene directly by electioneering. Tories did not expect him to do so, although there was some criticism that he did not issue a declaration repeating to the electorate what he had told parliament on 15 December and 4 January, drawing attention to the turbulent factiousness of the last session, deploring Whig intransigence, and making an explicit promise to consider all means of securing the Protestant religion, on condition that the succession was not altered.[4] Charles intended to say all these things in his opening speech to parliament at Oxford, but he had good reasons for not doing so earlier, and for not involving himself in the elections. Parliamentary numbers were not to be the instrument that he would use against the Whigs – his prerogative powers were to prove the decisive weapon. Furthermore electoral interventions were unlikely to have much effect, and popular defeats at the polls would damage his prestige and discourage his partisans.

Electorally, Charles was impotent. He was the first sovereign to face not only a formed party in parliament but in addition an efficient, centrally directed electoral machine, backed by an extremely extensive and persuasive propaganda campaign. In fact Whig electoral organization and journalism reached a peak of effectiveness in the general election of 1681.[5] A few far-sighted peers and former MPs prudently lapsed into inactivity, but the Whig party retained its hold on the electorate and the popular masses. Whigs achieved a series of unopposed returns and runaway victories, which the party leaders consolidated by giving the newly elected MPs instructions mandating them to insist on Exclusion at Oxford: these were drafted centrally to ensure disciplined behaviour in what Shaftesbury proclaimed would be the final and decisive struggle to achieve Exclusion. If, after so many statements that he would never consent, Charles could now be forced to concede Exclusion, his political credit would be annihilated, he would demoralize the Tories, and the Whigs would gain a monopoly of office and power.

Whig hopes were to be shattered. The Oxford parliament was a cleverly planned trap for the Whigs, contrived by Charles himself. He kept his intentions effectively secret – even James (in Edinburgh) did not know them, expressing real anxiety before the session about his brother's staunchness.[6] In the first place Charles offered a new and attractive alternative to Exclusion. He discarded the complex proposals of putting limitations on a Catholic successor, which would have been difficult and time-consuming to embody in legislation, and which had come in for damaging criticism by Whig constitutional lawyers during the 1680 session. Instead Charles launched the idea of a regency – a person or persons (clearly, but implicitly, Mary and William) were to take charge of government, leaving a Catholic sovereign with little more than his title. Two Court spokesmen, Ernle and Littleton, had the brief of developing this idea at length; significantly Charles made sure that the latter gained election, taking care to conceal the fact that he had royal encouragement. The regency proposal had the merits of simplicity and intelligibility. It would not reduce the powers of the monarchy, even temporarily, so

William could accept it. It is very doubtful whether Charles would finally have allowed it, but he knew that the Whigs would not accept any form of alternative to Exclusion; although they allowed the Tory spokesmen to expound the idea during an Oxford debate, they refused to be drawn into a discussion of its merits, persisting in the line that only an act of Exclusion could bring security.[7]

By insisting on Exclusion himself, and persuading the Whigs that Charles would give way, Shaftesbury relied on party discipline.[8] His supporters knew that having committed themselves to Exclusion they were irrevocably exposed to James's resentment and revenge, should he ever succeed to the throne. The Whigs dogmatically ignored unmistakable evidence of Charles's determination. He underlined his disapproval of Sunderland's 1680 vote for Exclusion by not only dismissing him (24 January 1681) but refusing to allow his successor (Conway) to pay him the customary sum for the secretary's place – a penalty of £6,000.[9] The removal of the new parliament to Oxford ought to have warned the Whigs. It represented a fresh assertion of the king's prerogative powers over parliament, the decisive weapon in the royal armoury. The Whigs did not expect a particularly long session, but they were to be taken totally by surprise by the early dissolution, and they then found that they had no alternative but to obey and disperse. Separation from their allies in London, and the presence of cavalry quartered in nearby towns, made it impracticable for the Whigs to consider using extra-legal tactics, such as remaining even temporarily in session.[10]

The switch to Oxford also demonstrated Charles's confidence at this critical time. Most contemporaries believed that Charles I had made a fatal error by quitting London in 1642, and James was to agonize over whether to stay and guard the capital or to move out to confront Monmouth in 1685 and William in 1688. By contrast Charles went to Oxford without hesitation, because he had ensured royal control over London during his absence. He brought military units up to strength, filling the gaps left by the need to send reinforcements in 1680 to defend Tangier. He gave command of the forces in and around London to the loyal Earl of Craven, an excellent choice. Craven knew the labyrinthine lay-out of London streets in detail through pursuit of his hobby (which made him one of the best-known London characters), personal attendance at fires in the City and suburbs. He would appear at any conflagration, day or night, riding a horse as celebrated as himself which could sniff out the location of fires and carry his pyrophile master to them. Craven carefully worked out routes by which troops could move to the Tower, to overawe the City, and he prepared to strengthen other key points – Gravesend and Sheerness (to block the Thames), and Lambeth Palace. Charles gave Craven secret powers to deal drastically with all forms of disorder. If there were riots, or tumultuous meetings that threatened to get out of hand, he was to suppress them, if necessary by 'killing, slaying or otherwise howsoever destroying those who shall so resist in the disturbance of the public peace'.[11] The lord mayor and sheriffs, as Whigs, could not be relied on, but they were given orders to keep the peace, so as to pin responsibility on them. In a more oblique move Charles sought to deprive the Whigs of any opportunity to exploit mass discontent. He ordered the London clergy to organize special collections for relief of the deserving poor, which meant conforming Anglicans amenable to their influence, and made a substantial contribution himself, giving as reason the particularly hard winter weather.[12]

Charles's strategy for the Oxford parliament depended on the successful negotiation beforehand of a subsidy treaty with Louis. The king had allowed the previous round of negotiations to lapse at the end of 1679. At that time it had appeared that Louis was preparing a major attack on the Spanish Netherlands. He had offered only a rather miserly subsidy in return for inaction on England's part that was certain to create serious difficulties for Charles. Inaction would mean an abrupt and open reversal of the so-called Protestant foreign policy which had been adopted as a means of reassuring public opinion. It would infuriate William, who would as in 1678 try to work through Charles's ministers to compel the adoption of an anti-French policy. If parliament had to be called there would be a serious danger of a repetition of the futile and acrimonious sessions of that year, with French, Dutch and Spanish agents working on, and with, factional groups and dividing the Court interest.[13] A French subsidy treaty could not be operated by the king so long as he might have to depend on parliament for anything. But by the beginning of 1681 Charles had decided not to call another parliament once he had used the Oxford session to discredit the Whigs. In addition the new direction of French expansion into Alsace and the adjacent areas made it less likely that a major crisis would erupt over incursions into the Spanish Netherlands, and it was with the immediate future that Charles was concerned.[14]

However, it has to be emphasized that throughout the course of these negotiations for a subsidy treaty the initiatives were French, not English. Louis opened the way by telling Barrillon (8, 15 November 1680) that if – as the ambassador reported was likely – Charles's position collapsed under Whig pressure, he would not give any support to Monmouth's pretensions.[15] Apparently putting ideological considerations before national interest, Louis said he would aid Charles even if William derived advantages from the king's survival. When serious negotiations began in January 1681 Barrillon employed an indirect approach, using as intermediary the elderly and life-long francophile the Earl of St Albans. Although the latter had a bad reputation as a former adviser to Henrietta Maria and member of the Louvre party, no one was better placed at this time. Charles was using him as manager of a clandestine negotiation with a group of

Whigs, headed by Montagu, who were angling for office in return for breaking with Shaftesbury's leadership. Significantly this negotiation was broken off as soon as Charles realized that aid might be forthcoming from France: as always he preferred to make concessions to Louis rather than to any section of his own subjects.[16] However, Charles did not at first rush to respond to the proposals transmitted by Barrillon, recognizing them as the usual French gambit of beginning with tough demands. Louis wanted Charles to withdraw openly from the 1680 treaty with Spain, to recall diplomats from northern Europe, where they were supposed to be negotiating treaties to check French advances, and to permit James to return to Court from Edinburgh. He also suggested that enforcement of the penal laws against Catholics should be suspended, and accompanied the offer of an inadequate subsidy with the condition that no new parliament should be called.[17]

Superficially these proposals could not have been accepted without wrecking Charles's entire political strategy, but Louis did not expect them to be accepted in their initial form. He had hidden reasons for each demand. By suggesting James's recall, and relief for the Catholics, he was warning Charles against sacrificing them as a way of reconciling himself with the Whigs. Paradoxically Louis' surprising statement that he would opt for William, not Monmouth, was aimed at dissuading Charles from turning as a last resort to William for aid, a course that several ministers were recommending. Louis knew that if William was invited to intervene in English affairs as an arbitrator, he would use the opportunity to push Charles into anti-French policies. Louis expected Charles to bargain for larger subsidies, and was prepared to be flexible about the terms, provided that they secured France against English intervention in Europe.

A treaty was agreed just before the opening of the Oxford parliament: Charles undertook the negotiation personally, assisted only by Hyde. They reached agreement in principle on 14/24 March, and concluded the secret treaty on 22 March/1 April. Although the French ambassador wanted a written document, for security reasons Charles insisted on a verbal agreement. Without formally abrogating his treaty with Spain, Charles undertook not to honour its obligations, and in vague language backed this by saying that he would not call parliament to give aid to Spain. In effect this was a promise not to call parliament again. On his side Louis did not pledge himself not to attack the Spanish Netherlands, but he gave Charles to understand that such an attack did not form part of his current strategy. Only on money matters was the agreement specific: Louis promised subsidies of an initial 2,000,000 crowns, with 500,000 in each of two succeeding years.[18]

This subsidy would not in itself make Charles financially independent, but the treaty coincided with another favourable development: the statutory prohibition of imports from France had expired on 20 March, and because of their concentration on passing an Exclusion Bill the Whigs had not tried to extend it. The consequent flood of luxury imports substantially improved the yield of customs duties, more than offsetting extraordinary taxes that were currently expiring, and also facilitating the transfer of funds from France. Import and export trade with other countries was also expanding, so that, with tight control over expenditure by Hyde, Charles could now expect to subsist without extraordinary taxes.[19]

In purely mercenary terms it is difficult to see how Louis could expect to get full value for the subsidies which he paid to Charles. As Barrillon advised him, he could paralyse England very much more cheaply by subsidizing his contacts among the Whigs to repeat their tactics of 1678, and so aggravating the crisis, make it impossible for Charles to intervene in Europe. Louis intervened primarily for ideological reasons, to save a fellow monarch and first cousin from ruin, just as he was to sponsor James II *after* 1688 and recognize James III in 1701. From the French angle the subsidy treaty of 1681 was largely a grace and favour arrangement.

Charles carefully prepared his opening speech at Oxford, which he published in London on the same day.[20] Laying heavy emphasis on the unreasonable behaviour of the previous Commons, he repeated his readiness to consider any expedients except Exclusion. He combined assurances of his own intention to rule constitutionally, and not to practise arbitrary methods of governing, with warnings that he would not tolerate arbitrary behaviour by others – meaning the Commons, who must 'make the Laws of the Land your Rule, because I am resolved they shall be mine'. It cannot have surprised or disconcerted him that the Whigs totally ignored his fresh dismissal of Exclusion – their intransigence served his strategy perfectly.[21] With hindsight it is obvious that this opening speech, with its warnings, promises and prohibitions, was composed deliberately in a form that could be repeated with great effect after the Whigs had failed to respond positively, and textual comparison of this speech with the royal declaration of 8 April shows that Charles, speaking explicitly for a record that he was preparing for use against the Whigs, confidently expected to be ignored, and planned to exploit Whig intransigence.

Only one unexpected development threatened to disrupt the king's plans for the Oxford parliament. The Duchess of Portsmouth employed a private agent, Fitzharris, to discover whether the Whigs, who had viciously attacked her in June 1680, were planning a repetition. Charles knew she was doing this, but probably attached little importance to the matter. In pursuit of information Fitzharris cultivated contacts with Whig radicals, and as a fellow-countryman worked himself into close association with the group of indescribably dishonest Irish witnesses and renegades recently imported by Shaftesbury to 'prove' the existence of an Irish plot. He did not scruple to 'improve' the inadequate gossip that he gathered, and fabricated an inflammatory pamphlet which he proposed to plant on Whig extremists, and then discover to the authorities as evidence of treasonable Whig activities. However when he showed the pamphlet to another political informer, Everard, the latter betrayed him to the last prominent Whig JP in London, Sir William Waller. After having been abandoned by the duchess, and facing treason charges, Fitzharris calculated that he could best save himself by going over to the Whigs and earning their protection by making sensational revelations about the duchess, James, the queen and leading Tories.[22]

Why should an obscure and incompetent spy threaten to upset the king's plans and intensify the crisis? The Whigs genuinely believed that Charles himself had been involved in commissioning Fitzharris to plant a libel on one of their radical leaders, Howard of Escrick, and to incriminate several other leading Whigs in treason, thus justifying their arrest in a dramatic coup arranged for Oxford – the reason why the Whig leaders were accompanied there by defensive bands of retainers, a curiously feudal touch. But the Whigs quickly appreciated how useful Fitzharris could be once he had changed sides. They proposed to impeach him, so as to try to ensure a longer session than Charles intended.[23] His imaginative and expansive revelations would provoke excitement and resentment. Charles's swift reaction shows how much he had learnt from his (and Danby's) mistakes in handling the original Popish Plot, and his behaviour reveals a severity, even brutality, that had not been apparent earlier but became even more pronounced in 1683. Charles removed Fitzharris from Whig reach and exploitation by removing him from the City prison of Newgate to the royal fortress, the Tower, where he kept him incommunicado. By this action he greatly reduced the impact of the affair. The hearsay allegations of Whig speakers in the Oxford debate that ended in a vote for Fitzharris's impeachment were no substitute for his personal presence at the bar, making sweeping and lurid allegations.[24]

Charles quite simply wanted Fitzharris dead, and he ruthlessly took advantage of an opportunity that now presented itself. Several of the Irish witnesses imported by Shaftesbury, with whom Fitzharris had associated, were defecting to the Court. They had been worked on by Warcup, a trusted magistrate, as part of the prosecution that Charles was already preparing against the most vulnerable Whig leaders, Shaftesbury and Howard. Unless silenced, Fitzharris might be used to discredit these witnesses. However, there was a complication: these Irish witnesses had earlier *sworn* informations against the Catholic Archbishop of Armagh, Oliver Plunkett. Charles knew that their allegations were perjured, but unless they stuck to this evidence they would not be believed when they came to make charges against the Whigs in the show trials that Charles planned for the period after the dissolution. The king did develop twinges of conscience about sending the innocent Plunkett to the gallows, but reason of state made it necessary if he was to achieve his immediate objective of putting Shaftesbury to death. As it happened Plunkett, the last victim of the Popish Plot trials, was to die on the same day as Fitzharris (1 July 1681) – and on the next day Charles had Shaftesbury arrested.[25]

With such plans for revenge and destruction in his mind, Charles played with the still-confident Whigs at Oxford. Their behaviour fulfilled all his expectations. Whig MPs cited the instructions presented by their constituents as mandating them to Exclusion.[26] Although allowing Littleton to expound the proposals for regency, the Whigs ignored these, and moved for a new Exclusion Bill on the first full day (24 March).[27] They voted to publish their proceedings, as an appeal to the nation. The Commons voted an impeachment of Fitzharris, but the Lords refused to proceed, which provoked shrill Whig indignation.[28] In short the Whig MPs behaved in exactly the way Charles desired, enabling him to argue later that such 'ill beginnings could not have a good ending'.[29] With malevolent care he prepared to surprise those whom he now saw as his enemies. He engaged in verbal sparring with Shaftesbury, who offered to make him 'easy' if he conceded Exclusion, concealing his anger in badinage.[30] When the Commons complained of cramped accommodation in the Schools he promised to make the Sheldonian Theatre available, and went through the farce of visiting it to urge the workmen to complete the structural alterations for the following week. Before then, on 28 March, the Commons while engaged in the debate on the first reading of the Exclusion Bill received a surprise summons to the Lords. There they found Charles enthroned, in his robes, to tell them that parliament was dissolved.[31]

The dissolution freed Charles from the necessity of acting cautiously. Earlier, subject to pressures and concerned not to provoke immediately hostile reactions, Charles had first prorogued and subsequently dissolved the Cavalier and both the Exclusion Parliaments. Now for the first time Charles told the full Whig Commons to their faces that they were dissolved and must disperse. He left immediately, and they had no alternative but to do the same.

Although the Whigs fought a stubborn rearguard battle for the next two years, and won some local successes, Charles had inflicted a decisive defeat upon them at Oxford. After this all the political initiatives came from him, and he systematically eliminated all the media that the Whigs needed in order to be able to function. On 8 April he appealed to the nation in a declaration which he required the clergy to read from their pulpits.[32] He castigated Whig conduct at Oxford, and in the previous parliament, characterizing it as 'unwarrantable', and contrasting it with his own readiness to consider all expedients, except Exclusion. Charles turned against the Whigs the kind of arguments that they had repeatedly made against the Court – accusing them of arbitrary and oppressive arrests of persons alleged to have infringed parliamentary privilege, of trying to suspend laws by mere resolutions, and of being motivated by ambition for office and influence. Charles justified the dissolution by claiming that the attempted impeachment of Fitzharris had so set the two Houses against each other that no public good could be expected from their continuing in session. He gave assurances, which time was to show were entirely tactical and insincere, that this unhappy experience would not put him out of love with parliaments, and that he intended to call them again and frequently. The declaration ended by drawing a partisan distinction between the 'restless malice of ill men who are labouring to poison our people', that is, the Whig militants, and the 'loyalty and good affections' of the sound elements in the nation, to whom Charles appealed with an evocative reminder of the past when 'religion, liberty and property were all lost and gone when the monarchy was shaken off, and could never be revived till that was restored'.

Charles effectively exploited the fears of another civil war or rebellion that were steadily replacing the anti-papist excitement on which Shaftesbury relied. With official encouragement, addresses poured in, thanking the king for the declaration.[33] Since the Anglican clergy played a large part in organizing these addresses, it is not surprising that many called for the energetic renewal of legal prosecutions against dissenters. Protestant dissenters had enjoyed virtual immunity while the Whig-dominated parliaments sat, but Shaftesbury had achieved nothing permanent for them. He had got one Bill passed, to repeal the statute (35 Elizabeth) that required attendance at church, but it had finally been lost by a royal trick. Charles had personally ordered the clerk to the Lords to 'lose' the Bill so that it was not presented with others for his assent or veto. The Whigs had failed to notice its omission until after the prorogation.[34] Charles's underhand trick was consistent with his general attitude: he favoured toleration if it was instituted by prerogative powers, but he resented any attempt by means of statute to force him to give concessions. Dissenters generally supported the Whigs in the hope of statutory relief, but their association with the struggle for Exclusion made Charles treat them as a danger to peace and his royal authority. He made an exception only for William Penn, who publicly disassociated himself from the Whigs; the Pennsylvania charter of 1681 was his reward, and was an example to other dissenters. After the Oxford dissolution repression of the dissenters began on an increasingly systematic and severe scale, with Charles's explicit encouragement. On the other hand, although he had pledged himself in the declaration 'to use our utmost endeavours to extirpate popery', he relaxed enforcement of the laws against Catholics, although he avoided attracting attention by formal statements or directives.[35]

Some historians have depicted Charles as coming under James's influence, or even domination, during this last phase of the reign.[36] However during the first and crucial part of the struggle against the Whigs Charles remained his own master. James returned from Scotland in February 1682, but his influence remained limited until Sunderland's return to Court in September, the month in which Charles completed the defeat of the Whigs.[37]

The first royal offensive against the Whigs, the prosecution of Shaftesbury and other notorious Whig activists, ended in failure. It is entirely apt to use military metaphors, since both Charles and the Whigs engaged in what a contemporary described as a form of civil war, but using the law in place of the sword. Charles was determined to convict, using any means, however dubious; the Whigs were equally resolved to clear their leaders at any price. The royal offensive began promisingly on 2 July 1681. Charles came up unexpectedly from Windsor to Whitehall. He and the council examined Shaftesbury, who had been arrested at dawn. Suspecting some reluctance to incur responsibility for committing the Whig leader, the king exerted pressure on all seventeen counsellors to sign the warrant. The council sent Shaftesbury to the Tower under contemptuously weak escort, and with no popular reaction. But difficulties soon began to cloud the prospect of putting him to death as a traitor. Charles could rely on the absolute dependability of his judges, but in Middlesex (which included London) the sheriffs were elected, whereas in all other counties the king nominated them. Those elected for 1680/81 and 1681/82 were staunch Whigs, who could be relied on to empanel grand and petty juries of Whig stalwarts, chosen for their determination to resist pressure beforehand and in the court-room.[38]

This obstacle to the judicial killing of prominent Whigs emerged in August, when a Middlesex grand jury cleared a minor Whig militant named College, and again, on 18 October, when a Whig organizer in the City, Rous, was similarly cleared.[39] Charles found a way to kill College, who had allegedly spoken treasonable words at Oxford during the parliamentary session: his case was reopened there in August; packed Tory juries presented and convicted him without question.[40] In Shaftesbury's case the necessity of a grand jury presenting him for trial tantalizingly provided the only obstacle to his judicial murder. Once presented, Shaftesbury would be tried by his peers, and since parliament would not be sitting this would be by a court consisting of the lord steward and thirty peers picked for their hostility to Shaftesbury. They would not need to be unanimous: a simple majority would convict. It would not matter that the evidence against Shaftesbury remained unimpressive, despite intensive work by the king's legal officers.

Although various alternatives were considered – moving the grand jury hearing to Oxford, or to Westminster with a jury returned by the bailiff, or to the royal court of the Verge at Whitehall – all faced formidable technical legal objections which even the politically most reliable judges would not be able to disregard.[41] But in his new style of ruthless determination Charles rejected the opportunity for an advantageous compromise. Depressed and ill, Shaftesbury sent a message via Arlington, offering to withdraw into private life if the prosecution was dropped, and to go to Dorset or into exile in Europe or even Carolina.[42] Charles was probably right in suspecting that Shaftesbury would repudiate any such undertakings (on the ground of coercion), and would never become politically inactive. He rejected the offer, saying that Shaftesbury must be left to the law, although in fact the chances of a conviction were fading. The Whig sheriffs empanelled a packed, but impressive and unimpressionable, grand jury for the hearing on 24 November. The charge against Shaftesbury, of intending to levy war against the king by compelling him by force to agree to Exclusion and the repeal of the laws against the dissenters, and of speaking treasonable words, rested solely on the unreliable evidence of disreputable witnesses. That had been good enough to convict Jesuits, Stafford and Plunkett, but the Whig grand jurymen tore it to shreds, defied judicial pressure and brought in an *ignoramus* – no case to answer.[43]

Charles took precautions to stifle demonstrations when he had to release Shaftesbury four days later. The general damage was to some extent reduced by the publication, just before the hearing, of Dryden's *Absalom and Achitophel*, commissioned earlier for the purpose of destroying Shaftesbury's reputation. It has certainly achieved this in influencing historical judgements, although the immediate contemporary impact appears to have been less damaging. The failure of the prosecution against Shaftesbury represented a major setback. Charles now had to set himself to destroy the Whig control over London, and for this he needed the Tories as active allies. Charles intervened personally to stiffen the Tory challenge to the dominant Whigs. His Ministers (particularly secretary Jenkins) and the Bishop of London assisted the Tory activists, systematically bringing pressure to bear on tradesmen who supplied the Court and the navy, and on licensees of coffee and ale houses. Charles also encouraged a vigorous press and pamphlet campaign to denigrate the Whigs. He attended and applauded Crowne's play *City Politics* which derided their leaders. The council directed JPs to intensify prosecutions of dissenting ministers and congregations. Great care was taken to supervise the City militia.[44]

Charles did not become master of his capital until, under his direction, the Tories won their decisive (if legally dubious) victory in the 1682 sheriffs' election. This achievement and the success of legal action, brought by writ of *quo warranto*, in which the judges declared the City's charter forfeit, at last freed the king from continuing dependence on his Tory allies. The installation of Tory sheriffs in September 1682 also belatedly eliminated Shaftesbury. Aware of his vulnerability now that he had lost the protection of Whig-nominated juries, he first went into hiding and then fled to Amsterdam, where he died in January 1683.[45]

The king's principal objective in the years after 1681 can best be described as the elimination of all parties, and of politics itself in the form of activity by people who did not hold any kind of responsible position. The unofficial and independent expression of opinions, in publishing, writing, preaching or even speaking privately, must be curbed. Only those appointed by the king, or by his deputies, to positions carrying specific responsibilities had the right to make public pronouncements. And these should be directly related to the sphere of activity of the body to which they belonged: for example, Charles told Tory aldermen and common councillors that he would listen to their representations concerning City matters, but would reject (and they must oppose) any on national affairs. Indeed this was one major reason for bringing actions of *quo warranto* against municipal charters, to gain permanent control over the members and officers of corporations.

The consequence, which suited Charles's overall strategy, was to channel Tory addresses (and also the Tory press) into denunciatory attacks on the Whigs for their past record and their continuing infringements of the laws. Addresses organized after Shaftesbury's *ignoramus* condemned the model of an association found among his papers – the only paper of substance that came to light. Grand juries called for legal action against dissenters. In several counties they also presented as disaffected and disturbers of the peace those Whigs who tried to keep the party alive. The Rye House Plot in 1683 inevitably stimulated floods of addresses from Tories denouncing the Whigs as rebels, and promising to stand by the king with their lives and fortunes.[46] But after this excitement subsided Charles did not encourage further addresses – they kept tensions alive, and fostered political consciousness even though of a favourable kind. Charles wanted political passivity and unconditional obedience from his subjects. He repeatedly snubbed Tory activitists who assumed that they had the king under a debt of obligation for services against the Whigs.

Politics continued after 1681–2 only at the highest level, among ministers, privy counsellors and holders of Court offices who, together with aspirants, formed a small enclosed political world at Whitehall. They became increasingly insulated from public opinion, in so far as it can be said to have continued, and it was this detachment of the Court from even the provincial Tories that foiled Edward Seymour's attempt to impose himself on Charles as his new chief minister. As former Speaker (and manager) in the Cavalier Parliament, and Tory spokesman against Exclusion, he knew much about the sentiments and interests of the provincial Tory gentry and clergy. During 1681 he formed a triumvirate, a framework for a new administration with himself at its head, as successor to

Danby; Conway as secretary would handle foreign affairs, and Ranelagh finance. They so arranged things that one of the three was always in attendance on the king. But Charles now had no need of another political manager and fixer.[47] Danby had been necessary only because of royal dependence on parliament. Charles had also made Seymour's self-appointed role as champion of militant Anglicanism superfluous, by establishing the commission for ecclesiastical promotions.[48] This exercised royal control over church patronage, and also checked the ambitious clerical politician Compton, Bishop of London. Handicapped also by his arrogant temperament and impatience, Seymour's influence steadily declined: by March 1683 he was reduced to seeking an alliance with Halifax, who wisely declined the offer.[49]

Hyde, who became Earl of Rochester in November 1682, also aspired to become chief minister, although on a rather different basis from his father, Clarendon. Competence as a financial administrator ensured his continuation as a minister (since Ranelagh's record in Ireland inspired distrust) until 1684, when Godolphin became available again, having purged himself of the error of voting for Exclusion. Rochester's achievement in making Charles financially secure had far more important benefits for the king than for himself. Most obviously it made it unnecessary to call another parliament.[50] It meant that Charles did not even have to consider using the extra-legal methods of raising revenue that his father had employed in the years after 1629. Moreover Rochester performed other important and delicate tasks. He negotiated the 1681 subsidy treaty with Louis. Charles delegated to him the maintenance of a correspondence with William, but in this he failed lamentably. Rochester's lack of subtlety, and especially the crass assumptions that he made about William's intentions, infuriated the latter, who preferred the pedestrian but factual reports of his other official correspondent, Charles's work-horse, the loyal and industrious secretary Jenkins. In addition Rochester, as Mary's uncle, painfully reminded William of his wife's plebeian origins. Rochester also acted as James's correspondent and representative, while the Duke continued in exile in Edinburgh, but after his return in February 1682 rapidly lost ground to Sunderland, who quickly established a personal ascendancy over James that lasted until 1688. This intimacy with James had a further consequence: Sunderland replaced Rochester as the minister with whom Louis preferred to do business.[51]

The in-fighting between Rochester, Sunderland and Halifax created divisions within the Court which actually fitted in with Charles's purposes and methods. Technically Rochester performed competently at the treasury, and he fought off two attacks by Halifax on his administration of the king's revenues: in October 1682 to February 1683, over the hearth tax; and in April 1683, over the new excise commission. But Charles was reminded of Rochester's father, Clarendon, when the son made an attempt to become chief minister in August 1684, and the king's harsh reaction showed how memories of the years of virtual tutelage still rankled. He refused to consider Rochester's appointment as lord treasurer but, after depriving him of his treasury commissionership, gave him the honorific post of lord president. In November Charles drove Rochester out of the central administration, nominating him to lucrative exile as lord-lieutenant of Ireland, although Rochester had not crossed to Dublin when the king died.[52]

Rochester's decline enhanced the influence of Sunderland with both Charles and James. It was not until July 1682 that Charles forgave Sunderland his vote for Exclusion and intrigues with William, but thereafter Sunderland's influence increased swiftly. This was not primarily a reward for sycophancy (although there was plenty of that), but the direct result of his ability to hold the confidence of both Charles and James and to ensure a smooth working relationship between them – abilities that no courtier had displayed so effectively since Falmouth in the 1660s. Sunderland facilitated the return of James to the inner group at Court on an informal basis. But it would be an over-statement to say that as a result of Sunderland's work James dominated Charles or eclipsed him in influence with courtiers and officials.[53] We know that Charles was to die soon, in February 1685, but in the three preceding years contemporaries had no reason to believe that James would outlive his brother. There is little evidence for the existence of a strong reversionary interest, and in the last months of the reign it was Rochester, not Sunderland, who attached himself exclusively to James – because he had lost Charles's confidence. Sunderland characteristically put his money on a both-ways bet, attentively serving both royal brothers, and made sure that he did not have to choose between them.

The revival of James's influence threatened Halifax's position, but in practice did him little damage. In assessing Halifax's influence with Charles it is necessary to discard his grossly inflated view of himself and his role. Halifax described himself memorably as the Trimmer, who always maintained a balance within the administration by acting as a counterweight. According to an extremely fashionable and pseudo-scientific concept of the time an approximate equilibrium was essential for the healthy operation of most systems – an administration, international affairs, the physiology of an individual. Halifax claimed to act as a corrective to imbalances, throwing his weight on the lesser side to counterbalance an undesirably predominant interest, just as Temple wanted England to follow a policy of maintaining a balance of power within Europe.

It is as the Trimmer, his own title, that Halifax has been seen by posterity.[54] The only reason not to accept him at his own estimation is simply that he never at any time during his career possessed sufficient weight to balance successively predominant influences – the Whigs in

1680–1, James after 1685, Danby and the Tories after 1688. As we have seen, he failed to secure Rochester's dismissal from the treasury in 1682–3, and for the significant reason that it did not (yet) suit Charles's purposes. Halifax should be seen primarily as the executant of royal policies, as in his resistance to Exclusion, and it must be said that his many negative characteristics fitted him admirably for this role. Almost alone among courtiers he never aspired to high office, and until October 1682 when he became lord privy seal held no office, acting in public affairs only as a privy counsellor. He made no attempt to form an interest, or group of supporters, as a power base. He rejected approaches from Seymour, who would bring one with him. Halifax worked as a lone operator.[55]

From Charles's viewpoint Halifax's unique characteristics were advantageous. He did not have to take seriously the minister's talk of calling a new parliament which would produce national reconciliation by passing a new act of indemnity and oblivion, and would also respond to appeals from Spain, the Dutch and the German princes to help contain French aggressions. Charles knew that Halifax could not manage parliament or organize elections, but his talk of a change of policies acted as a check on James and the 'French party'. Charles duped Halifax, particularly over foreign policy, and constantly manipulated him, correctly predicting that he would continue to cling to his new office. In so far as Halifax acted as a counterweight this was entirely the result of the tactical support which Charles gave him. Halifax was not the independent figure he thought he was. Constantly misled by Charles about his real intentions, constantly consulted but having little influence on decisions, Halifax unwittingly played a part in the king's overall manœuvres.

After 1677 Charles had to accept the way in which several of his ministers and advisers maintained close links with William. Although he could not legitimately deny William's personal right to concern himself with English affairs, after the Oxford dissolution in 1681 Charles set himself the objective of reducing William's ability to intervene. Rightly he saw that William's main purpose was to enlist British resources in his struggle against France. In 1678 this had meant dragging England into a dying and unsuccessful war against the odds. In the years after 1681 further French advances could ignite another general European war, but only if William could construct a credible alliance to fight one. Involvement in William's diplomatic preparations carried great dangers for Charles. As a minimum, even the prospect of war would require extraordinary votes of supply from parliaments that Charles could not be confident of controlling. He had to prevent himself becoming dependent on William, because the latter would single-mindedly try to involve him in anti-French policies. By contrast Charles found dependence on Louis a tolerable state. French subsidies helped to keep him solvent. In return Louis expected passive, not active, support and services. Pledges to remain inactive might appear to put Charles in an ignominious position, but after Oxford they enabled him to avoid falling into a much more dangerous dependence on a new parliament, which he feared would be exploited by William to gain a permanent control over English foreign policies.

Charles consistently overestimated the strength and closeness of William's links with the English politicians who opposed the Crown. Shaftesbury followed the tactic of waiting until Exclusion passed, and then negotiating with William. Consequently, as far as we know, the Whigs had no understanding with William, and some of their leaders (Montagu and Harbord) worked in close but secret co-operation with the French ambassador.[56] In addition radicals like Algernon Sydney and Papillon maintained close links with William's republican enemies in Holland, and shared their distrust of his intentions. They feared that William, like his father in 1650, would attempt to make himself absolute, and so would sympathize with Charles's attempts to increase his own authority.[57] In fact one of William's principal objectives during his visit to England in July 1681 was to dispel such false impressions, and persuade the Whigs to reduce their demands so as to unite with the Court in making possible an anti-French foreign policy. His chances of success were negligible. Charles did not want any form of compromise with the Whigs. He blocked all Whig attempts to extract advantages from the visit, prohibiting a reception that they planned to give William in the City. The king was even more concerned to prevent the visit being exploited by the Court group (Sunderland, Godolphin, Henry Sidney) who had advised William throughout the Exclusion crisis and now saw in him the means to recover their lost offices and influence.[58]

William knew perfectly well that, without exception, all those whom he encountered during his visit would try to use him for their own purposes. He never trusted Charles after the latter's cynical invitations to betray the Dutch republic in 1672, and he certainly believed that the king was really a papist at heart. He saw the danger that Charles would turn to France as the easiest escape from Whig pressure: in the summer of 1679, and again in April 1680 and January 1681, he reached the premature conclusion that Charles and Louis had made a secret agreement.[59] William detested limitations as a facile solution by which Charles would sacrifice the future (William's future, when Mary succeeded) to gain immediate ease.[60] In the autumn of 1680 William feared that Charles would eventually concede Exclusion, putting the Whigs in command. William greatly overestimated the possibility of a Commonwealth emerging from the crisis and, applying what he thought were the lessons of history, believed that a new republic would imitate the Rump in launching commercially inspired anti-Dutch policies, accompanied by an alliance with France.[61]

Throughout the Exclusion crisis William constantly represented to all his correspondents the urgent need for a settlement, because without union between king and parliament there could be no effective intervention in Europe, but he never had any ready-made solution to how this could be achieved. He did not act on Sunderland's advice to attend the 1680 session, but after the Lords rejected Exclusion he developed second thoughts. Sunderland cleverly alarmed him by reporting a surge in Monmouth's influence and prospects; and even more alarmingly the Dutch ambassador, van Leeuwen, forecast an early prorogation, with Charles consenting to Exclusion in a new session.[62] Charles revealed, in an angry interview with van Leeuwen, that he knew a great deal about these interchanges.[63] Sidney also outraged the king by soliciting a letter from the States General urging Charles to settle with parliament, which clearly implied his consenting to Exclusion. Although William had not initiated or even approved this intervention, Charles can be excused for thinking that he was adding his influence to those who urged him to abandon James[64] Relations with William deteriorated. The latter realized that no good would come of a visit to coincide with the Oxford parliament, and was disheartened by its dissolution. Charles recalled Sidney in disgrace, and provocatively proposed to replace him with Skelton, knowing that the latter was detested by William as little better than a French agent. Moreover by May 1681, when French forces began a new if limited incursion into the Spanish Netherlands, William's intelligence system was picking up indications of a secret treaty between Charles and Louis.[65]

Although pessimistic about the chances of success, William felt obliged to make a visit (the last before a more fortunate one in 1688), and venture into the labyrinth of English politics. Charles had a relatively easy task in containing William. He and his ministers explained the complex and uncertain political position to justify their concentration on domestic affairs. Charles rejected most of the advice William offered. He did not think it an appropriate time to call another parliament. He would not separate his interest from James's. He refused to send even a token force to protect Flanders. Peremptory royal orders stopped William dining in the City with the Whigs.[66] Significantly Charles took great care to keep Barrillon informed about his meetings with William, so as to substantiate his repeated and rather anxious assurances that the visit would have absolutely no effect on his treaty with Louis. He even felt it prudent to explain that he had permitted the visit (despite Barrillon's advice), because a prohibition would have persuaded everyone that he was tied to France by a secret treaty.[67]

During his visit William failed to get any undertakings from Charles. The king and his ministers subsequently had to devote a great deal of time, energy and skill to fulfilling the treaty obligations to Louis not to assist Spain against piecemeal advances, while concealing the real reasons for inaction. The first crisis came in October 1681 with a French blockade of

Luxemburg. Charles allowed Halifax, who knew nothing of the treaty with Louis, to negotiate with Dutch and Spanish diplomats. The resulting memorial was to be jointly presented to Louis by the Dutch and English ambassadors in Paris, but Louis refused to accept any joint remonstrance, and made Charles realize that he was incurring suspicions of double-dealing. Charles could not afford to offend Louis. He dropped the memorial.[68] Instead he agreed to play the leading role in the farce that Louis now arranged, nominating Charles as arbitrator (with a pre-arranged solution) in the dispute with Spain. Charles recommended Spanish retention of Luxemburg, but on condition that its fortifications were destroyed. As William protested, this left the southern Spanish Netherlands defenceless. In return for this service Charles got an increase in subsidy.[69]

Even this major check, and accumulating evidence that Charles had no intention of calling another parliament, did not end Dutch activities designed to obtain English assistance. Their main effect was to convince Charles that William was trying again to gain control over English policy. He believed (rightly) that William wanted to involve him in a European war, which would mean calling parliament. He suspected that William hoped to intervene in parliament in concert with Whigs and other disaffected politicians. Consequently for the remainder of the reign Charles kept William at a distance. He did not give even token sympathy or support when the French invaded Orange, William's hereditary territory.[70] Princess Anne's marriage to George of Denmark, arranged with the help of French diplomats, represented a snub to William: Denmark and the Dutch republic were on bad terms.[71] In 1683 Charles vetoed a new visit by William, because he suspected that its undeclared purpose was to drag England into a war that he believed William was trying to provoke. Charles clearly saw William, not Louis, as the main danger to European peace.[72]

Halifax did not share this view, but his efforts to persuade Charles of the need to join in an anti-French alliance that would have involved a general reversal of policy were not very convincing.[73] Charles could not risk either a breach with Louis or the calling of parliament. As far back as December 1679 Godolphin had accurately predicted the king's intentions – 'to keep himself quiet, if he can [and] not to think of the rest of the world'.[74] Acting on this maxim Charles stayed neutral (as he was entitled to do, since the 1680 treaty had a purely defensive character) when in December 1683 Spain declared war on France, hoping to ignite a general war in which support would be forthcoming from a new anti-French alliance. This gambit resulted in humiliating failure for Spain and William. No state came to Spain's assistance. William failed to persuade the States General to declare war. Charles remained a cynical spectator.[75]

The deterioration in relations between Charles and William was

accelerated by English protests against the harbouring of a new generation
of political fugitives in the United Provinces, men accused of being
involved in the Whig conspiracy known as the Rye House Plot, which
broke in sensational fashion in June 1683. Plotters who turned king's
evidence revealed two loosely linked conspiracies: one, by City radicals,
planned to assassinate Charles and James on the Newmarket–London road
at Hoddesdon, where the Whig Rumbold owned the Rye House. The
other, by aristocratic Whigs (Russell, Grey, Monmouth, Hampden and
Essex), envisaged a coup to overcome the Life Guards, seize Charles and
coerce him into conceding Whig demands.[76]

The discovery of the plot spurred Charles into intense activity, and also
provoked a new wave of Tory activism which eventually he had to check.
However, it is not accurate to interpret this as an isolated phase of
uncharacteristic royal attention to affairs of state. It was a mark of
Charles's success in restoring his authority that he could relax, and at the
same time control all aspects of government and decision-making. In the
1660s and 1670s Charles had taken his ease by delegating most governmental business to a chief minister – first Clarendon, then Danby. After
1681, choosing not to have a chief minister, Charles delegated what we
would call departmental business – finance to Rochester, foreign affairs to
Conway and the most difficult tasks (security, the corporations and the
church) to secretary Jenkins. Freed from detailed administrative chores
Charles enjoyed more leisure, spending long periods at Newmarket,
Windsor and Hampton Court, to which he intended adding Winchester,
where construction of a new palace began in March 1683: one advantage
was that few Whigs lived in its region.[77]

Charles returned to London to take personal charge of investigations
immediately the first informers came forward. Learning from the mistakes committed in 1678, he insisted that they should be subjected to
thorough and systematic examination by the council. Some of their evidence is by modern standards defective, but Charles took full advantage of
the opportunity to destroy the hard core of intransigent Whigs, retrieving
his failure against Shaftesbury in 1681. However, he set himself against
what he called a 'growing evidence', refusing to allow informers to
elaborate and expand their original allegations, as Oates had been allowed
to do in 1678–9. In concentrating on the Whig notables he ignored the
eagerness of the most partisan Tories to initiate a nationwide proscription
of all former Whigs, but he showed himself severe and even pitiless in his
treatment of the surviving Whig leaders. Very revealingly, he took care, in
interrogating the informers, to ask whether Oates had been implicated,
but unfortunately there was no evidence to hang him.[78] But such leading
Whigs as Russell, Armstrong, Rous and Essex had undoubtedly committed treason, as the law interpreted it after the statute of 1661. In
Russell's case the king was primarily concerned with the impact that his

conviction and execution would make. He ignored the pleas made on Russell's behalf by his connections and friends, giving public reasons for severity. Regarding Russell as a mortal enemy of the monarchy, Charles explained crudely that if he did not have Russell's head, the obstinate Whig leader would again attempt the king's death.[79]

More generally Charles and his propagandists lost no opportunity of demonstrating how the Rye House Plot exposed the rebellious principles of the Whigs, as true descendants of the party that had fought the king and brought about his death in 1649. Charles sneered that he found it 'strange that beggars should contend for Property, atheists for Religion, and bastards for Succession'.[80] However, his own bastard, Monmouth, posed embarrassing problems for him. Charles had tried repeatedly since Monmouth's disgrace in 1679 to reconcile himself with the son whom he loved more consistently than any other person. But he refused to allow his private feelings to override his political duty and judgement, insisting that as the price of restoration to favour Monmouth must reveal everything about his connections with the Whigs, and especially about Shaftesbury's promises. He must also break with his Whig associates, above all with his political mentor and friend, Sir Thomas Armstrong, whom Charles and James joined in detesting more strongly than any other disaffected subject, and whom they put to death (without trial) as an outlaw in 1684.[81] Monmouth's attempts to state his own conditions wrecked all the many attempts at reconciliation. In May 1682 Monmouth went so far as to say that he would submit to Charles, but not to James, provoking a peremptory royal order that no one in the king's service should communicate with Monmouth.[82] But Charles made another attempt at reconciliation in August, a time when Monmouth's bargaining position was stronger because he was about to depart on a pseudo-royal progress to Cheshire, where he actually received an enthusiastic reception comparable to that during his 1680 west-country tour, a time of Whig confidence and strength. For Charles the motive for renewing contact with Monmouth was the hope that the latter's submission would be followed by that of many other Whigs, but the king refused to 'capitulate', that is, bargain, with them. Submission must be unconditional, and the political penitents must renounce party affiliations and political activity.[83]

The discovery of the Rye House Plot destroyed Monmouth's bargaining position. It forced him into hiding. Charles knew where he was, but made no serious attempt to arrest him. However, when Monmouth asked for a pardon Charles stiffened the terms on public grounds. He demanded an admission of involvement in the plot, so as to authenticate the official version which the remaining Whigs strenuously contested. Monmouth surrendered after signing a submissive letter drafted for him by Halifax. Examined before the council, he made a confession, but asked that it should not be used in evidence at any trial.[84] Although in reality Monmouth's position in relation to Charles was that of a suppliant, the Whigs deliberately misrepresented what happened, claiming that Monmouth was being restored to favour at James's expense and that further changes would follow. Charles moved quickly to uphold James's credit. He had already involved his brother in investigations of the plot, instructing him to attend the committee of the council regularly. Now he published an account of Monmouth's submission in the *London Gazette*, cleverly designed to compromise Monmouth with the Whigs. Charles was demanding a straight choice by his son. He could either have a pardon, and a conditional return to royal as well as paternal favour, or he could keep his Whig connections. Charles also skilfully devalued Halifax's attempts to claim credit for acting as intermediary on Monmouth's behalf, and prevented his making use of the duke as a counterweight to James. Monmouth's vacillations brought him discredit. Charles personally drafted a letter in which Monmouth denied that he had meant to 'lessen the late plot and [had] gone about to discredit the evidence given against those who [had] died by Justice', and explicitly acknowledged having had a share in the conspiracy. Having signed the paper, Monmouth subsequently asked for it to be returned, but Charles entered it in the council record.[85]

Halifax's reputation suffered from his being associated with this humiliation of Monmouth, and some Court observers thought Charles was about to discard him. That would have given James a predominance that his brother did not intend. The Rye House Plot disclosures benefited James, who had been marked for assassination as well as the king. On Charles's orders James attended all council investigations of the plot, and he continued to attend council regularly afterwards, although he had not taken the oaths or the Anglican sacrament. In May 1684 Charles went further. He terminated the admiralty commission, in theory taking control over the navy himself. But in practice he restored James to the function of which the Test Act had deprived him in 1673. The previous month Charles increased James's influence by appointing Godolphin as secretary of State; he assisted Sunderland in advising the Duke.[86] In addition Charles's decision not to fulfil the legal requirements of the Triennial Act stipulating a parliament after an interval of three years – which meant one in March 1684 – seemed to testify to many a significant increase in James's influence over Charles. However, this important negative decision was entirely consistent with the king's long-term strategy. Elections would entail a revival of popular interest and participation in politics. Many Tories had already begun preparations, but they received no encouragement from any of the ministers, Halifax included, and there is little evidence of popular disappointment at the king's refusal to permit elections and a session.[87]

During the second half of 1684 Charles consciously strengthened Halifax's position within the administration. In July North and Thynne entered the treasury commission.[88] In August Charles removed Rochester, giving him as compensation the secondary office of lord president, only to remove him even further from power in November with nomination as lord-lieutenant of Ireland. It has been claimed that this move was to clear the way for Sunderland to become chief minister, a view that originates with Sunderland himself, but the continuing pattern of royal manœuvring argues that Charles had no intention of allowing any minister to achieve the kind of dominance that Clarendon and Danby had once thought they possessed.[89]

During his last months Charles continued to keep everyone at Court in a state of uncertainty. For a time he allowed Sunderland to believe, and spread reports, that Halifax was about to be dismissed, but nothing happened.[90] Two of Charles's major initiatives caused James considerable anxiety. The king made a first approach for some years to improve relations with William.[91] Much more sensationally he agreed to a secret visit in November by Monmouth, who lived in self-imposed exile in the Netherlands. We know nothing of the details, but Charles had a long interview with his son, and after returning overseas in December 1684 Monmouth started to correspond with Charles via an intermediary who most probably was Halifax.[92] It is now impossible to say what the king intended, and there is nothing to substantiate the later Whig assertions that he intended a complete revolution in his affairs – and that this was why James had him poisoned, a claim that Monmouth made in his declaration at the start of his rebellion in 1685. But undoubtedly knowledge of this intrigue greatly concerned James, who was due to depart again for Scotland where a parliament was to be convened in 1685. The fact that Charles had just appointed two of James's closest associates to positions of influence – Middleton as secretary of state, Jeffreys as a member of the cabinet council – was not enough to reassure him.[93] In the middle of these continuing manœuvres, the purpose of which only Charles had any real idea of, terminal illness suddenly struck him down on 2 February 1685. He lingered until the 6th, which gave him time finally to submit to the Catholic Church, when at last this move had only private and personal significance.

In terms of English politics these last two years of Charles's reign saw no significant developments. He had succeeded in reducing politics to a matter of movements of individuals – in and out of office, up and down in degrees of influence. No one at Court, not even his brother James, could bring sufficient pressure to bear on the king to make him undertake some specific action. During this last phase Charles can at last be described as easy, having achieved freedom from restrictions imposed by ministers, parliament and the church. Financial solvency formed the basis of this ease: although the French subsidies ceased early in 1684, his revenue now exceeded expenditure, and he even managed to put money aside for his new palace at Winchester. Unadventurously but safely, Charles set himself to continue in this comfortable fashion for as long as possible. He had broken the Whigs. For the time being there was no danger of a European war creating complications that might involve additional expenditure or even the calling of a parliament. He was about to pack off Rochester, the only minister to make an open bid to become chief minister, to a gilded exile in Dublin. By unfreezing relations with William, Charles served notice on both Louis and the so-called French party at Whitehall that he must not be taken for granted. His most independent move was discreetly to initiate a modest measure of relief for Catholic laymen. In October 1684 he ordered the release from prison of any recusant whose family had given Charles I loyal service during the Civil Wars. This was largely a token move, since few individuals benefited, but it reflected a desire to make amends for his failure to protect innocent Catholics during the hysteria of the Popish Plot.

The only new development of Charles's last years came in Ireland, where the policy that he initiated was to be continued and expanded by James after his accession. Charles planned changes from as early as June 1681 when, as a result of discussions about the Irish revenue (from which he excluded Ormonde), he stated his intention of 'modelling' the army in Ireland, but he did nothing until 1684. He permitted Richard Talbot, a close and long-standing associate of James, to return to Ireland in order to collect material giving a state of the kingdom from a Catholic point of view. Talbot had already done this in 1669 when he had used his information and contacts to attempt a wholesale revision of the Restoration land settlement. Then, he had made the mistake of raising the explosive land issue at the beginning: in 1684 he proposed to start with changes in administration which could subsequently be used to facilitate a new attempt to restore forfeited lands to their former Catholic owners. Charles knew what Talbot intended, and in the interim opened the land issue himself by establishing what proved to be an ineffective commission of grace, with powers to examine defective land titles and sell new patents to approved applicants.[94]

In October 1684 Charles informed Ormonde of his early recall. He issued Rochester with considerably modified powers as the next lord-lieutenant, depriving him of all control over the appointment and dismissal of army officers. He also made drastic changes in the composition of the Irish privy council and, just before his death, gave the command of regiments to Talbot and another Catholic, Justin Mac-Carthy.[95] These changes provoked a spate of rumours, but although Talbot certainly had in mind the policies that were to be introduced in 1685–8, there is no evidence to suggest that Charles had clearly formulated his objectives. James after his accession moved quickly, looking ahead as a *visionnaire* to the transformation of Ireland. It is impossible to know exactly what Charles intended, but the little evidence we have supports the view that he was looking backwards in time. Only in Ireland had a major Cromwellian interest survived the Restoration, with officers and soldiers retaining part of the land taken from Catholics. A few veterans, and many of their sons, filled commissions and served in the ranks of Ormonde's army in 1677–85. Charles explicitly stated his intention of sweeping rebels and rebels' sons out of the council and the militia as well as the army, a policy that James carried out. But it is doubtful whether Charles had even begun to think of transforming the government of Ireland. For him it was a question of honouring the promises that had been made by him to his faithful Irish Catholic partisans before 1660, but that Ormonde and Protestant opinion in both kingdoms had prevented him from carrying out.

In the last phase of the reign Charles was able to rule with a freedom that he had not previously experienced. He did not have to defer to James, or accept the advice offered by any minister or Court group. Apart from petitioning there was now no way in which any organized group outside Whitehall could influence royal policy, and petitions now concerned the cases of individuals or the interests of economic bodies, not matters of national politics. Charles retained Halifax, primarily as a check on James, but also because Louis wanted his dismissal. The king's refusal to take notice of the amended Triennial Act, and call a parliament in 1684, acted as a rebuff to Halifax – the public advocate of a new parliament – but, even more important, it cut down to size the Tory activists led by Seymour. Similarly Charles paid no attention to the political moves initiated by Danby immediately after his release from the Tower after four years' imprisonment.[96] By starting a new correspondence with Monmouth, Charles worried not only James but also William. The commission for ecclesiastical promotions was allowed to lapse, weakening James's ecclesiastical influence. A personally timid and politically inactive archbishop, Sancroft, ensured that Charles would not again encounter the kind of obstruction or opposition that he had experienced from Sheldon.

In his last year Charles was freer from restraints than ever before. Yet in a wider sense this was a limited achievement. He had not definitively settled any major issue. All the political and religious divisions that had caused major instability remained under the surface of a unity based on enforced obedience. Charles achieved complete success as a political tactician, concentrating exclusively on the immediate and the short-term. Consequently it is not surprising that this achievement proved to be short-lived. Charles never really concealed his contempt for 'la sottise de mon frère', but although James certainly lacked his brother's political flair, and was fatally compromised by his conversion to Catholicism, he inherited problems of fundamental intractability.

9 Conclusion

In the last phase of the reign Charles can be said to have finally achieved his
'objectives': he had preserved the rights and powers of the monarchy and
freed himself from domination by a chief minister. Charles had defeated
the Whig attempt to change the succession, dismantled the party and freed
himself from the need to call a session of parliament every year. He was no
longer obliged to act as a politician. Instead of having to solicit the support
of his subjects, he now commanded their obedience. When Charles died,
James was able to succeed without immediate challenge or disturbance,
something that would have been incredible a few years before.

Charles's achievement was personal, not institutional, and consequently
it can be described as both limited and precarious. He was able to rule
without calling parliament, but any future legislation would require parliamentary consent.[1] He had failed to obtain recognition of a power to suspend
statutes (in the one area of ecclesiastical affairs), and his power to dispense
with the law in individual cases had been defined, and so limited.[2] Royal
solvency depended on temporary factors: without a parliament it became
politically practicable to dismantle part of the patronage system built up
since 1673. An unusually long period of European peace made retrenchment in naval expenditure possible, and augmented the receipts from
customs revenues. However, royal credit still depended on improvisations:
unlike all other major European kingdoms, which were much less advanced
economically and commercially, England possessed no state bank.

In comparing his own position with that of his peers, the monarchs of
Europe, Charles was conscious of his particular susceptibility to pressures.
He had had mixed success in repulsing parliamentary invasions of areas
that were undoubtedly within his prerogative – foreign policy, including
peace and war, royal marriages, the succession. As the unexpected developments of the Popish Plot demonstrated, his administration continued to
be dangerously vulnerable to 'accidents'. The sum total of his achievement
was that he could actually rule, at least for the time being, without calling
parliament – something that all his predecessors had taken for granted.

Charles's victory over the Whigs in March 1681 was based on the
subsidy treaty that he had just concluded with Louis. The latter gave him
enough money on which to subsist, provided that all extraordinary expenditure could be avoided. This was virtually assured by the undertaking

that Charles gave Louis, that he would not intervene in Europe. Consequently a paradox underlaid the strength of royal authority during
Charles's last years: supreme over his subjects at home, the king surrendered to Louis all freedom of action in Europe. This acceptance of a
permanent orientation towards France was in keeping with two consistent
strands in Charles's attitude throughout his life. First, his family relationship with Louis (they were first cousins), his admiration for French
power and influence in Europe, and his envy of the strength of the
monarchy within France moulded his policies from the start. Although at
times he could not prevent ministers from foisting on him attempts to
check French expansionism, notably the Triple Alliance of 1668, Charles
always regarded an alignment with France as being in the best interests of
the monarchy.

Secondly, Charles himself saw a successful foreign policy as one that
would contribute towards the strengthening of his own authority at home.
This was the purpose of his major foreign policy initiatives – the sale of
Dunkirk, the two Dutch Wars, his intrigues with Louis in 1676–8. Like
Oliver Cromwell he was concerned to establish a close alliance with the
strongest power in Europe, because it was the strongest.[3] This would
minimize both risks and expenditure, whereas the alternative of opposing
France, so as to obtain a balance of power in Europe, meant participation in
difficult, even dangerous, defensive wars. That would (as his experiences in
1673 and 1678 showed) put him at the mercy of the Commons, who could
be expected to extract major political concessions, such as the Test Act, in
return for voting the large sums of money that would be needed.

Louis made it relatively easy in 1670 and 1681 for Charles to align
himself with France. The Dover treaty and the equally secret subsidy
treaty concluded just before the Oxford parliament gave the king the
means by which he could achieve independence from his subjects.
Charles, in return for subsidies, lost sight of all other considerations.
Before 1670 he had pretended to insist that France must accompany the
alliance with a commercial treaty that would give English traders major
concessions, but after the conclusion of the alliance at Dover he abandoned
the attempt, and also dropped his suggestions that Louis should limit the
size of his navy. Similarly he ignored the national interest in and after 1681,
by agreeing in advance not to intervene in Europe. He gave Louis a blank
cheque, not knowing or caring that the French were about to renew their
piecemeal aggression against the Spanish Netherlands, and thereby put
themselves into a position to take the whole territory when Carlos II died.

It is very noticeable that Charles seldom referred to the past, and particularly to his father's reign.[4] He also rarely spoke about the future. If ever a
sovereign lived in, and for, the present it was Charles II. In this respect he
differed fundamentally from his brother James, who always had a deep

sense of belonging to the Stuart dynasty.[5] Charles did not, especially after his restoration, probably because he had no legitimate descendants. Consequently while James formulated long-term objectives, above all the 'establishment' of Catholicism in a form that would survive his own death, Charles concentrated on defensive tactics designed to protect his prerogative and the succession. There is no evidence that he looked any further. Absorbed by short-term considerations, responding flexibly to rapidly changing situations during the years after 1672, Charles consistently rejected the advice which James offered during periods of crisis to adopt 'resolute courses', that is, to arrest opposition leaders, to dissolve parliament and to use the army to overawe his subjects. James treated each crisis as one of incipient rebellion. Charles by contrast saw that ill-considered repressive action might precipitate rebellion. He knew that an almost universal fear of civil war inhibited all but the most desperate leaders of opposition from planning to use violence, and that this fear represented one of his principal advantages.

The difference between the two brothers was starkest in matters of religion. Although apparently convinced of the claims of Catholicism from his years in exile, Charles regularly attended Anglican worship and communicated every Easter. Charles clearly shared the views of his maternal grandfather, Henri IV, that it was politically necessary for the sovereign to share the faith of the vast majority of the nation. Indeed it was said, as early as 1650, that he took Henri, not the gospel, as his guide.[6] Therefore he deferred his conversion to Catholicism until the last possible moment, when it could lead to no significant political consequences. By contrast James's conversion, from which all his major difficulties stemmed, remained the central event of his life, and by setting an example of personal devotion he tried to dispel anti-Catholic prejudices. He attempted to exploit Charles's conversion by publishing devotional treatises allegedly composed by him and found among his papers after his death.[7] But during his lifetime Charles never really tried to set anyone an edifying example. However, he extracted the maximum advantage from the religion that he continued to follow solely for reasons of state; had he not done so it would have been difficult to rally the clergy and the Tories to help defeat Exclusion. His pursuit of the machiavellian principles of *raison d'état*, and the need to keep up appearances as a Protestant, led him to take actions that would have seared his conscience, had he possessed one – authorizing the execution of innocent men convicted of being involved in the Popish Plot, ordering James to receive and listen to Anglican bishops attempting to reconvert him.[8]

Few, if any, leading personalities in Restoration England equalled Charles in cynicism and insincerity. Consequently it is tempting to conclude that while Charles's lack of political morality explains his survival, James lost his kingdoms because of his virtues – his enduring attachment to the Catholic Church, his constancy and honesty, his habit of plain if often tactless speaking. However, such a superficial comparison overlooks the most negative aspect of the difference between the two royal brothers. Charles's cynicism, opportunism and flexibility, his unsurpassed skill in dissimulation and in penetrating other men's thoughts and even intentions, gave him a clear margin of superiority over all ministers and politicians. The disadvantage was that he not only set the tone of politics in such a way that negative characteristics had to be acquired by politicians if they were to survive, but he 'educated' a whole generation of men in his methods. Danby, Seymour, Sidney and Sunderland could never fully match Charles, but they had little difficulty in outwitting and outmanœuvring James after 1685. Furthermore Charles's success, when he temporarily took on the role of a politician, misled his brother into emulating his example in 1687–8, although James lacked all the necessary skills.

After so much emphasis on Charles's many negative characteristics, it has to be added that in two vital matters he served the nation well. Both before and immediately after the Restoration he insisted on the paramount necessity of forgetting, and indeed effacing, the deep divisions and virulent hatreds generated by the Civil Wars. Without his stand it is doubtful that the Act of Indemnity and Oblivion would have passed (or been observed) in a sufficiently generous and comprehensive form to restore any lasting measure of national unity, and so prevent the recurrence of the earlier cycle of disturbances and instability. This early achievement was complemented by another of equal importance during his last years. Charles's skills enabled him to defeat Shaftesbury and the Whigs at their own and newly developed game of party politics. Charles as royal politician refuted the Whig claim to represent the nation, and mobilized so much support that Shaftesbury did not dare openly to challenge his use of the prerogative powers of the Crown. By using his political skills adroitly Charles saved the nation from the greatest catastrophe that could have overcome it – a destructive renewal of the Civil Wars of the 1640s. The Tory slogan claimed: 'Forty-one is here again'. If indeed the events of that year had been repeated, the nation would have been torn apart again with incalculable but calamitous consequences. Charles played on popular fears of another 'rebellion', but these fears were very real, and there are no reasons to suppose that a civil war would have had any outcome remotely resembling that of the Revolution of 1688, with a generally accepted political and constitutional settlement. Given the balance of forces in 1681, with Charles controlling the army, the militia, Scotland and Ireland, any Whig rebellion would have been easily crushed. By averting any danger of a new civil war Charles saved England from the fate of contemporary Scotland, a poor and deeply divided country, racked by recurrent rebellions, with a significant proportion of the nation alienated from each successive regime for over a century.

Notes

The place of publication is London unless stated otherwise.

1 Introduction

1 All dates in the text are old style, but with the calendar year beginning on 1 January. Where ambiguity might arise, the date is given in both styles, e.g. 1/10 January.

2 C. Hill, 'Some conclusions', in *Collected Essays* (Brighton, 1985), Vol. 1, pp. 322–3; C. Hill, 'A bourgeois revolution?', in J. G. A. Pocock (ed.), *Three British Revolutions* (Princeton, NJ: 1980), pp. 120–1, 122–3.

3 Eleven impressions appeared in its year of publication, 1931.

4 Despite its title, N. Sykes, *Church and State in the Eighteenth Century* (Cambridge, 1934), deals with the Restoration period. See also R. A. Beddard, 'The Restoration Church', in J. R. Jones (ed.), *The Restored Monarchy, 1660–1688* (1979), pp. 155–75.

5 Even the most trivial are printed in A. Bryant, *Letters, Speeches and Declarations of King Charles II* (1935).

6 J. R. Jones, *The First Whigs* (1961), pp. 35–48, 92–106, 159–74.

7 K. H. D. Haley, *William of Orange and the English Opposition* (Oxford, 1953).

8 C. L. Grose, 'Louis XIV's financial relations with Charles II and the English opposition', *Journal of Modern History*, vol. 1 (1929), pp. 177–204.

9 W. C. Costin and J. S. Watson (eds), *The Law and Working of the Constitution*, Vol. 1 (1952), pp. 29–33.

10 See C. Russell, *Parliaments and English Politics, 1621–1629* (Oxford, 1979).

11 These rights were still frequently as unclear as in the earlier period covered by D. Hirst, *The Representative of the People?* (Cambridge, 1975).

12 See D. Allen, 'The political function of Charles II's Chiffinch', *Huntington Library Quarterly*, vol. 39, no. 3 (1976), pp. 277–90.

13 J. Miller, 'The potential for absolutism in later Stuart England', *History*, vol. 69 (1984), pp. 187–207.

14 Largely the effect of Peter du Moulin's self-explanatory pamphlet, *England's Appeal from the Private Cabal at Whitehall to the Great Council of the Nation* (1673).

15 A. Browning (ed.), *English Historical Documents*, Vol. 8 (1953), pp. 185–8. *Lords Journals*, Vol. 13, pp. 745–6.

16 S. R. Gardiner (ed.), *Constitutional Documents of the Puritan Revolution* (Oxford, 1968), pp. 144–55. Costin and Watson, *Law and Working of the Constitution*, Vol. 1, pp. 33–4.

17 W. Cobbett (ed.), *State Trials*, Vol. 9, pp. 666–7, 688–818; Vol. 10, pp. 105–24.

2   *Charles in Scotland, and in Exile*

1   Edward Hyde, Earl of Clarendon, *History of the Rebellion* (Oxford, 1888), Vol. 3, pp. 450–1, 504–6; Vol. 4, pp. 14–34, 87–8, 107–9, 166–70.
2   ibid., Vol. 4, pp. 172–3, 174–82, 196–9, 199–200. E. Scott, *The King in Exile* (1905), pp. 9–11.
3   C. Oman, *Henrietta Maria* (1951), pp. 212–14.
4   Scott, *King in Exile*, pp. 42–3. H. L. Rubinstein, *Captain Luckless: James, First Duke of Hamilton* (Edinburgh, 1975), p. 190.
5   J. R. Powell, *The Navy in the English Civil War* (Hamden, Conn., 1962), pp. 154–5.
6   ibid., pp. 165–6, 167, 170.
7   Powell, *Navy in the English Civil War*, p. 178. Scott, *King in Exile*, pp. 54–5.
8   D. Stevenson, *Revolution and Counter-Revolution in Scotland* (1977), pp. 112–13.
9   Powell, *Navy in the English Civil War*, pp. 176, 181.
10   ibid., pp. 182–3, 186–8.
11   P. Geyl, *Orange and Stuart* (1969), p. 45.
12   *CSP*, Vol. 3, pp. 13, 19, 33. D. Nicholas, *Mr Secretary Nicholas* (1955), pp. 236, 242.
13   Stevenson, *Revolution and Counter-Revolution*, p. 157.
14   ibid., pp. 155–6. Scott, *King in Exile*, pp. 102–3, 118–21.
15   D. Stevenson, *Alasdair MacColla and the Highland Problem* (Edinburgh, 1980), pp. 82–4, 122, 204, 207–9.
16   M. Napier, *Memoirs of Montrose* (Edinburgh, 1856), Vol. 2, pp. 705–6.
17   ibid., Vol. 2, p. 750. E. J. Cowan, *Montrose: for Covenant and King* (1977), pp. 270–3, 278.
18   Scott, *King in Exile*, pp. 100, 284–6. Clarendon, *History of the Rebellion*, Vol. 5, pp. 33–7, 78–97, 233.
19   Napier, *Memoirs of Montrose*, Vol. 2, p. 750. Cowan, *Montrose: for Covenant and King*, p. 272.
20   Napier, *Memoirs of Montrose*, Vol. 2, p. 704. Cowan, *Montrose: for Covenant and King*, p. 268.
21   Stevenson, *Revolution and Counter-Revolution*, pp. 149–51.
22   ibid., p. 153.
23   Stevenson, *Revolution and Counter-Revolution*, pp. 155–6.
24   ibid., pp. 155–6. Nicholas, *Mr Secretary Nicholas*, pp. 248, 249.
25   Napier, *Memoirs of Montrose*, Vol. 2, p. 752.
26   ibid., Vol. 2, pp. 700–5.
27   Napier, *Memoirs of Montrose*, Vol. 2, pp. 753–4.
28   *CSPD, 1650*, p. 61.
29   Cowan, *Montrose: for Covenant and King*, pp. 284–90. Napier, *Memoirs of Montrose*, Vol. 2, pp. 743–6.
30   Stevenson, *Revolution and Counter-Revolution*, p. 160.
31   Cowan, *Montrose: for Covenant and King*, pp. 280–1. Napier, *Memoirs of Montrose*, Vol. 2, pp. 758–62.
32   Stevenson, *Revolution and Counter-Revolution*, pp. 166–7.
33   Napier, *Memoirs of Montrose*, Vol. 2, pp. 764–5. J. Willcock, *The Great Marquess* (Edinburgh, 1903), p. 235.

34 ibid., pp. 302, 305, 309, 311, 314, 319, 321–2.
35 *CSPD, 1650*, pp. 186–7. Clarendon, *History of the Rebellion*, Vol. 5, pp. 107–9.
36 Geyl, *Orange and Stuart*, p. 52.
37 *CSP*, Vol. 3, p. 19. Nicholas, *Mr Secretary Nicholas*, p. 248.
38 S. R. Gardiner, *Letters and Papers Illustating the Relations between Charles II and Scotland in 1650* (1894), p. 2.
39 Geyl, *Orange and Stuart*, pp. 50, 53–4, 60–1, 65–6. Clarendon, *History of the Rebellion*, Vol. 5, p. 108.
40 Geyl, *Orange and Stuart*, p. 63.
41 ibid., p. 54. Gardiner, *Letters and Papers*, pp. 44–5, 51, 55–6, 58, 67, 69, 79.
42 Gardiner, *Letters and Papers*, pp. 141–2. Stevenson, *Revolution and Counter-Revolution*, p. 169.
43 Scott, *King in Exile*, pp. 166–8. Willcock, *Great Marquess*, pp. 241, 243–4, 264–5, 267, 269.
44 Scott, *King in Exile*, p. 176. Stevenson, *Revolution and Counter-Revolution*, p. 174.
45 Stevenson, *Revolution and Counter-Revolution*, p. 175. Willcock, *Great Marquess*, pp. 246–7, 253. C. S. Terry, *The Life and Campaigns of Alexander Leslie* (1899), pp. 454, 474.
46 Stevenson, *Revolution and Counter-Revolution*, pp. 176–7. Scott, *King in Exile*, pp. 177–9. *CSPD, 1650*, pp. 291–2, 321.
47 Stevenson, *Revolution and Counter-Revolution*, pp. 183–5.
48 G. Burnet, *History of his Own Time*, ed. M. J. Routh (Oxford, 1823), Vol. 1, p. 99.
49 T. Carte, *An History of the Life of James, Duke of Ormonde* (1736), Vol. 1, p. 391.
50 Stevenson, *Revolution and Counter-Revolution*, pp. 195, 199–200, 201–2, 203–5. Willcock, *Great Marquess*, pp. 256–7, 258, 270, 272.
51 Stevenson, *Revolution and Counter-Revolution*, pp. 201–2, 203–5.
52 Willcock, *Great Marquess*, p. 270.
53 D. Laing (ed.), *The Correspondence of Sir Robert Kerr* (Edinburgh, 1875), Vol. 2, p. 360.
54 Stevenson, *Revolution and Counter-Revolution*, pp. 205–6.
55 D. Underdown, *Royalist Conspiracy in England* (New Haven, Conn., 1960), pp. 50–1. *CSPD, 1651*, pp. 320–2, 337, 367.
56 R. Ollard, *The Image of the King* (1979), pp. 87–8.
57 R. Ollard, *The Escape of Charles II* (1966), pp. 25–7, 32–3, 37–8, 43–56.
58 Ollard, *Image of the King*, p. 86.
59 C. P. Korr, *Cromwell and the New Model Foreign Policy* (Berkeley, Calif., 1975), pp. 44–6.
60 E. Scott, *The Travels of the King* (1907), pp. 92–4, 95–6.
61 ibid., pp. 105, 162.
62 *CSP*, Vol. 3, pp. 88, 90, 92, 172, 184–5. *Thurloe State Papers*, Vol. 1, p. 449.
63 Geyl, *Orange and Stuart*, pp. 99–100, 104, 116–22.
64 ibid., p. 109. *Thurloe State Papers*, Vol. 1, p. 371.
65 Geyl, *Orange and Stuart*, p. 135. Clarendon, *History of the Rebellion*, Vol. 6, pp. 227–8, 233.
66 Korr, *Cromwell and the New Model Foreign Policy*, p. 39.
67 ibid., pp. 40, 44–5.

68 Korr, *Cromwell and the New Model Foreign Policy*, pp. 160–7, 182–4.
69 Clarendon, *History of the Rebellion*, Vol. 6, pp. 14–15, 43–4. G. F. Warner (ed.), *The Nicholas Papers*, Vol. 3 (1897), pp. 232–3, 279.
70 Scott, *Travels of the King*, pp. 362–3.
71 *CSP*, Vol. 3, p. 10.
72 ibid., Vol. 3, pp. 153, 157, 165, 191, 243, 257–8, 260–1.
73 *CSP*, Vol. 3, pp. 260–1; Vol. 4, pp. 59, 71.
74 ibid., Vol. 3, pp. 290–1. *Thurloe State Papers*, Vol. 1, pp. 740–4.
75 *Cal. Clarendon SP*, Vol. 4, pp. 30, 49, 55, 56, 163–4.
76 Scott, *Travels of the King*, pp. 355, 413. D. Townshend, *George Digby, Second Earl of Bristol* (1924), pp. 181–2.
77 *CSP*, Vol. 3, pp. 170, 297, 387. Warner, *Nicholas Papers*, Vol. 4 (1920), p. 13.
78 J. R. Jones, 'Booth's rising of 1659', *Bulletin of the John Rylands Library*, vol. 39, no. 2 (1957), pp. 417–26.
79 Underdown, *Royalist Conspiracy in England*, pp. 87–8, 93–4.
80 ibid., pp. 235–7, 238–40.
81 Underdown, *Royalist Conspiracy in England*, pp. 131–3.
82 *Cal. Clarendon SP*, Vol. 4, p. 2.
83 *CSP*, Vol. 3, pp. 315, 316–17, 331, 341.
84 ibid., Vol. 3, pp. 331, 341. Warner, *Nicholas Papers*, Vol. 3, pp. 264–5.
85 *CSP*, Vol. 3, p. 316.
86 R. S. Bosher, *The Making of the Restoration Settlement* (1957), pp. 89–93.

3 The Restoration

1 Warner, *Nicholas Papers*, Vol. 4, p. 76. *CSP*, Vol. 3, pp. 428, 458.
2 *CSP*, Vol. 3, pp. 500, 561, 592. *Cal. Clarendon SP*, Vol. 4, pp. 229, 381, 427–8. M. Coate (ed.), *The Letter-Book of John, Viscount Mordaunt* (1945), pp. 87–8.
3 *CSP*, Vol. 3, pp. 605, 622. Coate, *Letter-Book of John Mordaunt*, pp. 73, 83.
4 *CSP*, Vol. 3, p. 663.
5 ibid., Vol. 3, pp. 498, 512–13, 514–15, 536–7. *Cal. Clarendon SP*, Vol. 4, pp. 216, 541. Coate, *Letter-Book of John Mordaunt*, p. 13.
6 Coate, *Letter-Book of John Mordaunt*, p. 169 n.
7 *CSP*, Vol. 3, p. 437. *Cal. Clarendon SP*, Vol. 4, 638–9, 664, 672, 681. Warner, *Nicholas Papers*, Vol. 4, pp. 180–1.
8 Underdown, *Royalist Conspiracy in England*, pp. 254–85. Jones, 'Booth's rising'.
9 Underdown, *Royalist Conspiracy in England*, pp. 260, 263, 264–72. Jones, 'Booth's rising', pp. 435–6.
10 *CSP*, Vol. 3, pp. 548–9. *Cal. Clarendon SP*, Vol. 4, p. 406. *Nicholas Papers*, Vol. 4, pp. 167–8. Coate, *Letter-Book of John Mordaunt*, pp. 66–7.
11 Coate, *Letter-Book of John Mordaunt*, pp. 74, 75.
12 F. J. Routledge, *England and the Treaty of the Pyrenees* (Liverpool, 1953), pp. 53–4.
13 ibid., p. 20.
14 *Cal. Clarendon SP*, Vol. 4, p. 293.

15 Routledge, *England and the Treaty of the Pyrenees*, pp. 57–8.
16 *Cal. Clarendon SP*, Vol. 4, p. 363.
17 ibid., Vol. 4, pp. 460–1. Coate, *Letter-Book of John Mordaunt*, p. 108. Routledge, *England and the Treaty of the Pyrenees*, pp. 57–9.
18 Routledge, *England and the Treaty of the Pyrenees*, p. 59. Warner, *Nicholas Papers*, Vol. 4, pp. 183–6.
19 *CSP*, Vol. 3, p. 597. *Cal. Clarendon SP*. Vol. 4, p. 420.
20 Routledge, *England and the Treaty of the Pyrenees*, pp. 65–7.
21 ibid., pp. 71–2, 74. *Cal. Clarendon SP*, Vol. 4, pp. 356, 385, 420.
22 *Cal. Clarendon SP*, Vol. 4, p. 687. Routledge, *England and the Treaty of the Pyrenees*, pp. 79–80, 82, 87–8, 97–8, 101.
23 *CSP*, Vol. 3, pp. 670–1.
24 ibid., Vol. 3, pp. 412–14, 417–18.
25 *CSP*, Vol. 3, pp. 543, 618. T. Skinner, *The Life of General Monck* (1724), pp. 98–9.
26 *CSP*, Vol. 3, pp. 533, 672.
27 ibid., Vol. 3, pp. 651, 654, 661. *Cal. Clarendon SP*, Vol. 4, pp. 638–9. Warner, *Nicholas Papers*, Vol. 4, p. 194.
28 *Cal. Clarendon SP*, Vol. 4, pp. 545, 555. Skinner, *Life of General Monck*, pp. 210–12, 213–14, 217.
29 *Cal. Clarendon SP*, Vol. 4, pp. 572, 573, 578.
30 Warner, *Nicholas Papers*, Vol. 4, pp. 200–1, 205. Skinner, *Life of General Monck*, pp. 253–4, 256.
31 *CSP*, Vol. 3, p. 702. *Cal. Clarendon SP*, Vol. 4, pp. 565, 595. Skinner, *Life of General Monck*, p. 248. T. Gumble, *Life of General Monck* (1671), pp. 265–6, 273.
32 *CSP*, Vol. 3, pp. 710–11. *Cal. Clarendon SP*, Vol. 4, pp. 621–2.
33 *Cal. Clarendon SP*, Vol. 4, p. 620.
34 *CSP*, Vol. 3, pp. 705, 729–30. Gumble, *Life of General Monck*, pp. 260–1.
35 Coate, *Letter-Book of John Mordaunt*, p. 111.
36 *CSP*, Vol. 3, pp. 437, 529.
37 *Cal. Clarendon SP*, Vol. 4, pp. 640–1.
38 ibid., Vol. 4, p. 650. Routledge, *England and the Treaty of the Pyrenees*, pp. 103–5, 108, 112, 114. Clarendon, *History of the Rebellion*, Vol. 6, pp. 200–1.
39 Skinner, *Life of General Monck*, pp. 267–9, 273, 274–5, 284. Gumble, *Life of General Monck*, p. 121.
40 C. H. Firth and G. Davies, *Regimental History of Cromwell's Army* (Oxford, 1940), Vol. 1, pp. 158–61. W. H. Dawson, *Cromwell's Understudy: the Life and Times of John Lambert* (1938), pp. 389–91.
41 Gumble, *Life of General Monck*, pp. 484–6. Browning, *English Historical Documents*, Vol. 8, p. 58.
42 *Commons Journals*, Vol. 8, p. 6. Gumble, *Life of General Monck*, p. 370.
43 Gumble, *Life of General Monck*, pp. 393, 406–7. *Cal. Clarendon SP*, Vol. 4, p. 670.
44 *Commons Journals*, Vol. 8, p. 5.
45 S. B. Baxter, *The Development of the Treasury, 1660–1702* (1957), pp. 6, 266.
46 *CSP*, Vol. 3, p. 736.

47 Baxter, *Development of the Treasury*, pp. 9–11, 174–8. Edward Hyde, Earl of Clarendon, *The Life of Edward, Earl of Clarendon, Being a Continuation of the History of the Rebellion* (Oxford, 1827), Vol. 2, p. 234.

48 As Chamberlain (Manchester); privy councillor and lord-lieutenant (Northumberland); and vice-treasurer of Ireland (Annesley).

49 HMC, xiith Report, Appendix, Vol. 7, p. 29. R. C. Latham and W. Matthews, *The Diary of Samuel Pepys* (1970–83), Vol. 3, pp. 42–3 (7 Mar. 1662).

50 *Lords Journals*, Vol. 11, pp. 189, 224. *Commons Journals*, Vol. 8, pp. 188, 200–1. Clarendon, *Continuation of the History*, Vol. 2, p. 2.

51 *Commons Journals*, Vol. 8, p. 150. C. D. Chandaman, *The English Public Revenue, 1660–1688* (Oxford, 1975), pp. 200–6, 262–4.

52 For contrasting interpretations see Bosher, *Making of the Restoration Settlement*; I. M. Green, *The Re-establishment of the Church of England* (Oxford, 1978); G. R. Abernathy, 'The English Presbyterians and the Stuart Restoration', *Transactions of the American Philosophical Society*, new series, vol. 55, pt 2, pp. 1–101 (1965).

53 Bosher, *Making of the Restoration Settlement*, pp. 117–18, 119–20. Abernathy, 'English Presbyterians and the Stuart Restoration', pp. 67, 75, 76, 77. *Cal. Clarendon SP*, Vol. 4, p. 654.

54 *Commons Journals*, Vol. 8, p. 47. Green, *Re-establishment of the Church of England*, pp. 39, 46–7, 50–1.

55 Beddard, 'Restoration Church', pp. 161–4. On clerical reconstruction, see A. Whiteman, 'The Re-establishment of the Church of England, 1660–1663', *Transactions of the Royal Historical Society*, 5th series, vol. 5 (1955), pp. 111–32.

56 Browning, *English Historical Documents*, Vol. 8, pp. 365–70.

57 *Lords Journals*, Vol. 11, pp. 179–82.

58 *Commons Journals*, Vol. 8, p. 176.

59 Browning, *English Historical Documents*, Vol. 8, p. 365.

60 ibid., p. 369.

61 *Commons Journals*, Vol. 8, p. 194.

62 Green, *Re-establishment of the Church of England*, pp. 83–97. Bosher, *Making of the Restoration Settlement*, pp. 179–84.

63 Bosher, *Making of the Restoration Settlement*, pp. 97–9, 125.

64 Green, *Re-establishment of the Church of England*, p. 89.

65 Beddard, 'Restoration Church', pp. 161–3.

66 ibid., pp. 157–9, 170–1.

67 *CSP*, Vol. 3, pp. 116–17, 291, 458–9, 522. *Cal. Clarendon SP*, Vol. 4, pp. 49, 55–6, 179, 253.

68 S. Prall, *The Puritan Revolution* (1968), pp. 286–305.

69 *State Trials*, Vol. 5, pp. 1230–1302; Vol. 6, pp. 539–63.

70 A general account is given in I. Morley, *A Thousand Lives: an Account of the English Revolutionary Movement* (1954).

71 J. Miller, *James II: a Study in Kingship* (Hove, 1978), pp. 44–5.

72 Oman, *Henrietta Maria*, p. 286.

73 C. H. Hartmann, *Charles II and Madame* (1934), pp. 19–20, 24–5, 26, 29–30.

4 Charles and Clarendon

1 *Lords Journals*, Vol. 11, p. 241.
2 Morley's partisan bias in *A Thousand Lives* results in an exaggerated estimate of the importance of the radicals.
3 V. Rowe, *Sir Henry Vane the Younger* (1970), p. 241.
4 *CSP, Venetian, 1659–61*, p. 297.
5 Coate, *Letter-Book of John Mordaunt*, p. 97. Latham and Matthews, *Diary of Samuel Pepys*, Vol. 3, p. 127 (30 June 1662); Vol. 4, pp. 134–9 (15 May 1663).
6 Article v of the impeachment (Cobbett, *State Trials*, Vol. 6, pp. 323–94). A. Grey, *Debates of the House of Commons from the Year 1667 to the Year 1694* (1769), Vol. 1, pp. 15, 28, 32. R. Hutton, *The Restoration* (Oxford, 1985), pp. 133–4. *CSP, Venetian, 1661–64*, pp. 97, 206. H. M. Margoliouth (ed.), *The Poems and Letters of Andrew Marvell* (Oxford, 1952), Vol. 1, pp. 143–6.
7 Bosher, *Making of the Restoration Settlement*, p. 270.
8 *Lords Journals*, Vol. 11, p. 303. *Commons Journals*, Vol. 8, pp. 249–50, 252, 271–2, 278, 295.
9 *Lords Journals*, Vol. 11, p. 495 (19 March 1663).
10 *Commons Journals*, Vol. 8, p. 285. Bosher, *Making of the Restoration Settlement*, pp. 224–5. Beddard, 'Restoration Church', p. 165.
11 *Lords Journals*, Vol. 11, p. 322. *Commons Journals*, Vol. 8, pp. 275, 279, 291, 301–2, 310–13, 337.
12 Beddard, 'Restoration Church', pp. 160–1.
13 *Lords Journals*, Vol. 11, pp. 478–9. *Commons Journals*, Vol. 8, pp. 440, 443.
14 *Commons Journals*, Vol. 8, p. 254.
15 Beddard, 'Restoration Church', pp. 165–6, 167.
16 *Lords Journals*, Vol. 11, p. 333.
17 Bosher, *Making of the Restoration Settlement*, pp. 250–2.
18 ibid., pp. 260–4.
19 Bosher, *Making of the Restoration Settlement*, pp. 266–7.
20 T. H. Lister, *The Life and Administration of Edward, First Earl of Clarendon* (1837–8), Vol. 3, pp. 198–201, 232–3. Browning, *English Historical Documents*, Vol. 8, pp. 371–4.
21 Browning, *English Historical Documents*, Vol. 8, p. 374. *Lords Journals*, Vol. 11, p. 474.
22 *Lords Journals*, Vol. 11, pp. 478–9.
23 *Commons Journals*, Vol. 8, pp. 442–3.
24 *Lords Journals*, Vol. 11, pp. 482, 484, 485, 487–9, 490, 491, 492.
25 R. A. Beddard, 'Sheldon and Anglican recovery', *Historical Journal*, vol. 19 (1976), pp. 1009–10. K. H. D. Haley, *The First Earl of Shaftesbury* (Oxford, 1968), p. 165. For Goffe see the entry in the *Dictionary of National Biography*.
26 HMC, Ormonde, new series, Vol. 3, p. 47. Lister, *Life of Clarendon*, Vol. 3, pp. 243, 244–5.
27 Lady Burghclere, *George Villiers, Second Duke of Buckingham* (1903), pp. 122–30.
28 C. H. Hartmann, *The King's Friend* (1951), pp. 72–83. Clarendon, *Continuation of the History*, Vol. 2, pp. 357, 395–6. H. C. Foxcroft, *A Supplement to Burnet's History of my Own Time* (Oxford, 1902), p. 65, Latham and

Matthews, *Diary of Samuel Pepys*, Vol. 3, pp. 121–3, 226–7, 302–3 (27 June, 17 Oct., 31 Dec. 1662); Vol. 4, pp. 255–6 (31 July 1663); Vol. 5, pp. 344–6 (15 Dec. 1664).

29 Haley, *First Earl of Shaftesbury*, p. 169.

30 Clarendon, *Continuation of the History*, Vol. 1, pp. 367–72. Lister, *Life of Clarendon*, Vol. 3, pp. 223–5, 225–7. V. Barbour, *Henry Bennet, Earl of Arlington* (Washington, DC, 1914), p. 57.

31 Clarendon, *Continuation of the History*, Vol. 2, pp. 197–8, 204–10. D. T. Witcombe, *Charles II and the Cavalier House of Commons, 1663–1674* (Manchester, 1966), pp. 21–2.

32 Clarendon, *Continuation of the History*, Vol. 2, p. 460.

33 Townshend, *George Digby, Second Earl of Bristol*, pp. 228–9.

34 *Commons Journals*, Vol. 8, pp. 502, 503, 511.

35 ibid., Vol. 8, pp. 511, 512, 514–15. Townshend, *George Digby, Second Earl of Bristol*, p. 226. Latham and Matthews, *Diary of Samuel Pepys*, Vol. 4, pp. 207–13 (1, 2 July 1663).

36 Townshend, *George Digby, Second Earl of Bristol*, pp. 229–30. *Lords Journals*, Vol. 11, pp. 547, 555–7.

37 *Lords Journals*, Vol. 11, pp. 555–6.

38 ibid., Vol. 11, pp. 559, 560. Townshend, *George Digby, Second Earl of Bristol*, pp. 228–9, 230–2. Latham and Matthews, *Diary of Samuel Pepys*, Vol. 5, pp. 88–9 (17 Mar. 1664).

39 H. Roseveare, *The Treasury, 1660–1870* (1973), pp. 20–1.

40 Witcombe, *Charles II and the Cavalier House of Commons*, pp. 9–22. P. C. Seward, 'Court faction and the parliamentary session of 1663', Fellowship dissertation, Christ's College, Cambridge (1984).

41 HMC, Ormonde, new series, Vol. 3, pp. 52–3.

42 *Lords Journals*, Vol. 11, pp. 579–80.

43 ibid., Vol. 11, pp. 582–3.

44 HMC, Ormonde, new series, Vol. 3, p. 78.

45 ibid., Vol. 3, pp. 89, 93.

46 W. D. Macray, *Notes which passed at Meetings of the Privy Council between Charles II and the Earl of Clarendon* (1896), p. 65.

47 HMC, Ormonde, new series, Vol. 3, pp. 103, 109, 118.

48 ibid., Vol. 3, pp. 104, 118, 123.

49 HMC, Ormonde, new series, Vol. 3, pp. 117–18. E. M. Thompson (ed.), *Correspondence of the Family of Hatton* (1878), Vol. 1, p. 34.

50 Hartmann, *The King's Friend*, pp. 72, 75, 79, 102, 174–5.

51 K. G. Feiling, *British Foreign Policy, 1660–1672* (1930), pp. 34, 46–9, 57–8.

52 ibid., pp. 59–62.

53 Feiling, *British Foreign Policy, 1660–1672*, pp. 93–7.

54 A. Bryant, *King Charles II* (1974), pp. 135–9.

55 Clarendon, *Continuation of the History*, Vol. 2, pp. 234, 235, 237–8, 240–1.

56 Hartmann, *Charles II and Madame*, p. 113.

57 *Commons Journals*, Vol. 8, p. 548.

58 Feiling, *British Foreign Policy, 1660–1672*, pp. 135–6. R. Ollard, *Man of War* (1969), pp. 86–7, 95.

59 Feiling, *British Foreign Policy, 1660–1672*, pp. 142, 144–5, 149–50.

60 *CSPD, 1664–5*, p. 460; *1665–6*, p. 366.
61 C. Robbins (ed.), *The Diary of John Milward* (Cambridge, 1938), pp. 20–1.
62 ibid., pp. 24, 38. *Commons Journals*, Vol. 8, pp. 636, 637–8, 640, 641.
63 HMC, Ormonde, new series, Vol. 3, pp. 53, 58. Carte, *Life of Ormonde*, Vol. 2, pp. 317–21, 322–3, 329–32. C. A. Edie, 'The Irish Cattle Bills', *Transactions of the American Philosophical Society*, new series, Vol. 60, no. 2, pp. 1–35 (1970).
64 Edie, 'Irish Cattle Bills', pp. 5, 6, 11–13.
65 ibid., pp. 23, 25, 28, 30, 33–4. Carte, *Life of Ormonde*, Vol. 2, pp. 333–4.
66 *Lords Journals*, Vol. 12, p. 81.
67 ibid., Vol. 12, pp. 56, 77–9, 94. *Commons Journals*, Vol. 8, pp. 666–7, 681, 684–6, 689.
68 Robbins, *Diary of John Milward*, p. 39. A. Browning, *Thomas Osborne, Earl of Danby* (Glasgow, 1944–51), Vol. 2, pp. 32–3. J. R. Jones, *Country and Court* (1978), p. 159. *CTB, 1667–8*, pp. xlviii–li, lxx.
69 Chandaman, *English Public Revenue, 1666–1688*, pp. 209–13. *Lords Journals*, Vol. 12, p. 110.
70 P. G. Rogers, *The Dutch in the Medway* (1970), pp. 53, 83–115, 133–43. *Commons Journals*, Vol. 9, pp. 11–14.
71 Latham and Matthews, *Diary of Samuel Pepys*, Vol. 8, pp. 92–4, 108, 330–1, 342–3, 362 (3, 11 Mar., 12, 17, 29 July 1667).
72 Clarendon, *Continuation of the History*, Vol. 3, pp. 252–8.
73 Robbins, *Diary of John Milward*, pp. 82–4. *Commons Journals*, Vol. 8, p. 692
74 *Lords Journals*, Vol. 12, p. 114. Robbins, *Diary of John Milward*, p. 84.
75 C. Roberts, 'The impeachment of the Earl of Clarendon', *Cambridge Historical Journal*, vol. 13, no. 1 (1957), pp. 3–5.
76 Witcombe, *Charles II and the Cavalier House of Commons*, pp. 66, 77, 78–81. Carte, *Life of Ormonde*, Vol. 2, pp. 361–2.
77 ibid., Vol. 2, pp. 362–3. Robbins, *Diary of John Milward*, pp. 214–22, 248–50.
78 Roberts, 'Impeachment of the Earl of Clarendon', p. 8.
79 ibid., pp. 5–6.
80 Robbins, *Diary of John Milward*, pp. 99–100.
81 *Commons Journals*, Vol. 9, p. 18. Grey, *Debates*, Vol. 1, pp. 29–32.
82 *Lords Journals*, Vol. 12, p. 135.
83 ibid., Vol. 12, pp. 137, 141.
84 *Lords Journals*, Vol. 12, pp. 158, 160, 167–8.
85 J. S. Clarke, *Life of James II* (1816), Vol. 2, p. 628.
86 *Lords Journals*, Vol. 12, pp. 332–3.
87 *Commons Journals*, Vol. 8, p. 377.
88 ibid., Vol. 8, pp. 500–1, 509.
89 *Commons Journals*, Vol. 8, pp. 672–3.
90 ibid., Vol. 8, p. 683. *Lords Journals*, Vol. 12, p. 111.
91 Roseveare, *Treasury, 1660–1870*, pp. 58–64. Baxter, *Development of the Treasury*, pp. 11–14, 39–44.
92 Witcombe, *Charles II and the Cavalier House of Commons*, pp. 36–7.
93 HMC, xiith Report, Appendix, Vol. 7, p. 42. Latham and Matthews, *Diary of Samuel Pepys*, Vol. 7, p. 271 (2 Sept. 1666).

5   *The 'Cabal' and its Projects*

1   Roberts, 'Impeachment of the Earl of Clarendon', pp. 15–18.
2   Latham and Matthews, *Diary of Samuel Pepys*, Vol. 9, pp. 336–7, 386–7, 462–3, 466–8, 471–2, 473, 475–6, 477–8 (23 Oct., 7 Dec. 1668; 1, 4, 6, 7, 9, 10 Mar. 1669). Hartmann, *Charles II and Madame*, p. 236.
3   Feiling, *British Foreign Policy, 1660–1672*, pp. 253–7.
4   *CSPD, 1667–8*, pp. 258–9. Foxcroft, *Supplement to Burnet's History of my Own Time*, p. 66.
5   *CSPD, 1667*, pp. 518, 523. Browning, *Thomas Osborne, Earl of Danby*, Vol. 1, pp. 60–1. H. Chapman, *Great Villiers* (1949), pp. 140–1.
6   Robbins, *Diary of John Milward*, p. 226. Burnet, *History of his Own Time*, Vol. 1, p. 501; Vol. 2, p. 1.
7   Grey, *Debates*, Vol. 1, pp. 3–5, 157–9, 163–4, 165–8, 169–70, 170–4, 178–9, 180–2, 213–15.
8   *Lords Journals*, Vol. 12, p. 181. HMC, xivth Report, Appendix, Vol. 4, p. 81.
9   Grey, *Debates*, Vol. 1, pp. 126–32. *Commons Journals*, Vol. 9, p. 77. F. Bate, *The Declaration of Indulgence* (1908), pp. 59–62.
10 Grey, *Debates*, Vol. 1, pp. 82–4. *Commons Journals*, Vol. 9, pp. 52, 70. Latham and Matthews, *Diary of Samuel Pepys*, Vol. 9, pp. 77–8 (18 Feb. 1668).
11 Browning, *Thomas Osborne, Earl of Danby*, Vol. 1, pp. 70–1, 74–5. Bate, *Declaration of Indulgence*, pp. 62, 65–6. Browning, *English Historical Documents*, Vol. 8, pp. 384–6. B. D. Henning (ed.), *The Parliamentary Diary of Sir Edward Dering* (New Haven, Conn., 1940), pp. 6–7.
12 *CSPD, 1673*, p. 62. Carte; *Life of Ormonde*, Vol. 2, pp. 413–15.
13 Carte, *Life of Ormonde*, Vol. 2, p. 372.
14 ibid., Vol. 2, p. 374. HMC, xiith Report, Appendix, Vol. 7, p. 61. W. Westergaard, *The First Triple Alliance* (New Haven, Conn., 1947), pp. 32, 37.
15 Latham and Matthews, *Diary of Samuel Pepys*, Vol. 10, pp. 77–8.
16 F. A. Mignet, *Négociations relatives à la succession d'Espagne sous Louis XIV* (Paris, 1835–42), Vol. 2, pp. 40, 43, 44–5; Vol. 3, pp. 31–2.
17 ibid., Vol. 2, pp. 515, 516–17.
18 Mignet, *Négociations*, Vol. 2, pp. 517–18, 520–1, 525, 527.
19 ibid., Vol. 2, pp. 513, 525, 527–8; Vol. 3, pp. 59, 60–1, 62–3, 64–5, 66–7. HMC, Buccleuch, p. 502.
20 Mignet, *Négociations*, Vol. 2, pp. 512, 529, 537–8.
21 Feiling, *British Foreign Policy 1660–1672*, pp. 249–56.
22 Mignet, *Négociations*, Vol. 2, pp. 561–2, 563, 564; Vol. 3, p. 9. H. H. Rowen, *The Ambassador Prepares for War* (The Hague, 1957), pp. 23, 28–9.
23 Mignet, *Négociations*, Vol. 3, pp. 9, 14–17, 45.
24 ibid., Vol. 3, pp. 10–11, 18. Hartmann, *Charles II and Madame*, pp. 200, 227, 229–32, 236–7, 240–2, 247–50, 254–60, 277–81, 292–5.
25 Mignet, *Négociations*, Vol. 3, p. 97. Hartmann, *Charles II and Madame*, p. 223. Sir J. Dalrymple, *Memoirs of Great Britain and Ireland* (1771–3), Vol. 2, p. 22. Clarke, *Life of James II*, Vol. 1, pp. 441–3.
26 Hartmann, *Charles II and Madame*, pp. 262–7. C. H. Hartmann, *Clifford of the Cabal* (1937), pp. 34–5. M. B. Curran (ed.), *The Despatches of William Perwich* (1903), pp. 17–18, 27, 101, 114, 115, 138.

27 Feiling, *British Foreign Policy 1660–1672*, pp. 292–3. Hartmann, *Charles II and Madame*, pp. 235, 258, 264, 266, 281–2. Mignet, *Négociations*, Vol. 3, pp. 86, 91, 100, 135, 144–5, 147–9.

28 Mignet, *Négociations*, Vol. 3, pp. 34–5, 36–7, 52–4, 84, 89, 90–1, 94. Hartmann, *Charles II and Madame*, pp. 231–2, 245, 255. Dalrymple, *Memoirs*, Vol. 2, pp. 24, 43, 76, 82.

29 Feiling, *British Foreign Policy*, p. 300.

30 Westergaard, *First Triple Alliance*, p. 249. H. H. Rowen, *John de Witt* (Princeton, NJ, 1978), pp. 731, 732, 744–5. *CSP, Venetian, 1669–71*, p. 178; *CSP, Venetian, 1671–72*, p. 23.

31 Mignet, *Négociations*, Vol. 3, pp. 117–23, 161–3. Browning, *English Historical Documents*, Vol. 8, pp. 863–7.

32 Mignet, *Négociations*, Vol. 4, p. 35.

33 ibid., Vol. 3, pp. 102–6, 229, 232. Dalrymple, *Memoirs*, Vol. 2, pp. 83, 84. *CSP, Venetian, 1671–2*, pp. 178, 179.

34 Arthur Capel, Earl of Essex, *Correspondence of Arthur Capel, Earl of Essex*, Vol. 1, ed. O. Airy (1890), p. 155.

35 HMC, viith Report, Appendix, pt. 1, pp. 267, 269, 270, 276, 404. Dalrymple published his *Memoirs of Great Britain and Ireland* in three volumes between 1771 and 1773.

36 Mignet, *Négociations*, Vol. 3, pp. 221–2, 247–50, 255–6, 256–65. *CSP, Venetian, 1669–71*, pp. 247, 278. HMC, Buccleuch, p. 496.

37 Mignet, *Négociations*, Vol. 3, p. 218. Geyl, *Orange and Stuart*, p. 324.

38 *Lords Journals*, Vol. 12, pp. 251, 287–8.

39 HMC, xivth Report, Appendix, Vol. 4, p. 84.

40 A. W. Thibaudeau, *The Bulstrode Papers* (1897), Vol. 1, p. 133. Clarendon, *Continuation of the History*, Vol. 3, p. 386.

41 *Commons Journals*, Vol. 9, p. 181. Westergaard, *First Triple Alliance*, pp. 348, 351–2. Henning, *Parliamentary Diary of Sir Edward Dering*, p. 27. *CSP, Venetian, 1669–71*, pp. 316–17.

42 *Lords Journals*, Vol. 12, pp. 515–16.

43 HMC, Buccleuch, p. 487.

44 Thibaudeau, *Bulstrode Papers*, Vol. 1, pp. 176–7. Henning, *Parliamentary Diary of Sir Edward Dering*, pp. 70–1, 80, 94, 95.

45 Miller, *James II: a Study in Kingship*, pp. 61–4.

46 Barbour, *Henry Bennet, Earl of Arlington*, pp. 155–7, 158–60, 162–3. M. Lee, *The Cabal* (Urbana, Ill., 1965), pp. 70–118.

47 Lee, *Cabal*, pp. 149, 156. Hartmann, *Clifford of the Cabal*, pp. 235, 248–9.

48 Lee, *Cabal*, pp. 119–60. K. G. Feiling, *A History of the Tory Party, 1641–1714* (Oxford, 1924), pp. 138, 139.

49 Hartmann, *Clifford of the Cabal*, pp. 153–5, 265. Barbour, *Henry Bennet, Earl of Arlington*, p. 140.

50 Lee, *Cabal*, pp. 151–5. Essex, *Correspondence of Essex*, Vol. 1, pp. 120–1. Thompson, *Correspondence of the Family of Hatton*, Vol. 1, p. 100.

51 Henning, *Parliamentary Diary of Sir Edward Dering*, pp. 143, 144. Westergaard, *First Triple Alliance*, pp. 382, 429, 434. HMC, Ormonde, new series, Vol. 3, p. 446.

52 *CSPD, 1671–2*, pp. 166, 185. See also *CSPD, 1671*, p. 432.

53 *CSPD, 1671–2*, p. 299. *CSPD, 1673*, pp. 62, 100–1, 558–9.
54 Robbins, *Diary of John Milward*, p. 215.
55 Westergaard, *First Triple Alliance*, pp. 255, 256. Bate, *Declaration of Indulgence*, p. 73. Thibaudeau, *Bulstrode Papers*, Vol. 1, pp. 140, 143, 145.
56 Browning, *English Historical Documents*, Vol. 8, pp. 387–8.
57 *CSP, Venetian, 1671–2*, pp. 162, 186.
58 Grey, *Debates*, Vol. 2, pp. 13–26, 26–37, 48–54, 54–60, 62–9, 91–2. Bate, *Declaration of Indulgence*, p. 115.
59 *CSPD, 1672–3*, pp. xxxvii–lxiv, 226, 232, 271, 282, 289, 381–2.
60 *CSPD, 1671–2*, pp. 76, 94, 105, 180, 189, 194.
61 ibid., pp. 469–70. *CSP, Venetian, 1671–2*, pp. 218–19, 243.
62 *CSP, Venetian, 1671–2*, pp. 290–1. Thibaudeau, *Bulstrode Papers*, Vol. 1, pp. 236–7, 238–9. Hartmann, *Charles II and Madame*, pp. 222, 338, 342.
63 Geyl, *Orange and Stuart*, pp. 349–50, 353. D. J. Roorda, *Partij en Factie* (Groningen, 1961), pp. 110–30, 256–8.
64 Geyl, *Orange and Stuart*, pp. 364–9. Mignet, *Négociations*, Vol. 4, pp. 45, 49. H. T. Colenbrander, *Bescheiden uit Vreemde Archieven* (The Hague, 1919), Vol. 2, pp. 141–2, 145, 146–8, 154–9, 164–5, 167–8.
65 Geyl, *Orange and Stuart*, p. 370. Mignet, *Négociations*, Vol. 4, pp. 48–9.
66 Geyl, *Orange and Stuart*, pp. 320–4. S. B. Baxter, *William III* (1966), pp. 55–6.
67 *CSPD, 1671–2*, pp. 42–3. Westergaard, *First Triple Alliance*, pp. 500–1.
68 N. Japikse (ed.), *Correspondentie van Willem III en van Hans Willem Bentinck* (The Hague, 1927–37), Vol. 1, p. 71.
69 ibid., Vol. 1, pp. 41, 43, 48.
70 Japikse, *Correspondentie van Willem III*, Vol. 1, pp. 62, 80: Vol. 2, pp. 40–1.
71 ibid., Vol. 1, pp. 72, 73–4, 86, 108–9. Colenbrander, *Bescheiden uit Vreemde Archieven*, Vol. 2, pp. 189–92, 193, 195.
72 Japikse, *Correspondentie van Willem III*, Vol. 1, p. 86. Haley, *William of Orange and the English Opposition*, p. 50.
73 Japikse, *Correspondentie van Willem III*, Vol. 1, pp. 115–16. Baxter, *William III*, p. 87. Geyl, *Orange and Stuart*, p. 419.
74 Japikse, *Correspondentie van Willem III*, pp. 114–15, 257–8, 259.
75 Haley, *William of Orange and the English Opposition*, pp. 50–1, 52–66.
76 *CSP, Venetian, 1671–2*, p. 9. J. Childs, *The Army of Charles II* (1976), p. 182.
77 Haley, *First Earl of Shaftesbury*, pp. 304–6, 319–22. Lee, *Cabal*, p. 221.
78 *Lords Journals*, Vol. 12, pp. 524–5.
79 ibid., Vol. 12, pp. 525–7. Haley, *First Earl of Shaftesbury*, pp. 316–17.
80 Henning, *Parliamentary Diary of Sir Edward Dering*, pp. 104, 105–6, 108–9.
81 *Commons Journals*, Vol. 9, p. 252.
82 Barbour, *Henry Bennet, Earl of Arlington*, p. 208.
83 *Commons Journals*, Vol. 9, p. 256. Henning, *Parliamentary Diary of Sir Edward Dering*, p. 131.
84 *Commons Journals*, Vol. 9, p. 257.
85 ibid., Vol. 9, pp. 259–60.
86 *CSP, Venetian, 1673–5*, pp. 19, 27.
87 ibid., pp. 22, 27. Mignet, *Négociations*, Vol. 4, p. 156. Dalrymple, *Memoirs*, Vol. 2, pp. 93–4. PRO, Baschet Transcripts, Colbert de Croissy, 20 Mar. 1673.

88 *CSPD, 1673*, pp. 24, 367–8.
89 W. D. Christie (ed.), *Letters Addressed from London to Sir Joseph Williamson* (1874), Vol. 1, pp. 2, 4, 6, 51. *CSP, Venetian, 1673–5*, p. 31. Colenbrander, *Bescheiden uit Vreemde Archieven*, Vol. 2, p. 283.
90 *CSP, Venetian, 1673–5*, pp. 100, 114, 121.
91 ibid., p. 183. *CSPD, 1673–5*, pp. 32–3. Mignet, *Négociations*, Vol. 4, pp. 225–6, 229–32.
92 Barbour, *Henry Bennet, Earl of Arlington*, pp. 222, 236–7. Lee, *Cabal*, pp. 234, 236–7.
93 Browning, *Thomas Osborne, Earl of Danby*, Vol. 1, pp. 110–11. *CSPD, 1673*, pp. 465, 477.
94 Haley, *First Earl of Shaftesbury*, pp. 260, 262, 296–9, 316–17.
95 Hartmann, *Clifford of the Cabal*, pp. 202, 221, 307–11.
96 *CSPD, 1673–5*, pp. 103–6. *CSP, Venetian, 1673–5*, pp. 106, 114. Essex, *Correspondence of Essex*, Vol. 1, pp. 132–3.
97 Miller, *James II: a Study in Kingship*, pp. 62–3.
98 *CSP, Venetian, 1673–5*, p. 187.

6 Charles and Danby: Crown and Church

1 *CSP, Venetian, 1673–5*, pp. 105, 121. *CSPD, 1673*, pp. 510, 524–5. Colenbrander, *Bescheiden uit Vreemde Archieven*, Vol. 2, pp. 309–10, 355–6, 356–8.
2 Thompson, *Correspondence of the Family of Hatton*, Vol. 1, p. 111.
3 *CSP, Venetian, 1673–5*, p. 40.
4 *Commons Journals*, Vol. 9, pp. 286–7.
5 *CSPD, 1673*, p. 37. Essex, *Correspondence of Essex*, Vol. 1, pp. 130–1.
6 Browning, *Thomas Osborne, Earl of Danby*, Vol. 1, pp. 90, 102. *CSPD, 1673–5*, p. 266. *CSP, Venetian, 1673–5*, p. 73. Christie, *Letters to Williamson*, Vol. 1, p. 99.
7 Haley, *First Earl of Shaftesbury*, pp. 342–7. *CSP, Venetian, 1673–5*, pp. 37, 161.
8 Browning, *Thomas Osborne, Earl of Danby*, Vol. 2, pp. 31–4. Christie, *Letters to Williamson*, Vol. 1, pp. 99, 102, 108. Essex, *Correspondence of Essex*, Vol. 1, pp. 132–3.
9 Essex, *Correspondence of Essex*, Vol. 1, pp. 258–9, 260.
10 Browning, *Thomas Osborne, Earl of Danby*, Vol. 1, pp. 167–73; Vol. 3, pp. 65–8, 68–71, 71–111.
11 ibid., Vol. 2, p. 70. Mignet, *Négociations*, Vol. 4, p. 237.
12 *CSPD, 1673*, pp. 463, 524–5, 598. *CSP, Venetian, 1673–5*, p. 72. Christie, *Letters to Williamson*, Vol. 1, pp. 106, 116–17, 143.
13 Christie, *Letters to Williamson*, Vol. 1, p. 106. *CSPD, 1673*, pp. 442, 448, 455, 498, 524–5. *CSP, Venetian, 1673–5*, pp. 76, 89.
14 Haley, *William of Orange and the English Opposition*, pp. 88–132.
15 ibid., pp. 97–8, 100–5.
16 Haley, *William of Orange and the English Opposition*, pp. 52–65.
17 *CSP, Venetian, 1673–5*, pp. 106, 163. Mignet, *Négociations*, Vol. 4, pp. 236, 253, 255, 259.
18 Essex, *Correspondence of Essex*, Vol. 1, p. 155.

19   *CSP, Venetian, 1673–5*, pp. 175, 176, 177, 206.

20   Browning, *Thomas Osborne, Earl of Danby*, Vol. 2, pp. 63–4, 65.

21   *CSP, Venetian, 1673–5*, pp. 69, 183. Essex, *Correspondence of Essex*, Vol. 1, p. 132.

22   Grey, *Debates*, Vol. 2, pp. 182, 189, 190–6, 214–15, 222. Henning, *Parliamentary Diary of Sir Edward Dering*, pp. 150, 155–6, 160–1.

23   *CSP, Venetian, 1673–5*, pp. 192–3. *CSPD, 1673–5*, pp. 131–2, 588. Thompson, *Correspondence of the Family of Hatton*, Vol. 1, p. 119.

24   Browning, *Thomas Osborne, Earl of Danby*, Vol. 1, p. 120. Essex, *Correspondence of Essex*, Vol. 1, pp. 153, 228, 232, 286.

25   *CSP, Venetian, 1673–5*, p. 84. Christie, *Letters to Williamson*, Vol. 1, pp. 73–119. British Library, Add. MSS, 29571, fols. 226, 228.

26   Browning, *Thomas Osborne, Earl of Danby*, Vol. 1, pp. 112–14. Essex, *Correspondence of Essex*, Vol. 1, p. 155.

27   Essex, *Correspondence of Essex*, Vol. 1, p. 161. *Commons Journals*, Vol. 9, p. 287.

28   Christie, *Letters to Williamson*, Vol. 2, pp. 105–6, 111–12, 115, 119. Grey, *Debates*, Vol. 2, pp. 248–53, 253–70.

29   Grey, *Debates*, Vol. 2, pp. 274–301, 301–17.

30   *Lords Journals*, Vol. 12, pp. 616–18. *Commons Journals*, Vol. 9, p. 298.

31   *Commons Journals*, Vol. 9, pp. 299, 307.

32   Mignet, *Négociations*, Vol. 4, pp. 319, 321. Essex, *Correspondence of Essex*, Vol. 1, pp. 180, 256, 259–60.

33   Browning, *Thomas Osborne, Earl of Danby*, Vol. 2, p. 63.

34   *CSP, Venetian, 1673–5*, p. 257. *CSPD, 1673–5*, p. 238. HMC, xiith Report, Appendix, Vol. 7, p. 110.

35   *CSP, Venetian, 1673–5*, pp. 206, 279.

36   *CSPD, 1673–5*, pp. 263–4, 275, 277, 284, 288, 299, 306, 320. Burnet, *History of his Own Time*, Vol. 2, p. 55.

37   Haley, *William of Orange and the English Opposition*, pp. 209–10, 213. Mignet, *Négociations*, Vol. 4, p. 325. *CSPD, 1673–5*, pp. 399–400.

38   Japikse, *Correspondentie van Willem III*, Vol. 1, pp. 338, 342.

39   Mignet, *Négociations*, Vol. 4, p. 315.

40   ibid., Vol. 4, pp. 321–2, 326. Carte, *Life of Ormonde*, Vol. 2, p. 449.

41   Mignet, *Négociations*, Vol. 4, pp. 322–3, 324, 327.

42   *Commons Journals*, Vol. 9, p. 314.

43   *CSP, Venetian, 1673–5*, pp. 316–17, 318, 324, 327, 337, 390. Essex, *Correspondence of Essex*, Vol. 1, p. 285. Miller, *James II: a Study in Kingship*, pp. 77–8.

44   Browning, *Thomas Osborne, Earl of Danby*, Vol. 1, pp. 147, 149. *CSP, Venetian, 1673–5*, pp. 353–4, 357. *CSPD, 1673–5*, pp. 390, 416, 548–9, 550–1. Essex, *Correspondence of Essex*, Vol. 1, pp. 293–5, 298.

45   Essex, *Correspondence of Essex*, Vol. 1, p. 298. *CSP, Venetian, 1673–5*, p. 368. *CSPD, 1673–5*, p. 571.

46   *Commons Journals*, Vol. 9, pp. 314–15. *CSP, Venetian, 1673–5*, p. 393. Thibaudeau, *Bulstrode Papers*, Vol. 1, p. 284.

47   Thibaudeau, *Bulstrode Papers*, Vol. 1, pp. 285, 286, 287, 289, 294, 296. Burnet, *History of his Own Time*, Vol. 2, pp. 54, 73–5. *Lords Journals*, Vol. 12, pp. 655, 664–6, 668–9, 673–4, 677, 691.

48 *Commons Journals*, Vol. 9, pp. 316–17, 321, 322–3, 324–6, 327–8, 328–9, 330–2. Grey, *Debates*, Vol. 3, pp. 24–9, 49–56, 57–69, 72–82, 83–96.
49 Thibaudeau, *Bulstrode Papers*, Vol. 1, p. 291.
50 *Lords Journals*, Vol. 12, p. 674.
51 ibid., Vol. 12, pp. 725, 726, 729. Thibaudeau, *Bulstrode Papers*, Vol. 1, pp. 290, 292–3, 296, 297, 298–9, 300, 301. *CSP, Venetian, 1673–5*, p. 416.
52 Thibaudeau, *Bulstrode Papers*, Vol. 1, p. 302.
53 A. Marvell, 'A Seasonable Argument' in Browning, *English Historical Documents*, Vol. 8, pp. 237–49.
54 Mignet, *Négociations*, Vol. 4, pp. 330–1, 332–3.
55 ibid., Vol. 4, pp. 368–70.
56 Mignet, *Négociations*, Vol. 4, p. 370.
57 Browning, *Thomas Osborne, Earl of Danby*, Vol. 1, pp. 191–4; Vol. 3, pp. 68–71, 71–111. *CSPD, 1676–7*, pp. 480, 488. Thibaudeau, *Bulstrode Papers*, Vol. 1, pp. 303, 314.
58 Thibaudeau, *Bulstrode Papers*, Vol. 1, pp. 315–16, 317–19, 320–1, 322–4.
59 Mignet, *Négociations*, Vol. 4, pp. 375–6, 377.
60 ibid., Vol. 4, pp. 426–7.
61 *CSPD, 1673–5*, pp. 559, 560–1, 562. HMC, xiith Report, Appendix, Vol. 7, p. 125.
62 HMC, xiith Report, Appendix, Vol. 7, p. 123. *CSPD, 1673–5*, p. 465. Browning, *Thomas Osborne, Earl of Danby*, Vol. 1, pp. 194–5. Haley, *First Earl of Shaftesbury*, pp. 403–4.
63 Browning, *Thomas Osborne, Earl of Danby*, Vol. 1, p. 199. *CSPD, 1676–7*, pp. 51, 75, 81. Bate, *Declaration of Indulgence*, pp. 139–43. HMC, xiith Report, Appendix, Vol. 7, p. 125. Thompson, *Correspondence of the Family of Hatton*, Vol. 1, pp. 128–9.
64 Thompson, *Correspondence of the Family of Hatton*, Vol. 1, pp. 132–3. *CSPD, 1676–7*, pp. 184, 194, 215, 232, 253–4. Essex, *Correspondence of Arthur Capel, Earl of Essex*, Vol. 2, ed. C. E. Pike (1913), pp. 60–1, 63, 69–70, 103–5.
65 Mignet, *Négociations*, Vol. 4, p. 405. British Library, Add MSS, 39672, fol. 41.
66 Mignet, *Négociations*, Vol. 4, pp. 440–1. Grey, *Debates*, Vol. 4, pp. 304–15, 332–4, 349–50, 355–61.
67 Mignet, *Négociations*, Vol. 4, pp. 430–1.
68 ibid., Vol. 4, p. 434. Dalrymple, *Memoirs*, Vol. 2, p. 110.
69 Mignet, *Négociations*, Vol. 4, pp. 434, 476–7, 479.
70 *Commons Journals*, Vol. 9, p. 401. *Lords Journals*, Vol. 13, p. 76. Browning, *Thomas Osborne, Earl of Danby*, Vol. 2, pp. 66–8, 69–71.
71 *Commons Journals*, Vol. 9, pp. 408, 409.
72 Grey, *Debates*, Vol. 4, p. 203.
73 *Commons Journals*, Vol. 9, p. 424.
74 ibid., Vol. 9, pp. 424–5. Grey, *Debates*, Vol. 4, p. 388.
75 Margoliouth, *Poems and Letters of Andrew Marvell*, pp. 203–4. Grey, *Debates*, Vol. 4, pp. 389–90.
76 Mignet, *Négociations*, Vol. 4, pp. 479–85, 485–96.
77 ibid., Vol. 4, pp. 497–500.
78 Mignet, *Négociations*, Vol. 4, pp. 503–5, 506, 508–10. Baxter, *William III*, pp.

148–50. Burnet, *History of his Own Time*, Vol. 2, pp. 120–4. Thompson, *Correspondence of the Family of Hatton*, Vol. 1, pp. 152–4.

79 Mignet, *Négociations*, Vol. 4, pp. 510–11, 512–13, 514. G. Groen van Prinsterer (ed.), *Archives ou Correspondance inédite de la Maison d'Orange-Nassau* (Utrecht, 1858–62), 2nd series, Vol. 5, pp. 354, 356, 357.

80 Baxter, *William III*, p. 151.

81 *CSPD, 1675–6*, p. 142. Bodleian, Clarendon State Papers, Vol. 87, fols. 297–305. HMC, Ormonde, new series, Vol. 4, p. 376. PRO, Baschet Transcripts, Barrillon, 16, 20 Dec. 1677.

82 Mignet, *Négociations*, Vol. 4, p. 510.

83 ibid., Vol. 4, pp. 506, 508–9.

84 Mignet, *Négociations*, Vol. 4, pp. 518–19.

85 ibid., Vol. 4, pp. 521–2, 532–3, 540. HMC, Finch, Vol. 2, p. 38.

86 Baxter, *William III*, pp. 151–3. For a new interpretation, see J. A. H. Botts, *The Peace of Nijmegen* (Amsterdam: Holland University Press, 1981).

87 Mignet, *Négociations*, Vol. 4, pp. 514–18.

88 Mignet, *Négociations*, Vol. 4, pp. 542–3, 553–4. HMC, Finch, Vol. 2, p. 38.

89 Mignet, *Négociations*, Vol. 4, p. 533. HMC, Ormonde, new series, Vol. 4, p. 410.

90 *Lords Journals*, Vol. 13, p. 130.

91 *Commons Journals*, Vol. 9, p. 430. Margoliouth, *Poems and Letters of Andrew Marvell*, p. 210. HMC, Ormonde, new series, Vol. 4, p. 419.

92 HMC, Ormonde, new series, Vol. 4, pp. 399, 403. *Commons Journals*, Vol. 9, pp. 431–2.

93 Mignet, *Négociations*, Vol. 4, p. 536.

94 Baxter, *William III*, p. 152. Margoliouth, *Poems and Letters of Andrew Marvell*, p. 219.

95 Mignet, *Négociations*, Vol. 4, pp. 540–1. HMC, Ormonde, new series, Vol. 4, p. 407. Thompson, *Correspondence of the Family of Hatton*, Vol. 1, p. 162.

96 Grey, *Debates*, Vol. 5, p. 119. Dalrymple, *Memoirs*, Vol. 2, pp. 148, 151, 176, 200. Childs, *Army of Charles II*, pp. 186–9.

97 PRO, Baschet Transcripts, Barrillon, 10 Oct. 1678. Margoliouth, *Poems and Letters of Andrew Marvell*, pp. 220–1. HMC, Ormonde, new series, Vol. 4, p. 413. Mignet, *Négociations*, Vol. 4, pp. 542–3.

98 PRO, Baschet Transcripts, Barrillon, 4 July 1678. Prinsterer, *Archives ou Correspondance Inédite*, 2nd series, Vol. 5, p. 360.

99 Mignet, *Négociations*, Vol. 4, pp. 541, 568, 571–2.

100 *Commons Journals*, Vol. 9, pp. 464–6.

101 ibid., Vol. 9, pp. 466, 471, 472–4, 475. HMC, Finch, Vol. 2, p. 41.

102 *Commons Journals*, Vol. 9, pp. 477, 479. Margoliouth, *Poems and Letters of Andrew Marvell*, pp. 231, 232–3.

103 Mignet, *Négociations*, Vol. 4, pp. 572, 575, 576–7, 578–81, 582. Dalrymple, *Memoirs*, Vol. 2, pp. 159–62, 165–8.

104 PRO, Baschet Transcripts, Barrillon, 2, 23 June 1678.

105 Mignet, *Négociations*, Vol. 4, pp. 595, 599, 601–3, 604–5. Dalrymple, *Memoirs*, Vol. 2, pp. 141, 172–3, 174, 176, 188–92. HMC, Ormonde, new series, Vol. 4, pp. 428, 439, 441.

106 PRO, Baschet Transcripts, Barrillon, 7 July 1678.

107 ibid., 18, 25, 29 Aug. 1678. Chandaman, *English Public Revenue 1660–1688*, pp. 242–4.
108 *Commons Journals*, Vol. 9, p. 499. Burnet, *History of his Own Time*, Vol. 2, p. 142. Margoliouth, *Poems and Letters of Andrew Marvell*, pp. 241–2. HMC, Ormonde, new series, Vol. 4, pp. 434–6.
109 HMC, Ormonde, new series, Vol. 4, pp. 454–7. HMC, xiith Report, Appendix, Vol. 7, p. 148. R. Halstead, *Succint Genealogies* (1687), p. 433.
110 Sir J. Pollock, *The Popish Plot* (Cambridge, 1944), pp. 74–5.
111 PRO, Baschet Transcripts, Barrillon, 10 Oct. 1678. HMC, Ormonde, new series, Vol. 4, pp. 454–5.
112 HMC, Ormonde, new series, Vol. 4, pp. 457–8, 460, 461. Bodleian, Carte MSS, Vol. 81, fol. 365. British Library, Add MSS, 38847, fols. 206, 219–20, 224–9. *Commons Journals*, Vol. 9, pp. 524–9.
113 Browning, *Thomas Osborne, Earl of Danby*, Vol. 1, p. 295. HMC, Ormonde, new series, Vol. 4, pp. 217, 457, 459, 461.
114 *Lords Journals*, Vol. 13, p. 293.
115 Bodleian, Carte MSS, Vol. 72, fol. 403.
116 PRO, Baschet Transcripts, Barrillon, 6 Oct., 24 Nov. 1678.
117 *Commons Journals*, Vol. 9, pp. 522, 532–3, 537. HMC, Ormonde, new series, Vol. 4, p. 461.
118 *Lords Journals*, Vol. 13, p. 345.
119 *Commons Journals*, Vol. 9, p. 543. PRO, Baschet Transcripts, Barrillon, 5 Dec. 1678. Bodleian, Carte MSS, Vol. 38, fols 604–9.
120 *Commons Journals*, Vol. 9, pp. 542, 545. PRO, Baschet Transcripts, Barrillon, 5 Dec. 1678.
121 HMC, Ormonde, new series, Vol. 4, pp. 257–8. Burnet, *History of his Own Time*, Vol. 2, p. 171.
122 HMC, Ormonde, new series, Vol. 4, pp. 257, 480.
123 PRO, Baschet Transcripts, Barrillon, 26 Jan. 1679.
124 ibid., 12, 22 Dec. 1678; 5, 9, 12, 30 Jan., 16 Feb. 1679.
125 PRO, Baschet Transcripts, Barrillon, 24, 27 Oct., 3, 14 Nov., 22, 29 Dec. 1678; 9, 12, 26, 30 Jan. 1679. Dalrymple, *Memoirs*, Vol. 2, p. 205.
126 *Lords Journals*, Vol. 13, p. 447. Bodleian, Carte MSS, Vol. 39, fol. 1. HMC, Ormonde, new series, Vol. 4, pp. 295, 297–9.
127 PRO, Baschet Transcripts, Barrillon, 6 Feb. 1679. Bodleian, Carte MSS, Vol. 39, fol. 5.

7 The Contest with the Whigs

1 PRO, Baschet Transcripts, Barrillon, 6 Feb. 1679. Browning, *Thomas Osborne, Earl of Danby*, Vol. 1, p. 313.
2 J. R. Jones, 'Shaftesbury's worthy men', *Bulletin of the Institute of Historical Research*, vol. 30 (1957), pp. 232–41.
3 Jones, *First Whigs*, p. 35. Miller, *James II: a Study in Kingship*, pp. 90–1. Burnet, *History of his Own Time*, Vol. 2, p. 197.
4 Browning, *Thomas Osborne, Earl of Danby*, Vol. 1, p. 324. PRO, Baschet

Transcripts, Barrillon, 17 Apr. 1679. Chandaman, *English Public Revenue, 1660–1688*, pp. 247–51.

5   Chandaman, *English Public Revenue, 1660–1688*, p. 247 n. 1. Feiling, *History of the Tory Party*, pp. 191–2.

6   H. C. Foxcroft, *A Character of the Trimmer* (Cambridge, 1946); this study now needs revision.

7   J. P. Kenyon, *Robert Spencer, Earl of Sunderland* (1958), pp. 24–6.

8   Haley, *First Earl of Shaftesbury*, pp. 512–14, 517–18.

9   Browning, *Thomas Osborne, Earl of Danby*, Vol. 1, p. 334; Vol. 2, pp. 82–4, 84–8. Dalrymple, *Memoirs*, Vol. 2, p. 207.

10 Feiling's study, *A History of the Tory Party*, deals almost entirely with 'high politics'; in my next study, *The First Tories*, I propose to examine the broader basis of the party's appeal.

11 Browning, *English Historical Documents*, Vol. 8, pp. 185–8 ('The Declaration of the King', 8 Apr. 1681).

12 Jones, *First Whigs*, pp. 59–61.

13 PRO, Baschet Transcripts, Barrillon, 1 May 1679; 21 Oct. 1680; 23 Jan., 28 July 1681. Dalrymple, *Memoirs*, Vol. 2, p. 220. R. W. Blencowe (ed.), *Diary of the Times of Charles the Second by the Honourable Henry Sidney* (1843), Vol. 2, p. 137.

14 *Lords Journals*, Vol. 13, p. 345.

15 Jones, *First Whigs*, p. 123. Kenyon, *Robert Spencer, Earl of Sunderland*, pp. 36–7, 40–2, 44–5. Burnet, *History of his Own Time*, Vol. 1, p. 287. Clarke, *Life of James II*, Vol. 1, p. 750.

16 Browning, *Thomas Osborne, Earl of Danby*, Vol. 1, pp. 312, 317. PRO, Baschet Transcripts, Barrillon, 9 Feb. 1679.

17 British Library, Add MSS, 28053, fol. 133.

18 PRO, Baschet Transcripts, Barrillon, 13, 16 Mar. 1679. PRO, Privy Council Registers, Vol. 67, fol. 121.

19 Browning, *Thomas Osborne, Earl of Danby*, Vol. 1, pp. 317–20. Jones, *First Whigs*, pp. 49–50. Grey, *Debates*, Vol. 6, pp. 403–4, 404–8, 409–24, 424–33, 433–9; Vol. 7, pp. 1–3.

20 Browning, *Thomas Osborne, Earl of Danby*, Vol. 1, pp. 320–1.

21 PRO, Baschet Transcripts, Barrillon, 3 Apr. 1679. HMC, Ormonde, new series, Vol. 4, p. 360. Thompson, *Correspondence of the Family of Hatton*, Vol. 1, pp. 183–4.

22 Browning, *Thomas Osborne, Earl of Danby*, Vol. 1, pp. 317, 322. HMC, Finch, Vol. 2, p. 46. Grey, *Debates*, Vol. 7, p. 19, Burnet, *History of his Own Time*, Vol. 1, pp. 200–2. *Commons Journals*, Vol. 9, p. 574.

23 Grey, *Debates*, Vol. 7, pp. 54–63.

24 Browning, *Thomas Osborne, Earl of Danby*, Vol. 1, p. 323.

25 ibid., Vol. 1, pp. 326–9. HMC, Finch, Vol. 2, pp. 48–50.

26 Haley, *First Earl of Shaftesbury*, pp. 510–11. PRO, Shaftesbury Papers, Vol. 6a, fol. 334.

27 PRO, Baschet Transcripts, Barrillon, 27 Apr., 1 May 1679. Jones, *First Whigs*, pp. 61–3. E. R. Turner, 'The Privy Council of 1679', *English Historical Review*, vol. 30 (1915), pp. 251–70.

28 Sir W. Temple, *Memoirs* (1714), pp. 318–23. Thomas Bruce, Earl of Ailesbury, *Memoirs* (1890), Vol. 1, p. 35.

29 PRO, Baschet Transcripts, Barrillon, 15, 18 May 1679. Browning, *English Historical Documents*, Vol. 8, pp. 100–3.

30 Chandaman, *English Public Revenue, 1660–1688*, pp. 247–51.

31 H. C. Foxcroft, *The Life and Letters of Sir George Savile* (1898), Vol. 1, pp. 148–9.

32 W. A. Aiken, 'The admiralty in conflict and commission, 1679–1684' in W. A. Aiken and B. D. Henning (eds), *Conflict in Stuart England: Essays in Honour of Wallace Notestein* (New Haven, Conn., 1960), pp. 203–25.

33 *Commons Journals*, Vol. 9, p. 605. Grey, *Debates*, Vol. 7, pp. 137–52.

34 *Lords Journals*, Vol. 13, p. 547.

35 Grey, *Debates*, Vol. 7, pp. 159–64, 174.

36 ibid., Vol. 7, pp. 236–60. *Commons Journals*, Vol. 9, p. 620.

37 Grey, *Debates*, Vol. 7, pp. 265–78. *Commons Journals*, Vol. 9, pp. 621–2.

38 Grey, *Debates*, Vol. 7, pp. 313–14. *Commons Journals*, Vol. 9, pp. 626–7.

39 PRO, Baschet Transcripts, Barrillon, 5 June 1679. HMC, Ormonde, new series, Vol. 5, p. 103.

40 PRO, Baschet Transcripts, Barrillon, 19, 22, 26 June, 3 July 1679. R. Clifton, *The Last Popular Rebellion* (1984), pp. 112–13.

41 *Lords Journals*, Vol. 13, pp. 594–5. HMC, Ormonde, new series, Vol. 5, p. 103. Haley, *First Earl of Shaftesbury*, pp. 524–6.

42 PRO, Baschet Transcripts, Barrillon, 13 July 1679. Browning, *Thomas Osborne, Earl of Danby*, Vol. 1, pp. 338–9.

43 *Lords Journals*, Vol. 13, p. 595.

44 HMC, Ormonde, new series, Vol. 4, p. 535.

45 PRO, Baschet Transcripts, Barrillon, 26 June 1679. Haley, *First Earl of Shaftesbury*, pp. 542–3. HMC, Ormonde, new series, Vol. 5, pp. 32, 136, 140, 144–5, 158. J. P. Kenyon, 'The acquittal of Sir George Wakeman', *Historical Journal*, Vol. 14 (1971), pp. 693–708.

46 HMC, Ormonde, new series, Vol. 5, pp. 140, 144.

47 Kenyon, 'Acquittal of Sir George Wakeman', p. 693. Bodleian, Carte MSS, Vol. 79, fol. 77.

48 Kenyon, 'Acquittal of Sir George Wakeman', pp. 698–700, 707–8.

49 Haley, *First Earl of Shaftesbury*, p. 537.

50 Blencowe, *Diary of Henry Sidney*, Vol. 1, pp. 37–8. Jones, *First Whigs*, pp. 90–1, 92–106.

51 PRO, Baschet Transcripts, Barrillon, 6 July 1679.

52 ibid., 13 July 1679.

53 PRO, Baschet Transcripts, Barrillon, 3 Aug. 1679.

54 ibid., 31 Aug. 1679.

55 Thompson, *Correspondence of the Family of Hatton*, Vol. 1, pp. 189–90, 191, 193, 194. Clifton, *Last Popular Rebellion*, pp. 113–15.

56 Clifton, *Last Popular Rebellion*, pp. 94–7, 105–6.

57 Jones, *First Whigs*, p. 88. E. D'Oyley, *James, Duke of Monmouth* (1938), 277–8. G. Roberts, *The Life, Progresses and Rebellion of James, Duke of Monmouth* (1844), Vol. 1, pp. 247–8.

58 PRO, Baschet Transcripts, Barrillon, 25 Sept. 1679. Thompson, *Correspondence of the Family of Hatton*, Vol. 1, pp. 194, 195. Clifton, *Last Popular Rebellion*, pp. 114–15.

59 Haley, *First Earl of Shaftesbury*, p. 549.
60 ibid., pp. 550–1. Jones, *The First Whigs*, p. 114.
61 Thompson, *Correspondence of the Family of Hatton*, Vol. 1, pp. 203–4, 205–6. PRO, Baschet Transcripts, Barrillon, 11 Dec. 1679. Jones, *First Whigs*, pp. 113–14. Clifton, *Last Popular Rebellion*, p. 115.
62 PRO, Baschet Transcripts, Barrillon, 7 Dec. 1679. Jones, *First Whigs*, pp. 109–13.
63 Thompson, *Correspondence of the Family of Hatton*, Vol. 1, pp. 212–13.
64 PRO, Baschet Transcripts, Barrillon, 30 Nov. 1679; 11 Mar. 1680. HMC, Ormonde, new series, Vol. 5, p. 242.
65 PRO, Baschet Transcripts, Barrillon, 21, 25 Dec. 1679. Thompson, *Correspondence of the Family of Hatton*, Vol. 1, pp. 212–13.
66 Jones, *First Whigs*, pp. 119–21.
67 ibid., pp. 115–19.
68 PRO, Baschet Transcripts, Barrillon, 2, 9, 26 Oct., 2, 30 Nov., 11 Dec. 1679.
69 ibid., 18, 21, 25, 28 Dec. 1679. HMC, Ormonde, new series, Vol. 5, p. 263. Prinsterer, *Archives ou Correspondance Inédite*, 2nd series, Vol. 5, pp. 375–6, 377–8, 463 (misdated).
70 Blencowe, *Diary of Henry Sidney*, Vol. 1, pp. 211–12, 219–20, 221–2.
71 Prinsterer, *Archives ou Correspondance Inédite*, 2nd series, Vol. 5, p. 385.
72 HMC, Ormonde, new series, Vol. 5, pp. 271, 274.
73 Bodleian, Carte MSS, Vol. 243, fol. 444.
74 HMC, Ormonde, new series, Vol. 5, pp. 269, 301.
75 L. J. K. Glassey, *Politics and the Appointment of Justices of the Peace* (Oxford, 1979), pp. 45–54.
76 *State Trials*, Vol. 7, pp. 926–32, 931–60, 1111–30.
77 PRO, Shaftesbury Papers, Vol. 50, pt 2. HMC, Ormonde, new series, Vol. 5, pp. 311–12. Prinsterer, *Archives ou Correspondance Inédite*, 2nd series, Vol. 5, pp. 388, 389–90. Bodleian, Carte MSS, Vol. 39, fols. 25, 66, 83, 100, 127, 140–1, 142, 146, 150, 152, 154, 158, 164, 168, 170, 186, 188, 200, 204–5, 213, 219, 225, 229, 231, 234, 240, 244; Vol. 243, fols. 385, 477, 498, 504, 516, 518; Vol. 219, fols. 184, 186, 188, 190, 192, 194.
78 Thompson, *Correspondence of the Family of Hatton*, Vol. 1, p. 225. HMC, Finch, Vol. 2, pp. 76–7. Clifton, *Last Popular Rebellion*, pp. 121–2.
79 Prinsterer, *Archives ou Correspondance Inédite*, 2nd series, Vol. 5, pp. 384–5, 391–2, 407, 414.
80 HMC, Ormonde, new series, Vol. 5, p. 349.
81 Haley, *First Earl of Shaftesbury*, pp. 580–1. Jones, *First Whigs*, pp. 127–8.
82 Jones, *First Whigs*, pp. 133–9.
83 HMC, Ormonde, new series, Vol. 5, pp. 454, 459. Prinsterer, *Archives ou Correspondance Inédite*, 2nd series, Vol. 5, pp. 426, 428, 430.
84 Prinsterer, *Archives ou Correspondance Inédite*, 2nd series, Vol. 5, pp. 435–6, 436–7. HMC, Ormonde, new series, Vol. 5, p. 496. J. P. Kenyon, 'Charles II and William of Orange in 1680', *Bulletin of the Institute of Historical Research*, vol. 30 (1957), pp. 97–101.
85 Foxcroft, *Life and Letters of Sir George Savile*, Vol. 1, p. 233. Kenyon, *Robert Spencer, Earl of Sunderland*, pp. 55, 57–8, 59–60.
86 Kenyon, *Robert Spencer, Earl of Sunderland*, p. 58.

87 Miller, *James II: a Study in Kingship*, p. 103.
88 *Lords Journals*, Vol. 13, pp. 610–11. HMC, Finch, Vol. 2, pp. 89–90.
89 Grey, *Debates*, Vol. 7, pp. 427–8, 429–30, 431–2.
90 ibid., Vol. 7, pp. 433, 439–45, 445–59.
91 Blencowe, *Diary of Henry Sidney*, Vol. 2, pp. 125–6. *Lords Journals*, Vol. 13, p. 666.
92 *Commons Journals*, Vol. 9, pp. 660, 663. HMC, Finch, Vol. 2, p. 97.
93 See Sir G. Sitwell, *The First Whig* (Scarborough, 1894) for a colourful but unhistorical description.
94 Prinsterer, *Archives ou Correspondance Inédite*, 2nd series, Vol. 5, pp. 442–3, 451–3, 458, 465. For James's attitude see Bodleian, Clarendon State Papers, Vol. 87, fols. 334–6.
95 *Lords Journals*, Vol. 13, p. 716. HMC, Finch, Vol. 2, p. 98.
96 *Commons Journals*, Vol. 9, pp. 660–1, 665–7. HMC, Ormonde, new series, Vol. 5, p. 511.
97 HMC, Finch, Vol. 2, pp. 100–1. *Commons Journals*, Vol. 9, p. 699.
98 HMC, Finch, Vol. 2, pp. 98–9. HMC, Ormonde, new series, Vol. 5, p. 541.
99 Prinsterer, *Archives ou Correspondance Inédite*, 2nd series, Vol. 5, pp. 458, 461–2.
100 HMC, Ormonde, new series, Vol. 5, pp. 512–16. Kenyon, *Popish Plot*, pp. 201–3. Cobbett, *State Trials*, Vol. 7, pp. 1293–1568.
101 *Commons Journals*, Vol. 9, pp. 703–4.
102 *Lords Journals*, Vol. 13, pp. 742, 743. HMC, Ormonde, new series, Vol. 5, p. 555.

8 The Years of Personal Rule

1 Browning, *English Historical Documents*, Vol. 8, pp. 185–6.
2 An ideal expressed by Tory grand juries; *CSPD, 1682*, pp. 467–8.
3 *CSPD, 1680–1*, pp. 250–1, 267, HMC, Ormonde, new series, Vol. 6, pp. 335–6.
4 Jones, *First Whigs*, pp. 159–67.
5 ibid., pp. 159–73.
6 HMC, xiith Report, Appendix, Vol. 5, p. 57. Prinsterer, *Archives ou Correspondance Inédite*, 2nd series, Vol. 5, pp. 475, 481–2.
7 *CSPD, 1680–1*, pp. 156–7. Burnet, *History of his Own Time*, Vol. 1, pp. 276–7.
8 Jones, *First Whigs*, pp. 121–2, 133–5, 157–8, 167–72.
9 PRO, Baschet Transcripts, Barrillon, 20 Feb. 1681. Kenyon, *Robert Spencer, Earl of Sunderland*, p. 73.
10 Bodleian, Carte MSS, Vol. 222, fol. 272. N. Luttrell, *A Brief Relation of State Affairs* (Oxford, 1857), Vol. 1, pp. 69, 121.
11 Luttrell, *Brief Relation of State Affairs*, Vol. 1, p. 70. *CSPD, 1680–1*, pp. 82, 86, 166, 204.
12 *CSPD, 1680–1*, pp. 127, 129–30, 199.
13 Kenyon, *Robert Spencer, Earl of Sunderland*, pp. 41–8, 50–2, 72.
14 PRO, Baschet Transcripts, Barrillon, 30 June, 9 Oct. 1681.

15   Dalrymple, *Memoirs*, Vol. 2, p. 277.
16   PRO, Baschet Transcripts, Barrillon, 9, 13 Jan. 1681.
17   ibid., 4, 11 Nov., 5 Dec. 1680; 3 Mar. 1681.
18   PRO, Baschet Transcripts, Barrillon, 24, 27 Mar. 1681.
19   Chandaman, *English Public Revenue, 1660–1688*, pp. 253–4.
20   *Lords Journals*, Vol. 13, pp. 745–6. Grey, *Debates*, Vol. 8, p. 291.
21   Grey, *Debates*, Vol. 8, pp. 295–9.
22   PRO, Baschet Transcripts, Barrillon, 3 July 1681. Jones, *First Whigs*, pp. 174–6.
23   Grey, *Debates*, Vol. 8, pp. 303–9. *Lords Journals*, Vol. 13, p. 755.
24   Luttrell, *Brief Relation of State Affairs*, Vol. 1, p. 70.
25   Bodleian, Carte MSS, Vol. 222, fol. 294. Bodleian, MS, Don, fol. 7. PRO, Shaftesbury Papers, Vol. 6a, fol. 374; Vol. 6b, fol. 401; Vol. 43, fol. 63. Cobbett, *State Trials*, Vol. 8, pp. 223–330, 330–93. *Commons Journals*, Vol. 9, p. 670. HMC, Ormonde, new series, Vol. 5, pp. 602, 609.
26   Grey, *Debates*, Vol. 8, pp. 309, 310, 325, 326–7.
27   ibid., Vol. 8, pp. 295–9, 317–20. Prinsterer, *Archives ou Correspondance Inédite*, 2nd series, Vol. 5, pp. 490–1, 492.
28   PRO, Baschet Transcripts, Barrillon, 7 Apr. 1681. *Lords Journals*, Vol. 13, p. 755. Grey, *Debates*, Vol. 8, pp. 303– 5, 332–8.
29   *Lords Journals*, Vol. 13, p. 757.
30   PRO, Baschet Transcripts, Barrillon, 7 Apr. 1681. HMC, Ormonde, new series, Vol. 6, p. 2.
31   Grey, *Debates*, Vol. 8, p. 340, 340 n.
32   *CSPD, 1680–1*, p. 237. Browning, *English Historical Documents*, Vol. 8, pp. 185–8.
33   *CSPD, 1680–1*, pp. 258, 267, 271. Prinsterer, *Archives ou Correspondance Inédite*, 2nd series, Vol. 5, p. 501. Luttrell, *Brief Relation of State Affairs*, Vol. 1, pp. 79, 85–6, 87–8, 91, 92–3, 97, 100, 103, 105, 109, 110, 114–15, 118.
34   Grey, *Debates*, Vol. 7, pp. 424–5; Vol. 8, pp. 290, 285, 300–2. *Lords Journals*, Vol. 13, pp. 748, 751, 756.
35   *CSPD, 1680–1*, p. 250. J. E. Illick, *William Penn the Politician* (New York, 1965), pp. 21–9, 38–40.
36   Foxcroft, *Life and Letters of Sir George Savile*, Vol. 1, p. 357.
37   Kenyon, *Robert Spencer, Earl of Sunderland*, pp. 80–3.
38   PRO, Baschet Transcripts, Barrillon, 14, 17 July, 4, 8 Sept. 1681. HMC, Ormonde, new series, Vol. 6, pp. 90–1. Luttrell, *Brief Relation of State Affairs*, Vol. 1, pp. 105–6.
39   Luttrell, *Brief Relation of State Affairs*, Vol. 1, p. 108. *CSPD, 1680–1*, p. 525. HMC, Ormonde, new series, Vol. 6, pp. 95–6. Bodleian, Rawlinson MSS, D, Vol. 384, fol. 74.
40   *CSPD, 1680–1*, pp. 394, 399, 412. *State Trials*, Vol. 8, pp. 549–717. Luttrell, *Brief Relation of State Affairs*, Vol. 1, pp. 110, 117–18. Bodleian, Rawlinson MSS, D, Vol. 384, fol. 69.
41   Bodleian, Tanner MSS, Vol. 36, fol. 173. British Library, Stowe MSS, Vol. 144, fol. 19, HMC, Ormonde, new series, Vol. 6, p. 226.
42   *CSPD, 1680–1*, p. 500. Bodleian, Clarendon State Papers, Vol. 88, fol. 5.
43   *CSPD, 1680–1*, pp. 497, 500, 510–11, 517, 589, 592. Cobbett, *State Trials*,

Vol. 8, pp. 808–16. PRO, Baschet Transcripts, Barrillon, 8 Dec. 1681.
44 *CSPD, 1680–1*, pp. 453–4, 456, 469, 638. *CSPD, 1682*, pp. 263–5, 268, 270, 272, 280–1, 286, 289, 292, 302, 403, 436, 536, 557. Jones, *First Whigs*, pp. 198–206.
45 PRO, Baschet Transcripts, Barrillon, 18, 20 Oct. 1683. HMC, Ormonde, new series, Vol. 7, pp. 49–50.
46 Mostly published in the *London Gazette*, and listed in Luttrell, *Brief Relation of State Affairs*, Vol. 1, pp. 265–95.
47 HMC, Ormonde, new series, Vol. 6, p. 59.
48 R. A. Beddard, 'The Commission for Ecclesiastical Promotions', *Historical Journal*, vol. 10 (1957), pp. 11–40.
49 PRO, Baschet Transcripts, Barrillon, 24 Nov. 1681. Foxcroft, *Character of the Trimmer*, p. 180.
50 PRO, Baschet Transcripts, Barrillon, 16 June 1681. Chandaman, *English Public Revenue, 1660–1688*, pp. 250–5, 276.
51 Burnet, *History of his Own Time*, Vol. 1, pp. 339–40. Kenyon, *Robert Spencer, Earl of Sunderland*, pp. 92–4, 98–100.
52 Foxcroft, *Life and Letters of Sir George Savile*, Vol. 1, pp. 380–6.
53 PRO, Baschet Transcripts, Barrillon, 1 Oct. 1682. Kenyon, *Robert Spencer, Earl of Sunderland*, pp. 79–83. Prinsterer, *Archives ou Correspondance Inédite*, 2nd series, Vol. 5, p. 559.
54 His *Character of a Trimmer* did not appear until late 1684, and then only in manuscript.
55 Foxcroft, *Life and Letters of Sir George Savile*, Vol. 1, pp. 361–2.
56 PRO, Baschet Transcripts, Barrillon, 14 Dec. 1679; 31 Oct., 5 Dec. 1680.
57 ibid., 1 Sept. 1681.
58 Baxter, *William III*, pp. 173–5.
59 Blencowe, *Diary of Henry Sidney*, Vol. 2, p. 161.
60 Prinsterer, *Archives ou Correspondance Inédite*, 2nd series, Vol. 5, p. 451.
61 Baxter, *William III*, p. 167.
62 Blencowe, *Diary of Henry Sidney*, Vol. 2, pp. 116–17, 119–20. Prinsterer, *Archives ou Correspondance Inédite,* 2nd series, Vol. 5, pp. 435–6.
63 Prinsterer, *Archives ou Correspondance Inédite*, 2nd series, Vol. 5, pp. 451–6.
64 PRO, Baschet Transcripts, Barrillon, 26 Dec. 1680.
65 Prinsterer, *Archives ou Correspondance Inédite*, 2nd series, Vol. 5, pp. 502, 505, 506, 508, 525.
66 PRO, Baschet Transcripts, Barrillon, 11 Aug. 1681. HMC, Ormonde, new series, Vol. 6, pp. 113, 114, 115, 119.
67 PRO, Baschet Transcripts, Barrillon, 21, 24, 28 July, 11 Aug. 1681.
68 Prinsterer, *Archives ou Correspondance Inédite*, 2nd series, Vol. 5, pp. 525, 526–7, 528–9.
69 ibid., Vol. 5, pp. 530–1, 534–5, 535–6, 545, 552, 569, 581–2, 583. PRO, Baschet Transcripts, Barrillon, 15 Dec. 1681. *CSPD, 1682*, pp. 132–3. W. D. Cooper (ed.), *Savile Correspondence: Letters to and from Henry Savile* (1858), p. 266.
70 Baxter, *William III*, pp. 185–6. *CSPD, 1682*, p. 454.
71 PRO, Baschet Transcripts, Barrillon, 6, 13, 17 May 1683. Baxter, *William III*, p. 187. D. Green, *Queen Anne* (1970), pp. 33–4.
72 PRO, Baschet Transcripts, Barrillon, 10 June 1683.

73 ibid., 18 December 1681. Prinsterer, *Archives ou Correspondance Inédite*, 2nd series, Vol. 5, pp. 524, 526–7, 528, 531, 534.

74 Prinsterer, *Archives ou Correspondance Inédite*, 2nd series, Vol. 5, p. 374.

75 Baxter, *William III*, pp. 190–2.

76 Luttrell, *Brief Relation of State Affairs*, Vol. 1, pp. 262, 263–4, 265–9. HMC, Ormonde, new series, Vol. 7, p. 53. D. Milne, 'The Results of the Rye House Plot', *Transactions of the Royal Historical Society*, 5th series, vol. 1 (1951), pp. 91–108.

77 Lady A. Fraser, *King Charles II* (1979), pp. 430–2.

78 Burnet, *History of his Own Time*, Vol. 1, pp. 365, 369.

79 ibid., Vol. 1, pp. 380 n., 388–9. PRO, Baschet Transcripts, Barrillon, 22, 26, 29 July 1683.

80 Bodleian, Carte MSS, Vol. 216, fol. 305.

81 PRO, Baschet Transcripts, Barrillon, 12, 15 July 1683. Luttrell, *Brief Relation of State Affairs*, Vol. 1, pp. 309, 310, 311, 312–13.

82 Carte MSS, Vol. 216, fols. 47, 53. Bodleian, MS Eng. letters, d 72, fol. 3.

83 PRO, Baschet Transcripts, Barrillon, 3 Sept. 1682. Clifton, *Last Popular Rebellion*, pp. 135–7. D'Oyley, *James, Duke of Monmouth*, pp. 195–201.

84 PRO, Baschet Transcripts, Barrillon, 5, 8, 15 July, 8 Nov., 5, 9, 13, 16, 20 Dec. 1683. Burnet, *History of his Own Time*, Vol. 1, pp. 411–15.

85 PRO, Baschet Transcripts, Barrillon, 5, 16, 20 Dec. 1683. HMC, Ormonde, new series, Vol. 7, pp. 164, 165, 169.

86 Prinsterer, *Archives ou Correspondance Inédite*, 2nd series, Vol. 5, p. 586. Kenyon, *Robert Spencer, Earl of Sunderland*, p. 97. M. F. Bond (ed.), *Diaries and Papers of Sir Edward Dering* (1976), p. 150.

87 A. Browning (ed.), *The Memoirs of Sir John Reresby* (Glasgow, 1936), p. 327. HMC, Ormonde, new series, Vol. 7, p. 3.

88 HMC, Ormonde, new series, Vol. 7, p. 267. Foxcroft, *Life and Letters of Sir George Savile*, Vol. 1, p. 421.

89 HMC, Ormonde, new series, Vol. 7, pp. 280–1, 282–3. Kenyon, *Robert Spencer, Earl of Sunderland*, pp. 98–100.

90 Kenyon, *Robert Spencer, Earl of Sunderland*, pp. 108–9.

91 ibid., pp. 105–7. Baxter, *William III*, pp. 199, 200.

92 Foxcroft, *Life and Letters of Sir George Savile*, Vol. 1, pp. 422–6, 433–4. Kenyon, *Robert Spencer, Earl of Sunderland*, p. 104. D'Oyley, *James, Duke of Monmouth*, pp. 257–9.

93 G. H. Jones, *Charles Middleton* (Chicago, 1967), pp. 68–71.

94 Carte, *Life of Ormonde*, Vol. 2, p. 116. Bond, *Diaries and Papers of Sir Edward Dering*, pp. 26, 128, 148. J. G. Sims, *Jacobite Ireland* (1969), p. 6.

95 Carte, *Life of Ormonde*, Vol. 2, p. 111, 115. HMC, Ormonde, new series, Vol. 7, pp. 267, 280–1, 282–3, 284. *CSPD, 1684–5*, p. 287.

96 Browning, *Thomas Osborne, Earl of Danby*, Vol. 1, pp. 358–63. Chapman, *Great Villiers*, pp. 266–71.

9 Conclusion

1 A new sovereign would have to call a parliament, to settle a revenue for life on him (or her).

2 In the case of *Thomas* v. *Sorrel*, 1674. W. C. Costin and J. S. Watson (eds), *The Law and Working of the Constitution* (1952), Vol. 1, pp. 249–51.
3 Korr, *Cromwell and the New Model Foreign Policy*, pp. 199–200, 208–9.
4 With the important exception of the events leading up to the outbreak of civil war (or rebellion) in 1642; Bodleian, Carte MSS, Vol. 39, fol. 1.
5 James frequently made references to 'our family' in his letters to William (in Prinsterer, *Archives ou Correspondance Inédite* and in HMC, xith Report, Appendix, Vol. 5, Dartmouth). I would evaluate these expressions as sincere and not tactical.
6 *CSPD, 1650*, p. 186.
7 James ordered the publication in 1686 of a pamphlet, *Copies of Two Papers written by the late King Charles II and one by the Duchess of York.*
8 PRO, Baschet Transcripts, Barrillon, 6 Mar. 1679.

Bibliography

1 Manuscript Collections

BRITISH LIBRARY
Additional Manuscripts (abbreviated in notes as Add. MSS).
Stowe Manuscripts.

BODLEIAN LIBRARY, OXFORD
Carte Manuscripts.
Clarendon State Papers.
Rawlinson Manuscripts.
Tanner Manuscripts.

PUBLIC RECORD OFFICE (PRO)
Baschet Transcripts of French Diplomatic Despatches.
Privy Council Registers.
Shaftesbury Papers.
State Papers Relating to the Reign of Charles II.

2 Printed Sources

The place of publication is London unless stated otherwise.
Browning, A. (ed.), *English Historical Documents*, Vol. 8 (Eyre & Spottiswoode, 1953).
Calendar of Clarendon State Papers, Vols 2 and 3 ed. W. D. Macray (1869 and 1876); Vols 4 and 5 ed. F. J. Routledge (1932 and 1970); (Oxford: Clarendon Press) (abbrev. in notes as *Cal. Clarendon SP*).
Calendar of State Papers, Domestic (abbrev. in notes as *CSPD*).
Calendar of State Papers, Venetian (abbrev. in notes as *CSP, Venetian*).
Calendar of Treasury Books (abbrev. in notes as *CTB*).
Christie, W. D. (ed.), *Letters Addressed from London to Sir Joseph Williamson*, 2 vols (Camden Society, new series, Vols 8 and 9, 1874).
Clarendon State Papers, 3 vols (Oxford: Clarendon Press, 1767–86) (abbrev. in notes as *CSP*).
Coate, M. (ed.), *The Letter-Book of John, Viscount Mordaunt* (Camden Society, 3rd series, Vol. 69, 1945).
Cobbett, W. (ed.), *State Trials* (1810–11).
Colenbrander, H. T. (ed.), *Bescheiden uit Vreemde Archieven* (The Hague: Nijhoff, 1919).
Cooper, W. D. (ed.), *Savile Correspondence: Letters to and from Henry Savile* (Camden Society, Vol. 71, 1858).

Costin, W. C., and Watson, J. S. (eds), *The Law and Working of the Constitution* (A. & C. Black, 1952).

Dalrymple, Sir J., *Memoirs of Great Britain and Ireland*, 2 vols (1771–3).

Essex, Arthur Capel, Earl of, *Correspondence of Arthur Capel, Earl of Essex*, Vol. 1 (ed. O. Airy, Camden Society, new series, Vol. 47, 1890); Vol. 2 (ed. C. E. Pike, Camden Society, 3rd series, Vol. 24, 1913).

Grey, A., *Debates of the House of Commons from the Year 1667 to the Year 1694*, 10 vols (1769).

Henning, B. D. (ed.), *The Parliamentary Diary of Sir Edward Dering* (New Haven, Conn.: Yale University Press, 1940).

Japikse, N. (ed.), *Correspondentie van Willem III en van Hans Willem Bentinck*, 6 vols (The Hague: Nijhoff, 1927–37).

Journals of the House of Commons, Vols 8 and 9 (abbrev. in notes as *Commons Journals*).

Journals of the House of Lords, Vols 11, 12 and 13 (abbrev. in notes as *Lords Journals*).

Latham, R. C., and Matthews, W. (eds), *The Diary of Samuel Pepys*, 11 vols (Bell & Hyman, 1970–83).

Mignet, F. A. (ed.), *Négociations relatives à la succession d'Espagne sous Louis XIV* (Paris, 1835–42).

Prinsterer, G. Groen van (ed.), *Archives ou Correspondance Inédite de la Maison d'Orange-Nassau* (Utrecht, 1858–62).

Robbins, C. (ed.), *The Diary of John Milward* (Cambridge: Cambridge University Press, 1938).

Thibaudeau, A. W. (ed.), *The Bulstrode Papers* (1897).

Thompson, E. M. (ed.), *Correspondence of the Family of Hatton*, 2 vols (Camden Society, new series, Vols 22 and 23, 1878).

Thurloe State Papers, 7 vols, ed. T. Birch (1742).

Warner, G. F. (ed.), *The Nicholas Papers*, Vol. 1 (Camden Society, new series, Vol. 40, 1886); Vol. 2 (new series, Vol. 50, 1892); Vol. 3 (new series, Vol. 57, 1897); Vol. 4 (3rd series, Vol. 4, 1920).

HISTORICAL MANUSCRIPTS COMMISSION (HMC)

viith Report, Appendix, Vol. 1, MSS of Sir H. Ingilby.

viiith Report, Appendix, Vol. 1, MSS of Sir F. Graham, Sir H. Verney, G. E. Frere; Vol. 2, MSS of Marquis of Ormonde.

xth Report, Appendix, Vol. 4, MSS of Earl of Westmorland, N. S. Maskelyne, Sir N. W. Throckmorton.

xith Report, Appendix, Vol. 2, MSS of House of Lords; Vol. 4, MSS of Marquis of Townshend; Vol. 5, MSS of Earl of Dartmouth; Vol. 7, MSS of Duke of Leeds.

xiith Report, Appendix, Vol. 5, MSS of Duke of Rutland; Vol. 6, MSS of House of Lords; Vol. 7, MSS of Le Fleming; Vol. 9, MSS of Duke of Beaufort.

xiiith Report, Appendix, Vols 1, 2, MSS of Duke of Portland.

xivth Report, Appendix, Vol. 2, MSS of Duke of Portland; Vol. 4, MSS of Lord Kenyon; Vol. 9, MSS of Earl of Lindsey, Earl of Onslow.

xvth Report, Appendix, Vol. 7, MSS of Earl of Ailesbury.

MSS of: Marquis of Ormonde; Marquis of Bath; A. G. Finch; Earl of Lonsdale; Mrs Frankland-Russell-Astley; Earl of Lindsey; Mrs Stafford Sackville; Duke of Buccleuch.

3 Secondary Works

The place of publication is London unless stated otherwise.

Abernathy, G. R., 'The English Presbyterians and the Stuart Restoration', *Transactions of the American Philosophical Society,* new series, vol. 55, pt 2 (1965).

Aiken, W. A. and Henning, B. D. (eds), *Conflict in Stuart England: Essays in Honour of Wallace Notestein* (New Haven, Conn.; Yale University Press, 1960).

Ailesbury, Thomas Bruce, Earl of, *Memoirs* (1890).

Allen, D., 'The political function of Charles II's Chiffinch', *Huntington Library Quarterly*, vol. 39, no. 3 (1976).

Ashley, M., *Charles II: Man and Statesman* (Weidenfeld & Nicolson, 1971).

Ashley, M., *General Monck* (Cape, 1977).

Barbour, V., *Henry Bennet, Earl of Arlington* (Washington, DC, 1914).

Bate, F., *The Declaration of Indulgence* (Constable, 1908).

Baxter, S. B., *The Development of the Treasury, 1660–1702* (Longmans, Green, 1957).

Baxter, S. B., *William III* (Longman, 1966).

Beddard, R. A., 'The Commission for Ecclesiastical Promotions', *Historical Journal*, vol. 10 (1967).

Beddard, R. A., 'Sheldon and Anglican recovery', *Historical Journal*, vol. 19 (1976).

Beddard, R. A., 'The Restoration Church' in J. R. Jones (ed.), *The Restored Monarchy, 1660–1688* (Macmillan, 1979).

Blencowe, R. W. (ed.), *Diary of the Times of Charles the Second by the Honourable Henry Sidney* (1843).

Bond, M. F. (ed.), *The Diaries and Papers of Sir Edward Dering* (House of Lords Record Office, Occasional Publications, Vol. 1, 1976).

Bosher, R. S., *The Making of the Restoration Settlement* (Dacre, 1957).

Botts, J. A. H., *The Peace of Nijmegen* (Amsterdam: Holland University Press, 1981).

Browning, A., *Thomas Osborne, Earl of Danby*, 3 vols (Glasgow: Jackson, 1944–51).

Browning, A. (ed.), *The Memoirs of Sir John Reresby* (Glasgow: Jackson, 1936).

Bryant, A., *The Letters, Speeches and Declarations of King Charles II* (Cassell, 1935).

Bryant, A., *King Charles II* (Collins, 1974).

Burghclere, Lady, *George Villiers, Second Duke of Buckingham* (1903).

Burnet, G., *History of his Own Time*, 6 vols, ed. M. J. Routh (Oxford, 1833).

Carte, T., *An History of the Life of James, Duke of Ormonde*, 3 vols (1736).

Chandaman, C. D., *The English Public Revenue, 1660–1688* (Oxford: Clarendon Press, 1975).

Chapman, H., *Great Villiers* (Secker, 1949).

Childs, J., *The Army of Charles II* (Routledge & Kegan Paul, 1976).

Clarendon, Edward Hyde, Earl of, *History of the Rebellion*, 6 vols (Oxford: Clarendon Press, 1888).

Clarendon, Edward Hyde, Earl of, *The Life of Edward, Earl of Clarendon, Being a Continuation of the History of the Rebellion*, 3 vols (Oxford: Clarendon Press, 1827).

Clarke, J. S., *Life of James II*, 2 vols (1816).

Clifton, R., *The Last Popular Rebellion* (Maurice Temple Smith, 1984).

Cowan, E. J., *Montrose: for Covenant and King* (Weidenfeld & Nicolson, 1977).

Curran, M. B. (ed.), *The Despatches of William Perwich* (Camden Society, 3rd series, Vol. 5, 1903).

Davies, G., *The Restoration of Charles II* (San Marino, Calif.: Huntington Library, 1955).

Davies, G., 'Charles II in 1660', *Huntington Library Quarterly*, vol. 39 (1956).

Dawson, W. H., *Cromwell's Understudy: the Life and Times of John Lambert* (Hodge, 1938).

D'Oyley, E., *James, Duke of Monmouth* (Geoffrey Bles, 1938).

Edie, C. A., 'The Irish Cattle Bills', *Transactions of the American Philosophical Society*, new series, vol. 60, no. 2 (1970).

Feiling, K. G., *A History of the Tory Party, 1641–1714* (Oxford: Clarendon Press, 1924).

Feiling, K. G., *British Foreign Policy, 1660–1672* (Macmillan, 1930).

Firth, C. H., and Davies, G., *Regimental History of Cromwell's Army* (Oxford: Clarendon Press, 1940).

Foxcroft, H. C., *The Life and Letters of Sir George Savile* (Longmans, Green, 1898).

Foxcroft, H. C., *A Supplement to Burnet's History of my Own Time* (Oxford: Clarendon Press, 1902).

Foxcroft, H. C., *A Character of the Trimmer* (Cambridge: Cambridge University Press, 1946).

Fraser, Lady A., *King Charles II* (Weidenfeld & Nicolson, 1979).

Gardiner, S. R., *Letters and Papers Illustrating the Relations between Charles II and Scotland in 1650* (Publications of the Scottish History Society, Vol. 17, 1894).

Gardiner, S. R., *Constitutional Documents of the Puritan Revolution*, 3rd edn (Oxford: Clarendon Press, 1968).

Geyl, P., *Orange and Stuart* (Weidenfeld & Nicolson, 1969).

Glassey, L. J. K., *Politics and the Appointment of Justices of the Peace* (Oxford: Oxford University Press, 1979).

Green, D., *Queen Anne* (Collins, 1970).

Green, I. M., *The Re-establishment of the Church of England* (Oxford: Oxford University Press, 1978).

Grose, C. L., 'Louis XIV's financial relations with Charles II and the English Parliament', *Journal of Modern History*, vol. 1 (1929).

Gumble, T., *Life of General Monck* (1671).

Haley, K. H. D., *William of Orange and the English Opposition* (Oxford: Clarendon Press, 1953).

Haley, K. H. D., *Charles II* (Historical Association, general series, Vol. 63, 1966).

Haley, K. H. D., *The First Earl of Shaftesbury* (Oxford: Clarendon Press, 1968).

Halstead, R., *Succint Genealogies* (1687).

Hardacre, P. H., *The Royalists during the Puritan Revolution* (The Hague: Nijhoff, 1956).

Harris, F. R., *The Life of Edward Montagu KG, First Earl of Sandwich* (Murray, 1912).

Hartmann, C. H., *Charles II and Madame* (Heinemann, 1934).

Hartmann, C. H., *Clifford of the Cabal* (Heinemann, 1937).

Hartmann, C. H., *The King's Friend* (Heinemann, 1951).

Hill, C., *Collected Essays* (Brighton: Harvester, 1985).

Hirst, D., *The Representative of the People?* (Cambridge: Cambridge University Press, 1975).

Hutton, R., *The Restoration* (Oxford: Clarendon Press, 1985).

Illick, J. E., *William Penn the Politician* (New York: Cornell University Press, 1965).

Jones, G. H., *Charles Middleton* (Chicago: Chicago University Press, 1967).

Jones, J. R., 'Shaftesbury's worthy men', *Bulletin of the Institute of Historical Research*, vol. 30 (1957), pp. 232–41.

Jones, J. R., 'Booth's rising of 1659', *Bulletin of the John Rylands Library*, Vol. 39, no. 2 (1957).

Jones, J. R., *The First Whigs* (Oxford: Oxford University Press, 1961).

Jones, J. R., *Country and Court* (Edward Arnold, 1978).

Jones, J. R. (ed.), *The Restored Monarchy, 1660–1688* (Macmillan, 1979).

Kenyon, J. P., 'Charles II and William of Orange in 1680', *Bulletin of the Institute of Historical Research*, vol. 30 (1957).

Kenyon, J. P., *Robert Spencer, Earl of Sunderland* (Longmans, Green, 1958).

Kenyon, J. P., *The Stuarts: a Study in English Kingship* (Batsford, 1958).

Kenyon, J. P., 'The acquittal of Sir George Wakeman', *Historical Journal*, vol. 14 (1971).

Kenyon, J. P., *The Popish Plot* (Heinemann, 1972).

Korr, C. P., *Cromwell and the New Model Foreign Policy* (Berkeley, Calif.: California University Press, 1975).

Laing, D. (ed.), *The Correspondence of Sir Robert Kerr* (Edinburgh, 1875).

Lee, M., *The Cabal* (Urbana, Ill.: Illinois University Press, 1965).

Lister, T. H., *The Life and Administration of Edward, First Earl of Clarendon*, 3 vols (1837–8).

Luttrell, N., *A Brief Relation of State Affairs* (Oxford: Clarendon Press, 1857).

Macray, W. D., *Notes which Passed at Meetings of the Privy Council between Charles II and the Earl of Clarendon* (Roxburghe Club, 1896).

Margoliouth, H. M. (ed.), *The Poems and Letters of Andrew Marvell* (Oxford: Clarendon Press, 1952).

Marvell, A., 'A seasonable argument', in A. Browning (ed.), *English Historical Documents*, Vol. 8 (Eyre & Spottiswoode, 1953).

Miller, J., *Popery and Politics in England, 1660–1688* (Cambridge: Cambridge University Press, 1973).

Miller, J., *James II: a Study in Kingship* (Hove: Wayland, 1978).

Miller, J., 'The later Stuart monarchy', in J. R. Jones (ed.), *The Restored Monarchy* (Macmillan, 1979).

Miller, J., 'Charles II and his Parliaments', *Transactions of the Royal Historical Society*, 5th series, vol. 32 (1982).

Miller, J., 'The potential for absolutism in later Stuart England', *History*, vol. 69 (1984).

Milne, D., 'The results of the Rye House plot', *Transactions of the Royal Historical Society*, 5th series, vol. 1 (1951).

Morley, I., *A Thousand Lives: an Account of the English Revolutionary Movement* (Deutsch, 1954).

Napier, M., *Memoirs of Montrose* (Edinburgh, 1856).

Nicholas, D., *Mr Secretary Nicholas* (Bodley Head, 1955).

Oliver, H. J., *Sir Robert Howard* (Durham, NC: Duke University Press, 1963).

Ollard, R., *The Escape of Charles II* (Hodder & Stoughton, 1966).

Ollard, R., *Man of War* (Hodder & Stoughton, 1969).

Ollard, R., *The Image of the King* (Hodder, 1979).

Oman, C., *Henrietta Maria* (Hodder, 1951).

Pocock, J. G. A. (ed.), *Three British Revolutions* (Princeton, NJ: Princeton University Press, 1980).

Pollock, Sir J., *The Popish Plot* (Cambridge: Cambridge University Press, 1944).

Powell, J. R., *The Navy in the English Civil War* (Hamden, Conn.: Archon, 1962).

Prall, S., *The Puritan Revolution* (Routledge & Kegan Paul, 1968).

Roberts, C., 'The impeachment of the Earl of Clarendon', *Cambridge Historical Journal*, vol. 13, no. 1 (1957).

Roberts, C., *The Growth of Responsible Government in Stuart England* (Cambridge: Cambridge University Press, 1966).

Roberts, C., *Schemes and Undertakings: a Study of English Politics in the Seventeenth Century* (Columbus, Ohio: Ohio University Press, 1985).

Roberts, G., *The Life, Progresses and Rebellion of James, Duke of Monmouth*, 2 vols (1844).

Rogers, P. G., *The Dutch in the Medway* (Oxford University Press, 1970).

Roorda, D. J., *Partij en Factie* (Groningen: Wolters, 1961).

Roseveare, H., *The Treasury, 1660–1870* (Allen & Unwin, 1973).

Routledge, F. J., *England and the Treaty of the Pyrenees* (Liverpool: Liverpool University Press, 1953).

Rowe, V., *Sir Henry Vane the Younger* (Athlone Press, 1970).

Rowen, H. H., *The Ambassador Prepares for War* (The Hague: Nijhoff, 1957).

Rowen, H. H., *John de Witt* (Princeton, NJ: Princeton University Press, 1978).

Rubinstein, H. L., *Captain Luckless: James, First Duke of Hamilton* (Edinburgh: Scottish Academic Press, 1975).

Russell, C., *Parliaments and English Politics, 1621–1629* (Oxford: Clarendon Press, 1979).

Scott, E., *The King in Exile* (Constable, 1905).

Scott, E., *The Travels of the King* (Constable, 1907).

Seward, P. C., 'Court faction and the parliamentary session of 1663', Fellowship dissertation, Christ's College, Cambridge (1984).

Sims, J. G., *Jacobite Ireland* (Routledge & Kegan Paul, 1969).

Sitwell, Sir G., *The First Whig* (Scarborough: privately pub., 1894).

Skinner, T., *The Life of General Monck* (1724).

Stevenson, D., *Revolution and Counter-Revolution in Scotland* (Royal Historical Society Studies in History, 1977).

Stevenson, D., *Alasdair MacColla and the Highland Problem* (Edinburgh: Donald, 1980).

Sutch, V. D., *Gilbert Sheldon* (The Hague: Nijhoff, 1973).

Sykes, N., *Church and State in the Eighteenth Century* (Cambridge: Cambridge University Press, 1934).

Sykes, N., *From Sheldon to Secker* (Cambridge: Cambridge University Press, 1959).

Temple, Sir W., *Memoirs* (1714).

Terry, C. S., *The Life and Campaigns of Alexander Leslie* (Longmans, Green, 1899).

Townshend, D., *George Digby, Second Earl of Bristol* (Unwin, 1924).

Turner, E. R., 'The Privy Council of 1679', *English Historical Review*, vol. 30 (1915).

Turner, F. C., *James II* (Eyre & Spottiswoode, 1948).

Underdown, D., *Royalist Conspiracy in England* (New Haven, Conn.: Yale University Press, 1960).

Westergaard, W., *The First Triple Alliance* (New Haven, Conn.: Yale University Press, 1947).

Western, J. R., *Monarchy and Revolution* (Blandford, 1972).

Whiteman, A., 'The re-establishment of the Church of England, 1660–1663', *Transactions of the Royal Historical Society*, 5th series, vol. 5 (1955).

Whiteman, A., 'The Restoration of the Church of England', in G. F. Nuttall and O. Chadwick (eds), *From Uniformity to Unity* (SPCK, 1962).

Willcock, J., *The Great Marquess* (Edinburgh: Oliphant, 1903).

Witcombe, D. T., *Charles II and the Cavalier House of Commons, 1663–1674* (Manchester: Manchester University Press, 1966).

Zee, H. and B. van der, *William and Mary* (Macmillan, 1973).

Zwicker, S., *Politics and Language in Dryden's Poetry* (Princeton, NJ: Princeton University Press, 1984).

Index